TRUE CRIMES

LADY KILLERS

TRUE CRIMES

LADY KILLERS

JOYCE ROBINS

ACKNOWLEDGEMENTS

The publishers wish to thank the following organizations for their kind permission to reproduce the pictures in this book:

The Hulton-Deutsch Collection Ltd: 45, 61, 98, 132, 205, 215, 229, 243, 253, 259, 263, 275, 307, 323, 339, 353, 361

Topham Picture Library Source: 7, 23, 85, 144, 166,173, 185, 327, 337, 371

Popperfoto: 11, 37, 74, 87, 113, 123, 195, 278, 288, 299, 318

The Associated Press Ltd: 337

First published in Great Britain in 1993 by
Chancellor Press (Bounty Books), a division of Octopus Publishing Group Ltd

This edition published in 2009 by Bounty Books,
a division of Octopus Publishing Group Ltd
2–4 Heron Quays, London E14 4JP
www.octopusbooks.co.uk

An Hachette Livre UK Company
www.hachettelivre.co.uk

Copyright © Octopus Publishing Group Ltd 1993

ISBN: 978-0-753717-44-8

A CIP catalogue record for this book is available from the British Library

Printed and bound in the UK by CPI Mackays, Chatham ME5 8TD

Contents

Introduction

THERE HAS always been something especially horrifying about murders committed by women – perhaps because women are still considered gentler and more caring than men or perhaps because their victims are so often within the family, among those they are expected to protect and nurture.

The murderesses who have stood in the dock fit no stereotype. They may be rich and spoiled or poor and desperate, voluptuous sirens or dumpy matrons. Few of them are sadistic killers. The notorious Myra Hindley, one of the 'Moors Murderers', the women of Nazi death camps and Elizabeth Brownrigg, who tortured a servant to death, are the exceptions. Most see murder as a practical way out of their problems, for example Sarah Jane Robinson who poisoned most of her family for insurance money and Kate Webster who battered to death the employer who was about to turn her out into the street and boiled the remains in the copper to prevent identification. Then, of course, there are the freaks who kill for their own twisted motives: Anna Zimmermann who decided that human flesh would be cheaper than butcher's meat, Denise Labbé who drowned her child at her lover's whim and Mary Bell, the 11-year-old killer who strangled two small boys.

The true stories told here reveal the darker side of the female nature; while the characters that parade through these pages may be pitiable, hateful or inscrutable, they are always intriguing.

Chapter One

REASONS TO KILL

Introduction

THE MOTIVES for murder are many and varied but most have their roots in greed, hate or a twisted form of love. One of the simplest and most straightforward is gain; many women have found murder easier than hard work as a way of making money or acquiring a home and some kill again and again, every time the bank balance runs low. The frail and elderly are especially vulnerable to a plausible woman whose kindly smile hides murderous intent.

Jealousy and rage can combine into a powerful urge to dispose of a hated rival, but those who murder in the grip of political fervour are equally passionate. Women terrorists can be just as fanatical and pitiless as their male colleagues and show as little remorse for those they kill in pursuing their cause.

Even more repulsive are those who murder for their own sexual gratification or for the thrill of power it gives them to have helpless human beings at their mercy. Though most sado-sexual killers have been men, there are women whose perverted tastes have led them to torture and kill.

Belle Gunness

BELLE GUNNESS, a personable Norwegian widow living in La Porte, Indiana, USA had a novel way of attracting the victims she killed for their money: she advertised. Her carefully worded advertisements, carried in selected local papers circulated in areas where numbers of Scandinavian immigrants had settled, were tempting, though the wary might have taken warning from the emphasis on money. One read:

> Wanted – A woman who owns a beautifully located and valuable farm in first-class condition wants a good and reliable man as partner in the same. Some little cash is required for which will be furnished first-class security.

And another:

> Personal – Comely widow, who owns large farm in one of the finest districts of La Porte County, Indiana, desires to make the acquaintance of a gentleman unusually well provided, with a view to joining fortunes. No replies by letter will be considered unless the sender is willing to follow an answer with a personal visit.

A stream of men arrived at Belle's door, impressed to find that the farm was so well-kept and charmed by the large blonde with clear blue eyes who could lay on a delicious meal and was not averse to a kiss and a cuddle. The townsfolk occasionally remarked that Belle's visitors never seemed to stay for long but she explained that they were acquaintances from the old country, men who had to return to their homes and families. In fact, few of them ever left.

On the night of 27 April 1908, the farmhouse caught fire and by

5

morning the building was completely gutted. When a party of townsfolk, under the supervision of two local deputies, began searching the charred ruin they found the remains of Belle's three children, 11-year-old Myrtle, 9-year-old Lucy and 5-year-old Philip. Nearby was the body of a woman without a head. The authorities decided that all four had been killed before the fire started and the most likely perpetrator was a labourer named Ray Lamphere, who had been seen nearby at the time the fire started. He had once worked for Belle and there had been talk of a more intimate relationship, but then there had been a complete split; at one point Belle had prosecuted him for trespassing and made other spiteful allegations. Lamphere had often hinted that he 'had enough' on Belle to keep her under his thumb but his listeners could only guess at what he meant. Belle had always been independent and no one knew much about her affairs.

Belle had arrived in America in 1883, joining her sister and brother-in-law in Chicago. Within a year she had married Mads Sorenson, a security guard. Financially they never did more than scrape by and the first time Belle had money to spend was after her husband died – suddenly, with convulsions that could well have been due to poison – when she benefited from two handsome insurance policies. With her two daughters Myrtle and Lucy and her foster-daughter Jenny, she moved to the farm at La Porte. She married a widower, Peter Gunness, who died nine months later when, according to Belle, a sausage grinder fell on him from a great height. He, too, was well insured. For a while after that she ran the farm with the help of a succession of hired men. One of them was Ray Lamphere, who shared her bed for a time but was given his marching orders when the well-dressed strangers began arriving for brief visits.

One of the visitors was Andrew Helgelein from South Dakota, who had corresponded with the understanding Scandinavian widow for 16 months before setting off to meet her at last. In December 1907 she had written to him:

'To the dearest friend in all the world – I know you have now only to

Belle Gunness

come to me and be my own. The king will be no happier than you when you get here. As for the queen, her joy will be small when compared with mine. You will love my farm, sweetheart. In all La Porte county, there's none will compare with it. It is on a nice green slope near two lakes. When I hear your name mentioned, my heart beats in wild rapture for you. My Andrew, I love you!

'Be sure and bring the three thousand dollars you are going to invest in the farm with you and, for safety's sake, sew them up in your clothes, dearest.'

The last time Andrew Helgelein was seen was when Belle drove him towards the farm in her pony and trap. When his brother Axel began to make enquiries about him Belle insisted that he had left her home happy and never returned, leaving her grief-stricken. If only Axel would sell all his brother's possessions and bring plenty of money they could mount a search together. Axel, less credulous than his brother, left his money safely behind but came to investigate. He arrived to find men sifting through the remains of the farmhouse in search of anything that could identify the dead woman as Belle. As they began digging in the yard they found Andrew, his limbs and head hacked from his torso and the pieces neatly wrapped in sacking. The diggers redoubled their efforts, unearthing the remains of four people under the rubbish dump and several more in the chicken pen. Most had been cut into pieces and sprinkled with quicklime so that there was little left to identify but one body was that of Belle's foster-daughter Jenny, who was supposed to have left home 18 months before at the age of 16.

As reports of the finds were published, the relatives of missing men began arriving in the town, all telling a similar story: their brothers, sons or fathers had journeyed to Indiana to marry a rich widow. The bodies of 10 men were recovered but when all the reports were in, another dozen were still unaccounted for. John Moo, a farmer from Wisconsin last seen drawing $1100 dollars from the bank, and Tonnes Peter Lien, who had sold his farm in Minnesota and brought with him

$1000, were both identified by their watches; Olaf Lindboe, who had arrived at the bank in the company of Belle to draw out $1800, was identified by his teeth. The others were thought to include George Berry, who travelled with $1500, Christian Hinkley with $2000 and Herman Konitzer with $5000.

It was estimated that Belle had netted herself at least $30,000 but the balance in her bank account was modest, leading many people to believe that Belle, far from dying in the fire, was enjoying her ill-gotten gains on her travels. The head belonging to the burnt corpse had never been found (though a section of Belle's bridgework had been recovered from the ashes), and the body itself seemed too small for Belle's large bulk. Belle had been seen driving to the farm with a smaller companion the day before the fire and, given her past history, it would have been easy enough for Belle to kill an unknown woman along with the children and render her unidentifiable by removing her head. Then she could have decamped with her money, charging Lamphere to set the fire and leaving behind her false teeth to allay suspicion. The doubts cast on Belle's death were enough to acquit Lamphere on the murder charge, though he was found guilty of arson and sentenced to 20 years in prison. From his cell, he always insisted that Belle was still alive. After his death the prison chaplain revealed that Lamphere had confessed to chloroforming Belle's three children and setting fire to the house while she made her escape. However, by this time he had told several different stories and it is impossible to know whether he was telling the truth.

Dorothea Waddingham

WHEN Dorothea Waddingham decided to call herself Nurse Waddingham and open a nursing home for 'aged and chronic cases' she may have only had an eye to a lucrative business which would bring in far more money than her menial job. However, she soon became greedy and decided that disposing of her patients would bring better returns. Dorothea had never been too particular about how she obtained what she wanted – in the past she had twice been given probation by the English courts for false pretences and she had served a three-month prison term for theft. She was a thin, dour woman with a far from winning personality and it is difficult to see why anyone would put themselves in her care, but presumably she could be persuasive when she chose.

She never obtained any nursing qualifications but she had worked as a ward maid in a workhouse infirmary, so she had a good idea of how nurses worked and could put on a convincing performance. When her husband, Tom Leech, died leaving her almost penniless, she fixed her eye on his easy-going friend, Ronald Sullivan, who had his own house in Devon Drive, Nottingham. She convinced him that she had all the expertise necessary to run a nursing home which would bring in a good income for both of them. Reverting to her married name, she advertised for patients who could look forward to care from an 'unregistered nurse'.

In January 1935 89-year-old Mrs Baguley saw the advertisement and decided that the nursing home might be just what she needed. She had been caring alone for her daughter Ada, who was 52 and suffering from disseminated sclerosis, but Ada was now confined to a wheelchair and Mrs Baguley was too frail to look after her properly.

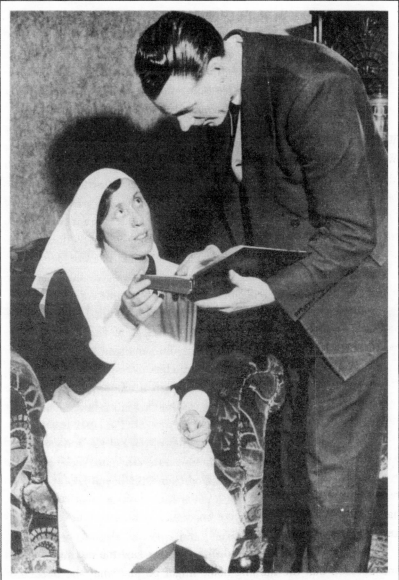

Dorothea Waddingham giving instructions for the day to Ronald Sullivan at the nursing home in Devon Drive, Nottingham

Dorothea, now Nurse Waddingham, agreed to take both women for the sum of £3 a week, which was the most they could afford. Dorothea's only other patient, Mrs Kemp, had died so she needed the money – but she soon found that looking after Ada was hard work, for the latter was a large, fat woman, scarcely able to move by herself. However, she put herself out to satisfy the Baguleys and must have succeeded, for on 6 May Ada made out a new will revoking a previous will in which she left her £1600 to her relatives and leaving it instead to Dorothea Waddingham and Ronald Sullivan. In return, the weekly payments would cease and the Baguleys would be looked after for the rest of their lives. It must have seemed like an advantageous arrangement to Ada and her mother at the time but in signing the will, Ada was signing their death warrants.

Little over a week later Mrs Baguley breathed her last, but there was no reason for the doctor to suspect that it was anything but the natural death of a very old lady. Four months later Ada died quite suddenly but again the doctor was quite happy and had no hesitation in issuing a death certificate, giving the cause of death as cerebral haemorrhage. Dorothea, anxious for a cremation to be arranged as soon as possible, dispatched to the medical officer in health a note (supposedly written by Ada and witnessed by Sullivan), expressing Ada's desire to be cremated and requesting that 'my relatives shall not know of my death'. It was never certain whether the letter was forged or obtained by Dorothea from the helpless Ada, but the last sentence was enough to ring alarm bells. Moreover, Dorothea made the mistake of giving her address as 'The Nursing Home, 32 Devon Drive' and Dr Cyril Banks, the health officer, knew that no nursing home was registered at that address.

Dr Banks contacted the coroner and a postmortem was ordered. It showed that there was no question of a cerebral haemorrhage; Ada had died from an overdose of morphine. When Mrs Baguley's body was exhumed sufficient traces of morphine were found to suggest that she had died in the same way. 'Nurse' Waddingham and Ronald

Sullivan were both charged with murder but Sullivan was discharged for lack of evidence at the beginning of the trial, leaving Dorothea alone to face the charge of murder.

Her defence was that she had only given her patient medicine as intimated by the doctor and that he had prescribed morphine for Ada, who was suffering from severe stomach pain, in five doses of two tablets at a time. Dr Manfield, who had attended the residents in Devon Drive, said that he had prescribed morphine for Dorothea's patients in the past but that Ada had never been in sufficient pain to warrant its use. She was found guilty but, for some unaccountable reason, the jury added a strong recommendation for mercy. This was disregarded by the judicial authorities. Dorothea's appeal was turned down and she was hanged at Winson Green prison, Birmingham, on 16 April 1936.

The Baby Farmers

THE NOTORIOUS baby farmers of the late 19th century plied a revolting trade. These women took illegitimate or unwanted babies for a fee, promising to provide foster care or find new homes. Then they quietly 'disposed' of the infants. Their terrible business was permitted by almost non-existent child protection laws in England at the time and encouraged by a moral code that left unmarried mothers as the outcasts of society.

The grim work of Amelia Elizabeth Dyer came to light in 1896, when she had already killed an unknown number of children. One day in March a bargeman hauled a brown paper parcel out of the Thames near Caversham. As the wet paper fell away, he found that he was holding the body of a baby girl. She had been strangled with a boot-lace, which was still around her neck. A few days later a carpet bag was fished out of the river near Reading and this time there were two murdered infants inside. A search of the river bed turned up several tiny bodies, in various stages of decomposition.

The first find had yielded an important clue, for one of the layers of brown paper bore the name and address of a Mrs Harding. Though Mrs Harding had moved from that address, neighbours revealed that she was always taking foster children and she was soon traced to a house where she had been living with her daughter and son-in-law, Polly and Arthur Palmer. The police set a trap, whereby a young woman posed as an unmarried mother wanting her baby adopted. She met Mrs Harding, a fat, elderly woman with an ingratiating manner, who agreed to take the imaginary child for £100 with a guarantee of no further problems for the mother. Instead of receiving the expected child she received a visit from a police inspector and his sergeant, who found a pile of baby clothes in a cupboard under the stairs, together with an unpleasant smell, which led them to believe that a decomposing body had been left there for some time. Mrs Harding, when questioned, admitted that her real name was Amelia Elizabeth Dyer.

Meanwhile, some of the dead infants had been identified and linked to Amelia Dyer. Evelina Marmon was a barmaid in Cheltenham, Gloucestershire, who had found it impossible to look after her illegitimate baby and keep her job. Consequently, she had answered a newspaper advertisement offering a caring home in return for a small payment. She was contacted by Amelia, posing as Mrs Harding, who said that she was thrilled at the idea of having 'a dear little baby girl' to bring up as her own. She assured Evelina that 'a child with me will have a good home and a mother's loving care'. On 31 March Evelina handed over baby Doris to her new 'mother', along with a payment of £10, and saw them off at Cheltenham railway station. Doris was one of the infants found in the waterlogged carpet bag with a knotted bootlace round her throat. Another of the bodies recovered from the river was that of Elizabeth Goulding's 10-month-old baby, who had been left with Amelia and a young man matching the description of Arthur Palmer.

Amelia had made a good business out of baby farming, always charging £10 or more for taking a baby and seldom keeping the child more than 24 hours. She operated under several names and from various addresses, always moving on before neighbours became suspicious or a parent started making enquiries about the welfare of a particular child. She had spent several short spells in lunatic asylums but it was suggested that sometimes she found this a convenient way of avoiding detection, knowing that she could demonstrate her sanity as soon as she was ready to resume her calling once more.

While awaiting trial, Amelia tried twice to kill herself, once with scissors and once with bootlaces, but she found suicide more difficult than killing babies and she was revived each time. Arthur Palmer was charged along with her but at the last moment Amelia wrote a confession in which she declared that, though her own days were numbered, she could not bear the thought of 'drawing innocent people into trouble' and that Arthur knew nothing of her crimes and had nothing to do with her wickedness. The authorities accepted her statement and released him.

The only possible defence was insanity and doctors testified that she suffered from extreme depression and delusions and was not responsible for her actions. For the prosecution, an eminent specialist in mental illness considered that there was no evidence of insanity and Dr James Scott, the medical officer of Holloway Prison, where he had seen Amelia on a daily basis, gave his opinion that her so-called delusions were all pretence. The jury rejected the plea of insanity and the judge, sentencing Amelia to hang, voiced the pious hope that the Lord would show more mercy to her than she had shown 'to these poor, innocent, unprotected infants'.

In 1902 another thriving baby-farming business was discovered. Amelia Sach, a personable 29-year-old redhead who ran a discreet nursing home in East Finchley, London, and Annie Walters, aged 54 and a great deal less personable, had a cosy little arrangement between them. Mrs Sach advertised her nursing services to expectant mothers with the tempting extra offer 'Baby can remain', thus attracting many young women desperate to leave the consequences of their little indiscretion behind and avoid the disgrace of admitting to an illegitimate baby. Whenever one of these young women gave birth Mrs Sach contacted Annie, who had lodgings in Islington, and Annie took away the baby.

Annie, who lodged with a policeman's family, told her landlady that she acted as a short-term foster mother, arranging suitable adoptions for the babies placed with her. She spoke so warmly of her charges and put up such a good pretence of doting on her 'little darlings' that her landlady was taken in for a while. However, she began to watch her lodger more closely after Annie, called away unexpectedly to collect another child, asked her to mind a baby girl for an hour, during which time the baby needed a nappy change and turned out to be a boy. At the same time, the landlady's policeman husband had begun to wonder about the speed with which Annie seemed able to arrange adoptions. No prospective parents ever came to the house, yet every baby disappeared with amazing rapidity. If questioned, Annie told highly coloured tales of the wealthy families with whom she placed the babies, handing them over to fine ladies in luxurious carriages, en route for their country estates.

On 15 November, a Miss Galley gave birth to a boy in Mrs Sach's nursing home and paid £25 to have the child adopted. Later that day, Annie Walters arrived to collect the baby and her share of the payment. The baby remained with her for two days, then on the third morning she was seen leaving the house carrying a well-wrapped bundle. This time she was followed and caught trying to dispose of the Galley baby's body. Among her baby-feeding equipment was found a supply of deadly chlorodyne, suggesting that the babies had met their end quickly once in the hands of their kindly foster-mother. Annie denied everything, repeating stories of rich but nameless adoptive parents and claiming that she had only used chlorodyne to keep her charges quiet, so that they would not disturb the household – but the more she talked, the more unlikely her story sounded.

She soon led the police to Mrs Sach of the Claymore House Nursing Home, who said that her only contact with Annie was when she had employed her for domestic work; there was no question of her being allowed to remove any babies from the nursing home. Her listeners remained unconvinced: it seemed far more likely that Mrs Sach was the brains behind the lucrative operation and that, though she might never have enquired about the method of disposing of the babies, she knew full well that they were going to their death.

The women went on trial before Mr Justice Darling at the Old Bailey on 15 January 1903. Both were sentenced to death and hanged at Holloway Prison less than three weeks later.

Euphrasie Mercier

IN THE spring of 1883 Elodie Ménétret confided in a neighbour that she was a little scared of her new companion, Euphrasie Mercier. She had known Euphrasie for a short time before engaging her, as she had been a customer in Euphrasie's shoe shop. The business had been failing fast and Euphrasie, who was nearing 60, had been looking for another job; meanwhile Elodie was feeling lonely and nervous, alone in her house near Paris. The arrangement had seemed perfect for both of them at the time but Elodie now felt she had made a mistake. She had asked Euphrasie to leave but her companion had flatly refused.

Following that conversation, the neighbour never saw Elodie again. When she enquired about her, Euphrasie told her that her employer had entered a convent and did not wish anyone to know the place chosen for her retreat. She told the same story to Elodie's family, adding significantly 'She is dead to the world.' A week later, Euphrasie made a trip to Luxembourg and went to a lawyer, introducing herself as Elodie Ménétret and saying that she had moved to Luxembourg and wanted to draw up a power of attorney in favour of her friend Euphrasie Mercier, who would be looking after her affairs in France. When she was told that two witnesses had to swear to her identity she brought in two strangers from the street and bribed them to vouch for her.

Back in France, she lost no time in installing her three sisters in the house: all of them were mentally deranged, suffering from religious mania, and she had been looking after them for years. The household remained undisturbed until 1885 when Alphonse Chateauneuf, son of one of the unbalanced sisters, moved in. Euphrasie doted on her shiftless nephew, who was too self-centred to return her devotion.

From the beginning, Alphonse sensed that his aunt had a guilty secret. When he questioned her about Elodie her answers were evasive and he found the story of her employer suddenly vanishing into a convent without a word to anyone unconvincing, to say the least. Then there was his aunt's extraordinary behaviour. More than once he saw her throw open the window and cry out 'Back, phantoms of the garden!' or 'Rest in peace, family of Ménétret!' At first he wondered if she was going the same way as her sisters but her strange obsession over the dahlia bed convinced him that her worries were not imaginary. The gardener was not allowed to touch that particular part of the garden and Euphrasie kept a close watch on it, making sure that she could see it from the dining table or from her armchair. Once, when a stray dog got into the garden and started digging in the dahlia bed, she ran out of the house screaming hysterically and belabouring it with her hoe.

Alphonse listened, too, to the strange mutterings of his mother and her two mad sisters who were always talking about the dead coming to life and 'misfortune' coming from the garden. He scoured the house for clues and eventually came up with the theory that Euphrasie had murdered Elodie, burned her body, then buried the remains in the dahlia bed. It was at this time that Alphonse asked his aunt for a substantial loan. When she turned him down he threatened to reveal a family secret, but still she refused. He then wrote to the police, outlining his suspicions and enclosing a plan of the garden, and to Elodie's uncle, claiming that she had been murdered by his aunt and even identifying the room in which the killing had taken place.

When the police dug up the dahlia bed they found charred human bones as well as several teeth. One of them had been filled with gold and was identified by Elodie's dentist as his work. A botanical expert was brought in to examine the bulbs and he concluded that they had been disturbed in the spring of 1883, at about the time of Elodie's disappearance. In the chimney of one of the bedrooms there was a greasy substance of the kind found in restaurant chimneys where meat had been cooked.

Though it was not possible to conclude how Elodie had met her death, Euphrasie was charged with murder and put on trial in April 1886. Alphonse, her beloved nephew, testified against her and a sad collection of her dead friend's bones stood in a jar on the courtroom table. She still insisted that Elodie was alive and living in a convent and, when she was told that investigators had contacted every religious house in the country and none of them had ever heard of Elodie, she countered by saying that the confusion could have arisen because her friend had changed convents frequently and that she had seen her several times. She said that the house had been bought with her money, not Elodie's, and she had nothing to gain from her death.

Euphrasie failed to convince the court and was sentenced to 20 years' imprisonment which, at her age, was to be a genuine life sentence. Alphonse, having failed to raise his loan, managed to make money out of her downfall by selling his account of the murder.

Barbara Graham

BARBARA GRAHAM'S path to the gas chamber of San Quentin began in childhood. When she was two years old her teenage mother was sent to a reformatory and she was left in the care of neighbours. A difficult and unhappy child, she was judged incorrigible at the age of nine and packed off to the same reformatory as her mother.

She married the first of four husbands in 1941 and subsequently had three children. She gathered convictions for vagrancy, disorderly conduct and prostitution and by 1947 was one of the call girls employed by Sally Stanford, San Francisco's most notorious madam. Her fourth husband, Harry Graham, introduced her to drugs and she became involved with a group of criminals headed by Jack Santos.

The Santos gang was made up of robbers who were ready to commit murder whenever it seemed expedient: in 1951 they tortured and robbed gold buyer Andrew Colner and his wife and in 1952 they murdered a gold miner, then a grocer and his two children. Barbara Graham could only be linked with certainty to the murder in 1953 of Mabel Monahan, a 63-year-old cripple who was reputed to keep a lot of valuable jewellery in her home.

The plan was for Barbara to trick her way into the widow's home by pretending an emergency and asking to use the phone. Then her three companions would crowd in, overpower Mrs Monahan and ransack the house. According to John True, a gang member who later turned state's evidence to convict Barbara, the idea was to leave the elderly woman unharmed – though on the past evidence of the gang's methods, this could be doubted. In fact, Barbara lost her temper and hit Mrs Monahan over the head with her gun butt. As the woman fell to the floor, crying 'Oh, no, no, no!', one of the men egged Barbara on,

21

urging: 'Give her more.' Barbara seized the woman's hair and laid about her again, cracking her skull. After that the gang turned the house upside down in search of valuables but were eventually forced to leave empty-handed. They had killed for nothing.

When arrested, Barbara came up with two different alibis in turn but both were easily proved false. While she was awaiting trial an undercover agent posing as another prisoner offered to provide her with an alibi for the right price and she agreed to pay $25,000. When a tape recording of the deal was played in court she cried out: 'Haven't you ever been desperate? Do you know what it means not to know what to do?' The tape recording weighed heavily against her, for the prosecution argued that only a guilty person would be willing to go to any lengths to furnish a false alibi.

The press called her 'Bloody Babs' and the prosecutor at her trial told the jury that the victim had looked 'as if she had been hit by a heavy truck travelling at high speed. The savage brutality of the attack is like nothing I have seen in my 20 years' experience. I can scarcely believe that human beings could do that to an elderly woman against whom they had nothing, merely because they wanted money.'

Barbara, now 32, and two of her male companions were sentenced to death; John True had saved his life by testifying against the others. For two years Barbara's lawyers battled for a reprieve and newspapers carried pictures of the tearful mother with her 19-month-old son, but it was in vain. As she was led into the gas chamber on 3 June 1955, she asked for a blindfold. 'I don't want to have to look at people,' she said.

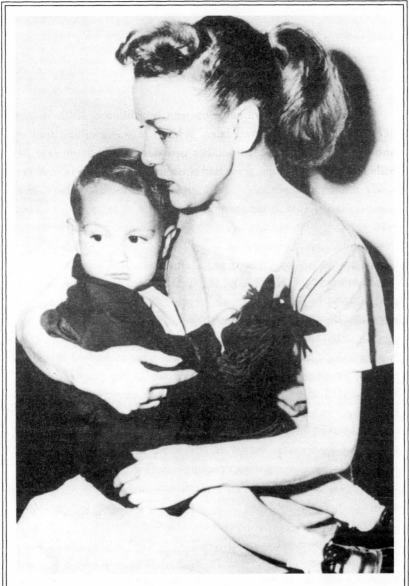

Barbara Graham holds her son Tommy in Los Angeles Jail, 14 October 1953, the day after she was sentenced to die in the gas chamber

Anna Hahn

ANNA HAHN, a German immigrant who had arrived in the USA in 1929, managed to make a lucrative business out of caring for the lonely and elderly in the German community of Ohio. Whenever a grateful patient died, Anna seemed to end up with extra money in her bank account. She had engineered a very comfortable lifestyle by the time the law caught up with her.

She first came to America as a housekeeper to her uncle, Max Doeschel, in Cincinnati. He had sent her the money for the fare but soon felt that he had made a bad bargain; Anna cared far more about her social life than about looking after the house. They soon came to a parting of the ways and she moved on to stay with a distant relative, Karl Osswald. Recently widowed, he was more interested in a wife than a housekeeper and within a few weeks he proposed. Anna explained that she had an illegitimate son, Oscar, who was living with her parents in Germany and that she would only consider marriage if she could bring him to join them in America. Osswald duly lent her the money for the fare but while she was still making plans for the journey she met a young telegraph operator, Philip Hahn, and decided to marry him instead. She used Osswald's cash to go back to Germany and collect Oscar but came back to Philip, with whom she opened a bakery.

Anna soon tired of the hard work of running a shop and looked around for a way out. She had become friendly with an elderly and reputedly well-off customer, Ernst Koch, and when he offered her a job looking after him she liked the idea. Philip objected but was soon too ill to enforce his objections – so ill that his mother had him taken into hospital. When he came out, he found that Anna had already moved in with Koch. It was only much later that anyone associated Philip's illness with the large quantity of croton oil, a fierce purgative, that Anna had bought from the chemist.

When Ernst Koch died, leaving a will naming Anna as chief beneficiary, his family contested the will and voiced strong suspicions over his death. A postmortem showed that the old man had died from cancer rather than from Anna's ministrations, but the episode must have shown Anna the way to easy money. She went to look after Albert Palmer, a retired railway worker in his seventies, and borrowed $2000 from him, supposedly to pay doctor's bills for her son. When Palmer died suddenly, early in 1937, Anna tore up her IOUs and moved on.

Her next patient was less cooperative. She managed to charm George Heiss into lending her money but he had serious doubts about his new housekeeper when he saw the flies that perched on the edge of his beer glass for a sip keeling over and waving their legs frantically in their death throes. He demanded that Anna should take a drink from the glass and when she refused, ordered her out of the house. Undeterred, she moved in with Jacob Wagner, who died very soon afterwards, leaving her $17,000.

Her next patient was George Opendorfer, a retired shoemaker, to whom she represented herself as the owner of a substantial ranch in Colorado. She persuaded him to take a trip there, in the course of which they travelled as man and wife, but when they got to Denver he fell ill. After a couple of days the hotel manager became worried and tried to persuade Anna to take him to hospital but when he became too pressing Anna took the sick man and boarded a train to Colorado Springs. At the other end, Opendorfer collapsed on the platform. He was taken to hospital and died a few days later. Anna refused to pay for his funeral, saying that she had met him on the train and had posed as his wife at his suggestion.

The authorities decided to investigate when they found that she had managed to draw several thousand dollars from the bank while pretending to be Mrs Opendorfer. Quantities of both croton oil and arsenic were found in Opendorfer's system and when the bodies of Jacob Wagner and Albert Palmer were exhumed, the cause of death was shown to be just as unnatural. When Anna was arrested, substantial quantities of both croton oil and arsenic were found among her possessions.

According to the prosecution at her trial, her ministrations had netted her as much as $70,000. Even the defence admitted that she had looted the bank accounts of her patients and even stolen jewellery belonging to their dead wives, but that was as far as it went: Anna had never harmed any of them, much less committed murder. 'I am as innocent as a new-born babe,' Anna announced to the court. The evidence of the pathologists, of George Heiss and his lucky escape and of Philip Hahn, who had been taken ill with stomach pains and vomiting as soon as he tried to cross Anna, weighed too heavily on the other side. Anna Hahn became the first woman to be executed in the electric chair in the state of Ohio.

Eva Coo

EVA COO, keeper of a roadhouse near Coopertown, USA, had reported Harry Wright missing on the night of 15 June 1934. He was a helpless alcoholic in his fifties and Eva had been looking after him for four years, ever since his mother died, during which time she saw that he had enough food and stood over him while he took an occasional wash. Later that evening Harry's body was found in a ditch not far from the roadhouse, and it was at first assumed that he had been hit by a car as he staggered drunkenly along the road.

Facts soon came to light that cast doubt on the hit and run explanation of Harry's death. It seemed that several insurance policies totalling some $3000 had been taken out on Harry's life shortly before his demise. On the first policy examined by the sheriff, Harry's age was given as 49 – though most of the townsfolk believed him to be 54 – and the policy contained an extra indemnity if he died before the age of 50. Harry made a will in May, leaving the benefits from all his insurance policies to Eva.

More detailed investigations indicated that Harry had not been run over on the road where his body was found but had been killed somewhere else and dumped there to make his death look like an accident. The local medical examiner decided that he had been hit over the head with a blunt instrument before being run over by a car. All the evidence that detectives collected pointed to the guilt of Eva and her friend Martha Clift.

Both women were taken in for questioning and when Eva was told that Martha had confessed and spilled the whole story, she said: 'I didn't have my hand on the wheel of the car. Martha Clift drove it. Martha ran over him. She went back over him a third time.' Later Eva made another confession which her lawyers argued had been forced from her when she had been deprived of food and sleep and compelled to take part in a gruesome reconstruction of the crime, involving manhandling Harry's corpse. At her trial the judge ruled that it was inadmissible in evidence, but the jury was well aware that it had been made.

Eva was charged with first-degree murder and Martha, who was to become the chief witness against her, was to be tried separately. There were suggestions afterwards that Eva had been railroaded. She was well-known in the town; the 'hostesses' at her roadhouse provided all manner of services to many of the outwardly respectable local worthies and she knew too much about too many of them. She received no support from those she thought to be her friends and it seemed that many of them were happy to see her discredited and removed.

The prosecution contended that Eva had obtained a second-hand car and, with Martha, had used a pretext to take Harry up Crumhorn mountain to the old Scott home, now deserted, where she had attacked him with a mallet. Afterwards he had been run over by the car and his body had been taken down to the foot of the mountain and rolled into the ditch. The defence, in the opening address, put forward a completely different story: the insurance policies had been taken out because doctors said that Harry had only a short time to live and he wanted to leave Eva something in return for all her care. On the evening of 15 June, Harry had died of natural causes but Eva had taken his body up the mountain and run over it, so that she would be able to claim a double indemnity on the policy following an accidental death. However, no evidence was introduced into the trial to support the idea of death from natural causes.

Martha Clift, the star witness, who had been promised that she could plead to second-degree murder if she testified, said that some weeks before Harry died Eva had said that she had kept Harry for long enough and that she would like to leave him in the car and let it roll down the hill and crash. Later she talked about leaving him in the car inside the garage with the engine running. Finally she had decided to buy an old car and 'bump him'. Martha had gone with her for a demonstration drive in the second-hand car and had agreed to pick it up from the dealer the following day. In the late afternoon, Eva told Harry that she wanted him to go with them to collect some little cherry trees from a property on Crumhorn mountain. They drove up to the Scott home and Martha stayed with Harry, talking and smoking, while Eva went into the house and collected the mallet, which she concealed under her coat. She came up behind Harry and hit him over the head.

Martha had then driven the car over Harry's body, to make his death look like a road accident. At that moment they had seen another vehicle approaching and Eva had signalled to Martha to reverse the car so that it was positioned over the body. The occupants of the other vehicle were the owners of the deserted house, Mrs Ida Fink, her daughter and son-in-law, and for a time they had chatted with Eva. After they left, Eva had put the body into the car and the two women drove down the mountain, throwing Harry's corpse out at the bottom. Eva had said she was tired out; it was the hardest night's work she had ever done.

Two witnesses – Eva's lover Harry Nabinger and one of her hostesses, Gladys Shumway – told of a trip they had made with Martha and Eva to the Scott home a fortnight before Harry's death. Eva had obviously been familiar with the property and at one point she had swung the mallet over her head, saying: 'Wouldn't this be good for hitting somebody?' Gladys remembered asking an insurance agent to call and discuss a policy for Harry with Eva. Nabinger said he had helped Eva to choose the insurance policies and had driven Eva and Harry to a lawyer so that Harry could make his will. It had been Eva's idea; she had convinced Harry that he should make a will in her favour.

The defence attempted to throw up a smokescreen by casting doubt on the movements of Harry Nabinger. He claimed that he had spent all evening drunk in a neighbouring town and had heard about Harry's death when he phoned Eva at 9.30 pm. However, three defence witnesses testified that they had seen Nabinger that evening and he had been sober. Two others swore that they had seen Nabinger driving towards Eva's roadhouse at about the time Harry was killed. One of the hostesses there said that he had told her that he had seen Harry not five minutes before he died.

The evidence was confusing but the confusion was not enough to save Eva who, on the advice of her lawyers, chose not to give evidence. She was found guilty and went to the electric chair in Sing Sing.

Marie Witte

As WINTER turned to spring in 1984, the townsfolk of Trail Creek in Indiana, USA, saw weeds taking over from flowers in the little garden that Elaine Witte had always tended so carefully. It reminded them that the 74-year-old widow was still on her travels. According to her daughter-in-law Marie she had taken off for California between Christmas and New Year and had decided to stay on and use it as a base for visiting parts of the country she had never seen. Her friends thought it odd; she had departed without a word to anyone and sent not a single postcard in five months.

Elaine Witte was well-known in the town, where she was president of the local group of Pioneers, retired employees of the Bell Telephone Company. The last time they had seen her was at the Christmas party, of which she had been one of the organizers, and everyone had congratulated her on a successful evening. But when the spring meeting came and went with no word from their president, the members became uneasy. They talked to the town marshal, who had known Elaine Witte for years, and he agreed to make some discreet enquiries.

Marshal Chastain had also known Mrs Witte's son Paul, who had died in a tragic accident at the age of 43. Paul had been a steelworker for some years but he had latterly set up a kennel, breeding Siberian huskies. He had met his wife Marie in a nudist camp in Florida and they had married when she was only 16. They had two sons, Butch, who was now 15, and Eric, three years older. After Paul's death Marie and her two sons had moved in with Mrs Witte, though Eric had now left home and was serving in the Navy.

When the marshal made enquiries at the Witte house he found

31

Marie's explanation of Mrs Witte's departure unconvincing, so he passed on his doubts to the state police – only to find that they had been contacted by a friend of Mrs Witte from another town who said he did not believe she was still alive. A few weeks later Marie got wind of the enquiries about her mother-in-law and left Trail Creek suddenly, telling no one of her destination. She was traced to a mobile park in San Diego, where Eric was stationed. They had rented a post office box in the name of Elaine Witte so that they could receive her social security cheques and had opened a bank account in the names of Elaine, Marie and Eric Witte, then forged Mrs Witte's signature to obtain the cash. The police soon discovered that all the signatures endorsing Mrs Witte's cheques from January onwards had been forged. As Marie and Eric tried to deposit the most recent cheque at the bank, they were arrested.

The police then went back to the mobile home to question Butch about the whereabouts of his grandmother. They could hardly believe their ears when the boy coolly admitted that he had killed her. His mother had told him it had to be done, he explained, because she had been cashing cheques on grandma's bank account and the old lady had found out. He had been selected as the killer because, as a juvenile, he would not suffer the full weight of the law if the murder was discovered. His mother had suggested suffocating grandma with a pillow or perhaps strangling her, but Butch had elected to use his wooden crossbow. He had crept upstairs while his grandmother was sleeping and shot her while she lay in her bed. When the horrified officers asked how he felt after killing the old lady, he said unconcernedly: 'I felt neutral about it. I didn't care one way or the other.'

He went on to relate the extraordinary story of the disposal of the body. The boys and their mother set to work with knives, a chain-saw and a chisel. Parts of the body went into the waste disposal unit, others into the trash compactor or the microwave and tasty morsels were fed to the dog. Sections of the corpse were parcelled up and stored in the freezer then scattered around the countryside a bit at a time. When the family left Trail Creek they took the final remains along in the freezer and disposed of them on rubbish tips in San Diego.

Butch's account of his grandmother's fate set the authorities thinking about his father's 'accidental' death. One afternoon in 1981, Paul Witte had been sleeping on the living room sofa when he was shot by his son Eric, then 15 years old. Eric had sobbed bitterly as he explained how he had been crossing the room, carrying a small pistol that seemed to have jammed. He was fiddling with the gun when he tripped on a ruck in the carpet and the gun went off. Butch, Marie and her mother, Margaret O'Donnell, had all seen the incident and all seemed very distressed, so the police had no reason to regard the death as anything but accidental. Now they had to think again.

Meanwhile, it had been decided that Butch should be tried as an adult, which meant that he could face the death penalty if convicted. Realizing that his mother's assurances about his invulnerability had been false, he quickly turned state's evidence and told what he knew about both crimes. His mother had master-minded his father's murder, he said, just as she had plotted his grandmother's death. The first time it had been Eric, the older boy, who had carried out her instructions and the rest of the family had been drilled in the story they would tell the police. It had worked so well that when his mother proposed the second murder he had had no hesitation about it.

Marie's mother, Margaret O'Donnell, was brought in for questioning and, faced with Butch's detailed confession, she too decided that it was in her interests to make a clean breast of the affair. She said that at first Marie had planned to murder Paul by putting large amounts of tranquillizers in his food. As suspicion was less likely to fall on Paul's mother-in-law than on his wife, she was the one who was charged with mixing the drug into his dinner. Though this had made him unusually sleepy there was no sign that it was doing him permanent harm, so then Marie had to plan a more direct method of murder.

Marie and Eric, who had been imprisoned on charges of forgery, were brought back to Indiana to face charges of murder. Both boys testified against their mother and the court accepted that they had acted under her influence. On the charge of murdering her mother-in-law she was sentenced to 90 years in gaol, with 30 years for conspiracy to commit murder to run consecutively. In a separate trial she was sentenced to a further 50 years for the murder of her husband.

Kim Hyon Hui

ON THE afternoon of 29 November 1987, Korean Air Flight 858 exploded over the Andaman Sea while on a flight from Abu Dhabi to Bangkok. All 115 passengers on board, most of them South Koreans, were killed. From the beginning the authorities assumed that the explosion was the result of sabotage, probably carried out by agents of North Korea as part of the bitter conflict between the two Koreas.

Flight 858 had previously flown from Baghdad and a number of passengers had left the plane in Abu Dhabi, so rigorous checks were carried out. When one of the passengers, a 27-year-old Japanese woman, Mayumi Hachiya, was found to be travelling on a false passport, she became top of the list of suspects. She had been accompanied by her elderly father and they had checked in no luggage; moreover, they had chosen a roundabout air route to reach their destination, Bahrain, when they could have taken a more direct flight. They were traced to the Regency Intercontinental Hotel in Bahrain, where South Korean embassy officials approached them with some preliminary questions, treading delicately in case they were, in fact, Japanese nationals.

The 'father and daughter', who were North Korean agents Kim Hyon Hui and 70-year-old Kim Sung, knew that they had to make their escape and planned to fly to Rome early next morning. They were arrested at the airport and put under guard to await a flight to Japan, where they would be taken for questioning. The two agents knew that this was the end of the road: they believed that they would be tortured into betraying their North Korean masters and that they must die rather than talk. They both carried cyanide capsules secreted in the filter tip of a cigarette, and as Kim Sung put his cigarette in his mouth, he whispered a goodbye. Kim Hyon Hui was not quite quick enough; something must have alerted her guard, who snatched the cigarette from her mouth before she could bite hard enough into the filter. Her elderly companion died immediately but Kim awoke in a Bahrain hospital, full of hatred for herself because she had failed to die.

Kim was the product of a strict totalitarian regime, where children were drilled in loyalty to the party and taught to hate the South Koreans and their toadying to the wicked American imperialists. At the age of six she was pretty enough to be chosen to appear in an important propaganda film and later, at university, she was a bright student who excelled in her Japanese language studies. It was her skill in languages, in addition to her unquestioned devotion to the Party, that led to her being chosen as an agent.

After seven years of rigorous training she was chosen for the bomb mission, which aimed to prove to the world that South Korea was not a safe place to host the Olympics, which were to be held in Seoul the following year. Kim's overwhelming feeling was one of pride that she had been chosen for such an important task. She did not allow herself to think about the innocent people she would be killing; a good agent is thoroughly brainwashed to remove all such thoughts.

On 28 November the two agents waited in Baghdad airport for the flight to Abu Dhabi, carrying two airline bags and a plastic carrier containing a radio and a bottle of 'whisky', which was actually liquid explosive. At the security check an official removed the batteries from the radio, saying that they were not permitted on the flight. The batteries were an essential part of the explosive device and for a moment it looked as though their mission was doomed, but Kim Sung gave such an impressive performance as an outraged passenger protesting at his daughter's treatment that the batteries were given back to them.

When they disembarked from the aircraft, each breathed a huge sigh of relief; they had been told that if anything went wrong they must

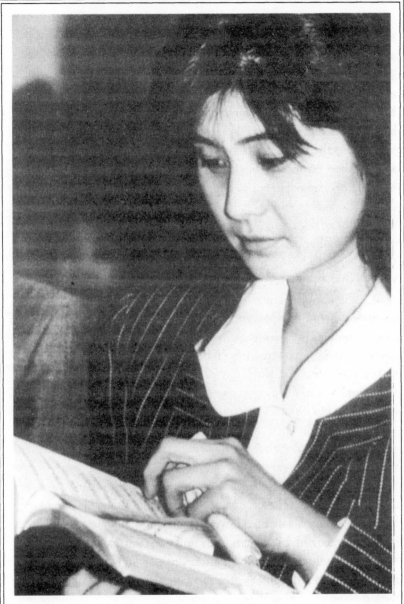

Kim Hyon Hui in South Korea

stay on board and share the fate of the other passengers, but all had gone smoothly. At Abu Dhabi, they faced the first hitch in their plans. They had tickets for Bahrain but this was merely a bluff – they actually planned to catch a plane for Rome, where they felt they would be safe. However, airline officials at the airport examined their tickets and they found themselves ushered out to a plane for Bahrain. They were forced to smile politely and thank the over-helpful officials, knowing that any protest would attract suspicion. They hoped to travel on to Rome immediately but found that there were no seats available until 1 December so they had no choice but to lie low in the hotel in which they were eventually discovered.

Following her suicide attempt, Kim was distraught. She was to be taken to South Korea which, in her eyes, was the worst thing that could happen to her. She tried desperately to bite through her tongue so that she would not be able to answer her captors' questions, but she was then gagged to prevent her from harming herself. The South Korean authorities were determined that she should arrive alive and well so that they could use her for their own propaganda purposes.

For the first eight days of her captivity she refused to eat and continued to insist that she was Japanese, saying that she had been adopted by her elderly companion, who had been taking her on holiday. Eventually she confessed and the South Koreans set about de-programming their captive, introducing her to a more westernized society and parading her on television where she wept publicly. She was put on trial in 1988 and sentenced to death, though she was later pardoned on the grounds that she had been brainwashed and could not be held responsible for her crime. Though theoretically free she remains under the protection of the security authorities, officially to ensure her safety, for many South Koreans still feel that she should have been put to death and North Koreans regard her as a traitor whose name remains high on their death list.

Ulrike Meinhof

IN THE early 1970s Ulrike Meinhof was regarded as the most dangerous woman in Europe. With her partner Andreas Baader, she led a fearsome terrorist group whose aim was to achieve world revolution and establish Marxism in place of capitalism. They committed so many crimes that by the time they were arrested the list ran to over 350 pages. Though Andreas Baader was the charismatic leader of the group Ulrike was the brains, the driving force behind it.

Ulrike was an attractive red-haired girl from an intellectual upper-middle-class family in Lower Saxony, Germany. By the time she was 14 both her parents were dead and she was fostered by a woman professor, a formidable intellectual with radical views. At university she proved to be an outstanding scholar and a natural leader, campaigning against the atom bomb and the American presence in Vietnam. She went to work on a left-wing literary magazine, *Konkret*, and married the editor. She gave birth to twin girls, then returned to work and established a reputation as a brilliant writer and a television personality. In 1968 she divorced her husband on the grounds of adultery.

It was when she interviewed Gudrun Ensslin who, with Andreas Baader and Thorwall Proll, had planted bombs in a Frankfurt department store as a protest against American activities in Vietnam that she decided to do more than write in favour of the cause. Though Ensslin and Proll had escaped, Baader was serving a prison sentence for his part in the bombing and in May 1970 Ulrike led a daring raid to free him. The leaders of the raid then fled to the Middle East to train with the Palestine National Liberation Front, but the Arabs thought the

Germans cold and arrogant and summed them up as rebels without a true cause.

When Ulrike returned to Germany she decided to send her two nine-year-old daughters to Jordan, where they would be trained along with Palestinian children to fight against Israel. Her plans were foiled when her ex-husband, who had engaged private detectives to find his daughters, heard that they were being kept in a gang hideout in Palermo, and arranged to have them snatched back in the nick of time. The children had been brainwashed into hating their father but he eventually managed to win back their trust and affection and give them a normal family life.

The gang was now some 150 strong, most of its members being from prosperous backgrounds. They had large stocks of small firearms, submachine guns, handgrenades and bombs and set out on a series of bank raids to fund the movement. In one particularly violent robbery, at the Bavarian Mortgage and Exchange Bank in Kaiserslauten in December 1971, a police officer was shot dead. It was only when the gang reckoned that their finances were healthy enough that they turned their attention to political targets and had a set of explosive devices manufactured to order, including bombs designed to be worn under a woman's clothing so that she looked pregnant.

A reign of urban terror ensued. In a single month in 1972 bombs planted in a US army headquarters in Frankfurt killed a lieutenant-colonel and injured 13 others; 5 policemen were injured by a bomb at police headquarters in Augsburg; 17 employees were hurt in explosions in a Hamburg publishing house; bombs planted in cars driven into the US army headquarters in Heidelberg killed three Americans and wounded several others. Ulrike Meinhof now displayed a complete disregard for human life, dismissing the police and US soldiers as 'pigs'.

The German public was horrified and the government intensified security precautions while the police concentrated their manpower in an all-out effort to smash the gang. Their first big break came early in 1972 when an anonymous tip-off sent them to a garage in a quiet Frankfurt street which was used by the gang as a bomb factory. Bomb-disposal experts worked to neutralize every device while marksmen took up their positions at strategic points and the whole area was surrounded. Early on the morning of 1 June 1972 a lilac Porsche drove up to the garage with Andreas Baader at the wheel, in the company of two other terrorists. Carl Raspe, Ulrike's lover, realized that they had walked into an ambush and fired on the police before making a run for it, but he was quickly arrested. Baader and another gang member, Holger Meins, barricaded themselves in the garage but after a long, tense siege, Baader was shot in the thigh and both men were forced to surrender.

A few days later Gudrun Ensslin was arrested in a Hamburg dress shop. She had taken off her jacket in order to try on a sweater and a shop assistant had found a gun in the pocket. Ulrike was now the only gang leader left at large and even her former friends began to shy away, feeling that she was too dangerous to know. She planned a getaway from Hanover airport, arranging through friends to stay over-night with a teacher in the suburban village of Langenhagen, near the airport. The teacher had left-wing leanings but had a respected posi-tion as Federal President of the Teachers' Union and was appalled to realize that his houseguest was a wanted terrorist. He phoned the police and on the evening of 15 June a band of officers entered the flat and overpowered her. Her suitcase, packed ready for the flight, contained three pistols, two hand grenades, a submachine gun and a 4.5 kg (10lb) bomb.

The remainder of Ulrike's life was to be spent in prison. The trial of the Baader-Meinhof gang began at Stammheim on 21 May 1975. The terrorists were confined in the nearby top-security prison, where special cells had been constructed. Such was the fear of rescue attempts or terrorist reprisals that armed guards with attack dogs patrolled the perimeter of the goal, anti-bomb netting was fixed on the roof and machine gunners were ready to counter any helicopter attack from above. The courtroom, where Ulrike screamed abuse and shouted political slogans at her judges, was also heavily fortified.

In the prison, the gang members turned against one another and Ulrike began to feel increasingly isolated. When Gudrun Ensslin eventually admitted that the gang had carried out several of the bombings, it was obvious that there was no hope of acquittal. It must have been the last straw for Ulrike, and on the morning of 6 May 1976, she was found hanging in her cell; she had been dead for several hours. Her followers refused to believe that she had committed suicide and were convinced that she had been murdered with the connivance of the authorities. Revenge attacks followed and in the most serious the Chief Federal Prosecutor was killed. Four thousand sympathizers marched in her funeral procession in Berlin, many of them masked to prevent identification.

A priest who had known Ulrike Meinhof when she was still a deeply religious young woman said after her death: 'I think she finally decided that she had come to the end of the wrong road.'

Charlotte Corday

CHARLOTTE CORDAY saw herself as a new Joan of Arc, a sort of avenging angel who could remove from the earth a wicked tyrant who daily condemned innocent men and women to the guillotine. When she plunged a knife into the breast of Jean Paul Marat, one of the leaders of the French Revolution, on 13 July 1793 she thought she was committing a noble act for the sake of the country. In fact, by disposing of Marat, a notable scientist turned politician, she may well have unleashed a wave of indiscriminate killing that cost hundreds more French lives, for following Marat's death Robespierre could proceed with his brutal reign of terror. Marat, who had always eschewed power and opposed those who craved it, was the one man who might have held him in check.

The undoubted beauty of the young woman from Normandy probably played a part in the near-worship with which she was regarded in the last century. Her hair was red-gold, her figure curvaceous and her eyes were grey and deepset. She was an intelligent, well-educated girl from a poor but aristocratic family in the town of Caen, where support for the Girondists, a middle-class party who opposed any idea of power for the people, was passionate. When the Girondists were routed in Paris and forced to flee into the country they blamed Marat, the 'friend of the people', for their downfall. They raised a force of volunteers and as Charlotte watched them marching through Caen she began hatching her own plan of revenge. She decided that it was wrong for so many brave men to risk their lives to defeat the tyrant. 'He did not deserve the honour,' she wrote later. 'A woman's hand was enough!'

Without telling anyone of her plan she set off by coach for Paris, taking with her a single change of clothes, and took a room at a hotel. She had hoped to get into the Convention and kill Marat there, in public, but when she found that he was unwell and remaining at home she decided that she would have to bluff her way into his house. First she bought a kitchen knife with a long, razor-sharp blade and an ebony handle from a shop in what is now the Palais Royal. Then she took a horse-drawn cab to No. 20 Rue des Cordeliers, where Marat lived with his mistress Simone Evrard, and asked to see him. She did not manage to get further than the doorstep, where she was told that Marat was too ill to see anyone, now or in the immediate future.

She returned to her hotel and penned a letter to Marat which read:

'I come from Caen. Your love of your country must make you wish to know the plots that are hatching there. I await your reply.

Charlotte de Corday, Hôtel de la Providence.'

She had no intention of awaiting his reply, for as soon as she was sure that the letter would have been delivered, she made ready to call on him again. She dressed in her best clothes – an Indian muslin gown and a hat with a black cockade and green ribbons – and carried gloves and fan, probably thinking that the smarter she looked, the more likely she was to get into the house without arousing suspicion.

She arrived at the house at 7 pm and at first was no more successful than before. This time she stood her ground, protesting that she had to see Monsieur Marat, it was a matter of life and death. Marat, on hearing the argument and being told that it was the lady from Caen who had written to him, decided that her mission must be important and asked her inside. A strange sight met her eyes. Marat was seated in a slipper bath – bathing for hours on end was the only way of relieving his painful skin complaint – with a dressing gown round his shoulders and a board across the bath so that he could work on his papers. A towel soaked in vinegar was wrapped round his head to soothe his headache.

He questioned Charlotte about the plots among the Girondists in Caen and asked for the names of the ringleaders. When she supplied a

Charlotte Corday and the death of Marat

list of fictitious names he wrote them down and promised that they would be rounded up and sent to the guillotine. While he was still absorbed in making his death list Charlotte drew the knife from her bodice and lunged at him, plunging it into his body up to the hilt. Marat's scream brought Simone running and she tried to stop the blood with her hands but it was too late; by the time Marat was lifted from the bath, he was dead.

Two servants knocked Charlotte to the floor and bound her hands. Soon the house was full of police and soldiers and the news of the killing spread quickly through Paris. A mob of furious citizens gathered outside the house, ready to tear the assassin to pieces, but Charlotte remained calm and self-possessed. Four members of the Convention were sent to question her and spent several hours doing so, as they could not believe that she had acted alone and were determined to discover the names of her accomplices. How was it, they asked her, that she had managed to kill her victim with a single blow if she had not been taught how to kill. Charlotte replied: 'The anger in my own heart showed me the way to his.'

At last she was driven away to the Abbaye Prison through the jeering crowds. Four days later she was put on trial, a mere formality with the verdict never in doubt. At the tribunal she remained clear-headed and defiant and, when asked what she had hoped to gain by killing Marat, she replied: 'Peace for my country. . . . I know that he was perverting France. I killed one man in order to save a hundred thousand.' The defence lawyer had been instructed to put in a plea of insanity, on the grounds that the young woman's judgement had been impaired by her political fanaticism. By portraying her as a madwoman, the revolutionaries hoped to prevent her from becoming a martyr.

She was condemned to death on the guillotine that same day. As she waited for the appointed time the artist Jean Jacques Hauer made a sketch for a portrait, so overcome by the tragedy of the situation that he could hardly see through his tears to complete his work. She also wrote a final letter, saying: 'I have hated only one person in my life and I have proved the strength of my hatred.'

As she made ready for execution her beautiful hair was cut off and she gave a lock to Hauer, who burst into tears as he took her last gift. She put on the simple red shift that all condemned murderers had to wear and calmly mounted the cart that was to take her through the streets to the Palace de la Revolution.

During the journey a thunderstorm broke, with great rolls of thunder and flashes of lightning adding a special drama to the scene. Rain poured down, plastering her shift to her voluptuous body, but she stood with her head held high, showing no sign of fear. As she mounted the scaffold, some members of the crowd cheered her and one young man even threw a rose at her feet.

When the guillotine had done its work the executioner's assistant held up the head for all to see, punching it gleefully, but the crowd booed and hissed so angrily that he quickly dropped it into the basket. The romantic martyrdom of Charlotte Corday was already under way.

The Price Sisters

In 1973, after the British government had decided to hold a referendum in Northern Ireland on the future of the Province, the IRA launched a bombing campaign on the British mainland. On 8 March bombs exploded outside the Central Criminal Court at the Old Bailey and the army recruiting office in Whitehall. One man was killed in the blast and over 200 people were injured. Several other bombs were traced and defused after an anonymous phone call gave clues to their locations.

The bombers, a group of IRA stalwarts led by two sisters, Dolours and Marian Price, were arrested as they tried to board a plane to Dublin. Their plan had been simple: they had driven several stolen cars loaded with explosives to London, parked them outside pre-arranged targets and primed the bombs. Their task completed by 8.30 am, they immediately caught the coach to Heathrow airport in the hope of being on their way back to Ireland before the security authorities were alerted.

The terrorists were unaware that warnings from Belfast had alerted Scotland Yard to a possible outbreak of bombings and security at airports had already been stepped up. Policemen on the beat were also extra-vigilant and at 9 am two officers stopped to check a car parked in Victoria because the numberplate did not match the year of manufacture. A bomb was found under the back seat, its clock already ticking, and explosives experts were called to defuse it. The word went out immediately to all airports and Special Branch detectives began checking every passenger on a domestic flight. The nine suspects were held because they had given false names and addresses and had consecutively numbered tickets showing that, though they denied any connection with one another, all the tickets had been bought at the same time.

From the beginning Dolours Price, an intelligent and articulate 22-year-old, stood out as the leader of the group. Her 19-year-old sister Marian was second in command. Both girls were students at one of Belfast's leading teacher training colleges; Marian was in her first year and Dolours was completing her Bachelor of Education thesis. They had been steeped in the Republican cause since childhood, for their father had spent 10 years in internment for his IRA activities, and by 1972 Dolours was already a brigade courier. She was thought to have had a hand in planning the Bloody Friday bombings when 20 devices exploded in Belfast and she had spent the previous summer in Italy, whipping up support for the IRA at meetings organized by Marxist groups. Marian was just as committed to the cause and had a reputation as a first-rate marksman, earning her the nickname of the 'Armalite Widow.'

At the trial, when Dolours and Marian were accused along with seven other defendants, counsel for the sisters argued that they were the type of people to engage in reasoned arguments to promote their cause, rather than resorting to bombings. He accused the police of planting incriminating evidence: a strip of Green Shield stamps obtained from a garage in Liverpool on the night before the bombings, a list of names and initials, including those of the other defendants, and a J-cloth identical to one found in the timing mechanism of a bomb defused outside New Scotland Yard. The prosecution firmly denied any such interference with the course of justice and said that the defendants were all officers or volunteers in one of the Provisional IRA's three Belfast battalions.

The trial lasted for 44 days and when the jury was ready to return a verdict the already stringent security precautions in the court were stepped up even further. Everyone entering was searched and once the court was in session the doors were locked. The defendants were surrounded by police officers and four rows of plain-clothes detectives sat behind the dock.

One of the defendants, the only one to deny on oath being a member of the IRA, was found not guilty and the rest expressed their feelings by humming the dead march from *Saul* in unison. The other eight were found guilty, with the Price sisters and another student teacher, Hugh McFeeney, held to be the ringleaders.

The judge, preparing to pronounce sentence on the two women, began by calling their actions evil and wicked, whereupon Dolours Price called out: 'May we be removed from the dock? We don't want to listen to a lecture.' The judge told her to stay where she was and sentenced her to life imprisonment, a sentence greeted by shouts of 'Up the Provos' and clenched fist salutes from her supporters in the gallery. Dolours simply remarked: 'That's a death sentence.'

When Marian was sentenced she announced: 'I stand before you as a volunteer of the IRA. I consider myself a prisoner of war. From this moment on I shall be on hunger strike until I am sent home to Ireland.'

Even in the face of the verdict the Price sisters remained as cheerful as they had been throughout the trial and their months on remand. Their supporters explained that they had no reason to be unhappy: they had made history for their cause and they had done right by their lights. Moreover, they did not believe they would be in prison for long; either their friends would find a way to free them or they would be granted an amnesty.

The Price sisters made good their threat to stage a hunger strike in support of their right to serve their sentences in Ireland and in March 1975 they were transferred to Armagh prison. After seven years Marian was freed on licence, as she was suffering from physical and psychological illness which could be life-threatening if she remained in prison. Dolours has also been released on licence.

Emma LeDoux

SOMETHING in the baggage room at the Southern Pacific railway station was smelling very unpleasant. The baggage handler, Mr Vizelich, thought he recognized the smell; he had handled plenty of coffins over the years and it was only too familiar. When he traced the offensive odour to an unlabelled trunk which had arrived at the station while he was off duty, he called the police. The trunk was broken open to reveal the body of a stocky man with a luxuriant black moustache.

The police soon discovered that the trunk had been delivered to the station at Stockton, 112km (70 miles) from San Francisco, by expressman Charles Barry on 24 March 1906. He had first collected it from Rosenbaum's store for an attractive young woman and had taken it to the California Rooming House, where the woman, saying she planned to pack a set of dishes, asked him to return for the trunk later in the day and take it to the railway station. She warned that it was likely to be very heavy so he took along an assistant and together they manhandled it out of the building, remarking that it was much heavier at one end than the other. Mr Barry could give a good description of the woman, as could the shop assistant who had sold her the trunk for $10 – and the assistant who sold her a length of stout rope, saying 'Look out now – don't hang yourself with it!' The landlady at the California Rooming House identified the mystery woman as Mrs Albert McVicar. She had checked in with her husband, whose description matched that of the dead body in the trunk.

The woman was quickly traced to a hotel at Antioch, a small town a couple of stops down the line towards San Francisco, where she was registered as Mrs Jones. When the police arrived she admitted that her real name was not Jones or McVicar, but Emma LeDoux. On the journey back to Stockton she told a strange story: at one time she had been married to McVicar but she had left him and married a farmer called LeDoux over a year before. She admitted that she had been with McVicar at the rooming house but said that he had been killed by a man called Joe Healy, a San Francisco plumber, who had given him carbolic acid. It was Healy who had sent her out to buy the trunk and, when it arrived, he had forced her to help pack the body inside.

When Emma was formally taken into custody the straw suitcase she carried with her was opened and found to contain, besides some men's clothing and a picture of Emma with McVicar, a bottle of morphine pills, a half-full bottle of cyanide of potassium, a bottle of carbolic acid and a bottle of chloral hydrate. An autopsy found no trace of carbolic acid in McVicar's body, but he had swallowed a large quantity of morphine and also chloral hydrate. In the opinion of the autopsy surgeon he had been alive, though thoroughly drugged, when he was put into the trunk. Though there were bruises and abrasions on his head, these were superficial and had probably been caused when he was rammed into the trunk. The cause of death had been asphyxiation. The inquest verdict was that McVicar had been murdered, that Emma LeDoux was probably responsible and that 'as far as we have been able to determine, she was unaided'.

Even when she was committed for trial, Emma's cheerful demeanour remained unaffected. 'The woman is beyond me,' said the District Attorney. 'I never saw an accused person more cool and unconcerned. She seems to take everything as a matter of course, and is as much interested in what goes on about her as though she were on a pleasure trip or sightseeing.'

At her trial on 16 April 1906, Emma appeared soberly dressed in a white shirtwaist with black tie and skirt and a large black hat with a veil. However, the account that emerged of her past was anything but sober. Even as a teenager, she had had a bad reputation for changing her men frequently. At 17 she had married for the first time, but her husband had died some time afterwards. She married again, this time to a miner called Williams who suffered from tuberculosis. He too died, leaving Emma his insurance money, which she squandered on a spree with McVicar, whom she married and divorced – though the details of her divorce were always hazy and the court was left with a strong impression that it had never taken place.

A year ago she had married LeDoux, a respectable farmer who seemed to allow her total freedom. When he was first questioned about Emma's whereabouts he said that she was somewhere in San Francisco, but could not produce an address. She often went away, he said, but she would be back in her own good time. Emma's life was now comfortable and enjoyable, so when McVicar appeared again and threatened her new-found security she decided to kill him. McVicar had been working as a lumberman and had left his job a fortnight before his death; his boss said that he was 'lured away' by Emma LeDoux, a woman known to have low moral standards.

Emma claimed that Joe Healy had threatened her with a revolver and a knife 'sharpened on both sides' to force her to help dispose of the body. He planned, she said, to send the trunk to San Francisco and store it for a year. When Joe Healy took the stand, he admitted that he had visited Emma in San Francisco but he had an unshakeable alibi for the night of the murder. He had known Emma for some time and when they were talking of marriage he had given her a diamond ring. Then he had discovered that she was already married and had come poste-haste to reclaim his ring.

Emma was found guilty and sentenced to hang on 19 October, but her lawyers appealed and she was granted a new trial on a technicality. This was set for 25 January 1907 but Emma claimed that her health had been badly damaged and she could not stand the strain of a new trial, so she was forced to plead guilty. The defence pleaded for leniency and Emma was sentenced to life imprisonment.

Emma was paroled after serving 10 years of her sentence but she found it impossible to keep out of trouble. After a few months her parole was revoked on the grounds that she had been drinking (these were the days of Prohibition) and seducing young men and she was returned to San Quentin. Four years later she was paroled again and this time she married and set up a matrimonial agency. Even then, Emma failed to achieve respectability. She was charged with passing dud cheques and her parole was revoked for a second time. She died in Tehachapi prison in 1941.

The Sadistic Nazis

THE NAZI creed, as propagated by Hitler and his followers, promoted the belief that certain races and groups of people were inferior beings who could be persecuted and killed by members of the master race, and gave many sadistic monsters an outlet for their own perverted sexual tastes in torturing and killing their helpless prisoners. Most were men, but among them were a handful of loathsome women who found no difficulty in equalling the cruelty of their male colleagues. Among them were the 'beast of Belsen', Irma Grese, and the 'witch of Buchenwald', Ilse Koch.

Irma Grese, born in 1923, came from a family with little sympathy for Hitler's ideals, but she was subjected to Nazi brainwashing in her formative years. Her father opposed her participation in the Hitler Youth and gave her a severe beating when he found that she had volunteered for work in the concentration camps but he had no influence over the determined young woman. She learned her trade at Ravensbruck, then in 1943 she was moved to Auschwitz and later to Belsen. In these camps, whose names are synonymous with horror, she was free to indulge every sadistic whim. She would patrol the camp with two vicious German shepherd dogs, who were set on inmates at the slightest excuse. Once the dogs had brought them down, she would kick them to death with her heavy boots. She always carried a whip and delighted in slashing the breasts of large-bosomed women, then watched with pleasure while the camp doctor sewed up the cuts without anaesthetic.

When she was in charge of the work detail she would deliberately leave a tool just outside the barbed wire enclosure and order one of the Jewish women prisoners to fetch it, laughing when the woman was mown down by machine-gun fire from one of the watchtowers. When she was rounding up prisoners to be sent to the gas chambers she would taunt them, pretending to select those whose names were not on the list, then telling others that they had a few weeks of life left, only to change her mind at the last moment and send them off to their deaths. Witnesses at her trial had seen her shoot those who tried to hide when their time came to join the gas chamber lines with her pistol, though she claimed that the weapon was only for show and was never loaded.

At the end of the war her main defence to the charges against her was that it was Himmler, who had set up the camps, who was responsible for all that went on in them and that anything she did was to maintain discipline when she was responsible for several thousand women at a time.

Ilse Koch was more robust in her own defence: her husband might have been commandant of Buchenwald, she said, but she was nothing more than a wife and mother. She had seen no atrocities in the camp and she had certainly never committed any: witnesses who told a different story were enemy stooges, engaged to play a part. She even pretended to have a fit in the witness box, to convince the court that she was a sick woman, not fully responsible for her actions.

Ilse Koch may have looked the part of a typical German wife – plump, blonde and blue-eyed, with a pleasant smile – but, not content with holding sex orgies with the young SS officers of the camp, she had taken advantage of her position to satisfy her sadistic urges. One of her 'games' was to sunbathe naked in full view of the male inmates, then if any of them dared to look at her she had them beaten to death. She thought up the novel idea of having the skin of dead prisoners made into gloves and lampshades for her home. Her mantelpiece was also decorated by the shrunken heads of camp inmates.

When the guards indulged in a killing spree, setting a crowd of prisoners loose in the compound and taking pot shots at them as they ran desperately to and fro, Ilse took part gleefully, managing to shoot several men herself. At her eventual trial she was charged with murdering 45 people as well as being an accessory to scores of other killings, but unlike Irma Grese she was spared the noose and died in prison in 1971.

Elizabeth Brownrigg

THE BRUTISH women of the concentration camps may have refined the art of cruelty but they were not the first to find that having complete power over a helpless human being brought out all their sadistic urges. In the 18th century young apprentices were delivered into the hands of a master and mistress who would have control over their lives from then onwards, with no outside supervision or inspection; consequently, they were at the mercy of any man or woman with a twisted personality.

Elizabeth Brownrigg and her husband James were both upstanding members of the community, with a substantial house in the City of London and a second home in Islington, used as a weekend retreat. James was a prosperous plumber and Elizabeth was a midwife who had been appointed by the parish of St Dunstan's to look after the female inmates of the workhouse. More fortunate women were looked after in her own home and she had a high reputation for kindly care of both mothers and infants.

In 1765, needing help with the private cases she took into her home, Elizabeth took her first apprentice, 14-year-old Mary Mitchell, a child from the workhouse. Shortly afterwards she took another teen-ager, Mary Jones, from the Foundling Hospital. For each child she paid £5 and in return received the services of an unpaid servant who would, in theory, be taught a trade. Elizabeth's idea of training her apprentices was to work them for 18 hours a day, dress them in rags and feed them on scraps, and beat them regularly until the blood ran down their backs.

Mary Jones tried to escape from her miserable existence but was caught and brought back. As a punishment she was stripped naked and laid across two chairs in the kitchen then viciously whipped by Elizabeth, who only gave up when she was faint from exhaustion. After a whipping, Elizabeth would revive the child by dipping her head in a pail of water and, finding that Mary had a special fear of drowning, she devised a new game, shared by her husband and son, whereby one of them would hold the girl up by her ankles with her head in the bucket of water while she fought for breath.

In spite of her fear of the Brownriggs, Mary Jones made a second bid for freedom and this time she succeeded in stealing out of the house, wandering the streets for hours until she found her way to the Foundling Hospital. Here she poured out her story and showed the terrible wounds she had received from the savage beatings. The hospital authorities wrote to the Brownriggs, threatening prosecution unless they received an explanation and financial compensation for the treatment handed out to Mary Jones. The Brownriggs ignored the letter, probably confident that the hospital authorities would not want to court a scandal by making the matter public, and no action was taken, beyond the termination of the apprenticeship.

Meanwhile, Elizabeth had applied to a workhouse in a different parish for another apprentice and 14-year-old Mary Clifford joined the Brownrigg household. Poor Mary Clifford was a dim girl with a slight physical infirmity and instead of giving her a bed, Elizabeth made her sleep on a mat in the coal-hole with a collar and chain round her neck so that she would have no chance of escaping like her predecessor. Throughout the day she was repeatedly punched, kicked and beaten about the shoulders with a cane. Elizabeth had found a splendid new way of whipping her apprentices: she tied their hands with cord which was strung over a waterpipe that ran across the kitchen ceiling, then as they dangled there naked, their feet swinging in mid-air, she would horsewhip them for the entertainment of Brownrigg father and son. When the waterpipe broke through over-use, James fixed a stout hook in the ceiling so that the whippings could continue.

A Frenchwoman who was spending her confinement in the house

took pity on the ill-treated Mary Clifford, who sobbed out her story and begged her for help. But her intervention, when she reproved Elizabeth for her brutality, only made matters worse: Elizabeth held Mary down while she slashed her tongue with scissors, threatening to cut it out if she told tales again.

One morning in July 1767, an aunt of Mary Clifford had called to see her niece, having been given the address by the parish. Elizabeth denied that any apprentices lived in the house and shut the door in her face. However, when the aunt made enquiries among the neighbours, a Mrs Deacon told her that the Brownriggs did have young apprentices and that she had been worried about them for some time. At weekends, when the Brownriggs went to Islington, the girls were left behind in the cellar and she had heard them crying. When the family was in residence she had often heard the children screaming in pain. A servant girl was set to watch for the girls through a skylight in the Brownrigg house and she saw the naked, bleeding body of Mary Clifford, but she was unable to rouse her.

At last the parish officials were forced to take notice and Mr Grundy, an overseer of the parish, arrived at the Brownrigg door with the police, demanding to see the girls. They found James Brownrigg alone in the house and at first he maintained that they had only one apprentice, Mary Mitchell. When the girl was brought forward, the rags of her dress were stuck fast to her shoulders by dried blood; they later had to be soaked from her body in hospital. A full-scale search of the house followed and Mary Clifford was found hidden in a cupboard, scarcely conscious, her body covered with cuts, bruises and festering sores. She died of her injuries in St Bartholomew's Hospital a few days later.

James Brownrigg was taken into custody, protesting all the time that he had never ill-treated the girls, it was all his wife's doing. Elizabeth and her son John had taken all the money they could find and fled, disguising themselves in second-hand clothes. After moving lodgings several times, they registered under assumed names at an inn in

Elizabeth Brownrigg awaiting trial

Wandsworth. Public feeling against Elizabeth was running high and newspapers carried her description prominently: a woman of medium size, around 50 years old, with a swarthy complexion and 'remarkably smooth of speech'. Her landlord, who had noticed that his new guests had not left their room and were exceptionally nervous, reported them to the police and both were arrested. At the subsequent trial, where Mary Mitchell gave evidence, James and his son John escaped with a mere six months in prison but the loathsome Elizabeth was sentenced to death.

Vast crowds assembled to see her executed and the hangman did the job as quickly as possible, afraid that the angry mob might snatch the prisoner and tear her limb from limb. Her corpse was taken to the Surgeon's Hall in the Old Bailey, where the bodies of all murderers were dissected at that time. Afterwards her skeleton was displayed for all to see.

Genene Jones

IN 1981 the paediatric unit of Bexar Hospital in San Antonio, Texas, was plagued with emergencies: unexpected cardiac arrests and sudden unexplained bleeding episodes. Some of the babies lived but far too many died and a number of investigations were mounted before it was discovered that the bleeding episodes were caused by someone adding an anti-coagulant to the intravenous drip bottles. Everything pointed to the guilt of a particular nurse, Genene Jones. Her shift, lasting from 3 to 11 pm, had become known as the 'death shift', as that was when all the emergencies had occurred. It was noticeable that when she had a day off all remained quiet and when she was away for a fortnight no babies died.

Genene Jones was a licensed vocational nurse, keen and energetic, quick to make decisions and act on them. She had been dismissed from her first job after complaints about her bossy ways and joined the staff at the Bexar Hospital at a time when there was an acute shortage of nurses, so that her past record was overlooked. She often ignored instructions, thinking that she knew better than the doctors, and had complete faith in her own instincts. Some of the senior staff rated her highly, admiring her confidence and initiative; others thought that she was a menace. No one denied that she was devoted to her small patients. She always made time to sit with them and answer all their parents' questions. When a baby died she would cradle the little body against her, crying and talking to the dead infant.

Even after the investigation identified Genene as the likely culprit the hospital authorities hesitated to make any accusations for fear of lawsuits, so instead they decided to replace all the licensed vocational nurses on the paediatric unit with registered nurses and dispose of the problem that way. Genene Jones went on her way with a reference saying that she was 'loyal, dependable, and trustworthy' and had been an asset to the hospital.

Next, Genene went to work at a newly opened clinic in Kerrville, run by Dr Kathleen Holland, and as soon as she arrived, the dramas began. One child, brought in because she had a cold and left with Genene for a few minutes while her parents completed the paperwork, went into cardiac arrest and needed resuscitation. A seven-year-old boy with a heart defect went into seizures and was rushed to hospital in San Antonio. On the way a paramedic saw Genene inject something into the child's intravenous line and a few minutes later he stopped breathing and had to be resuscitated. Genene maintained that the child was already having breathing troubles and had turned blue before she injected a drug to help open the airways. A five-month-old baby went into cardiac arrest after Genene had taken blood samples for tests.

In September 1982 17-month-old Chelsea McClellan was brought to Dr Holland's clinic for routine immunizations. After the first injection her breathing was irregular, but Genene reassured her mother that this was a normal reaction. The nurse went ahead with the second injection, whereupon the baby went into seizures and stopped breathing. Chelsea was revived and seemed to have recovered, but on the way to hospital in the ambulance with Genene she arrested again and was dead on arrival. Genene insisted on carrying the body all the way to the hospital mortuary herself, tears streaming down her face.

At Kerrville hospital there was a good deal of gossip about the number of babies coming from Dr Holland's clinic, all admitted as emergencies. Most of them seemed surprisingly well after their initial treatment and there seemed no good reason for their sudden collapse. The staff resented the high drama that Genene Jones always managed to create when she arrived with a patient, issuing orders and behaving as though she was running the hospital. One of the doctors shared his worries with a colleague who had recently worked in the paediatric unit in San Antonio. When the name of Genene Jones was mentioned he was told: 'You've got a baby-killer on your hands.'

When questions were asked, Dr Holland began her own investigation. She found discrepancies in the records of drugs she had ordered and discovered that bottles of succinylcholine – a drug which could produce symptoms similar to seizures, often called the 'doctor's poison' because its presence in the body is so difficult to detect – had been tampered with. Moreover, Genene's notes on her young patients often differed from Dr Holland's recollection of the cases.

Genene Jones was sacked, while newspapers trumpeted news of 'tot deaths probe' and talked of enquiries into 47 deaths. On 25 May 1983 she was arrested and charged with murder. She failed a lie detector test but a psychiatrist who examined her at the request of defence counsel decided that she was not suffering from any major psychiatric disorder and that she was convinced of her own innocence. Her letter to Dr Holland substantiated this view: 'I have never hurt a child or given a child anything that might hurt them. But if, as low man, I take the fall, I still don't think I can hate you. . . . But believe me, I won't go down alone.'

At the trial Dr Holland testified that pharmacy invoices at the clinic showed that unauthorized drugs had been ordered by Genene and that a bottle of succinylcholine lost by Genene and then found again had needle holes in the top. When she examined the contents, she found that the drug had been replaced by salt water. Though she had diagnosed seizures in Chelsea McClellan's case, she now thought that the baby's symptoms might have been the result of the drug.

Genene's attorneys, who did not call her to the stand, maintained that Dr Holland was responsible, suggesting that as she was new to working in a clinic she could have overreacted and prescribed unnecessary treatment for her young patients, then when things went wrong tried to put the blame on her nurse. Genene Jones, they insisted, was simply a scapegoat, 'victimized because she was aggressive and bossy and stepped on people's toes'.

The jury did not accept this version of events and she was sentenced to 99 years' imprisonment. Later she faced a second trial, this time for injuring a child by administering an anti-coagulant drug, and was sentenced to 66 years to run concurrently. Genene's motive was one of the strangest of reasons for murder: she seemed to live on the rush of excitement she got from dealing with emergencies, so she had to manufacture more and more of them. Several witnesses remembered how she looked when a child went into cardiac arrest: her white face, forehead beaded with sweat, her eyes glittering. The more dramatic the situation, with nurse Genene as the centre of attention, the more important and powerful she could feel.

Anna Zimmermann

OF ALL the motives for murder, the desire to cut the household shopping bills must surely be the most bizarre. Yet in 1984 Anna Zimmermann, a 26-year-old mother of two from Münchengladbach, West Germany, admitted to murdering her friend Josef Wirtz and slicing up his flesh to fill her freezer. By the time of her capture she had become expert at preparing goulash, stew and meat pies and serving rare steaks and well-cooked chops, all made from human flesh.

The crime was first uncovered when police were called to a gruesome discovery in a park in the northern part of the town. A girl bending down to look at the summer flowers had found herself face to face with a rotting human head. It had apparently spilled out of an open black plastic rubbish bag and there were two other bags, still safely tied up. When the contents were examined, they turned out to be the remains of a man in his early thirties with thick black hair and moustache. His flesh had been sliced from his bones with a sharp knife and some of the bones had been carved into pieces, probably by a power saw, so that the marrow could be extracted.

The mutilated body was identified as that of a 34-year-old barber, Josef Wirtz, who had been reported missing a month earlier. He had disappeared one weekend, leaving his employer without a word of explanation and his landlord with a month's rent owing. Everyone was puzzled that he had left behind all his clothes, a cupboard stocked with food and his razor and toothbrush in the bathroom, but there was no reason to suspect foul play and he had no relatives to harass the police so enquiries were soon dropped. Now the police examined Wirtz's possessions, still stored in the basement of his apartment house. It became obvious that he was a horror film addict and apparently hired films from a nearby video shop.

A detailed hunt began, which included tracing everyone who had taken horror films from the shop over the weekend of Wirtz's disappearance. One of the scores of hirers on the list was Anna Zimmermann, who was separated from her husband and lived with her two children, aged six and four. The police visit might have been purely routine if they had not noticed the deep bloodstains on the wooden kitchen table. This led to a search of the apartment, during which they found a stack of boxes filled with what looked horribly like human flesh in the freezer.

When Anna's estranged husband Wilhelm was questioned, he confirmed that Anna had known Josef Wirtz for over two years. They were both devotees of horror films and their close friendship had been one of the reasons why Wilhelm had left. He was still on reasonably good terms with his wife and on the weekend that Wirtz disappeared he had lent her a power saw for some jobs she needed to do around the apartment.

At last Anna confessed that while Wirtz was enjoying one of their usual horror film sessions she had given him brandy laced with sleeping pills. Before he passed out she helped him into the bathroom, where she held his head underwater in the bath until he drowned. The films she was in the habit of watching had taught her how to slice up a body and she had filled the freezer boxes in the kitchen while her children slept peacefully in the next room. Meat, she explained, was beyond her budget and this would ensure a long-term supply. She had packed the useless remains into sacks and taken them to the park late at night, in her four-year-old's pushchair.

Anna was charged with murder and confined to a mental hospital, where doctors would decide whether or not she would ever be able to stand trial.

Jean Harris

JEAN HARRIS was known as a refined and dignified woman, highly educated and the headmistress of a well-known girls' school in Virginia, USA, where she was a strict disciplinarian who laid so much emphasis on integrity that her pupils nicknamed her 'integrity Jean'. When she was tried for murder, her defence counsel described her as 'a very fine lady, of the kind you don't see much any more'. Yet she had another side – the jealous mistress about to be pushed aside, who pumped four bullets into her lover of 14 years.

Her lover was the world-famous Dr Herman Tarnower, known as 'Hi', the originator of the Scarsdale diet, which was followed by millions. The doctor, who lived in a fashionable section of New York's Westchester suburb, had helped to found the highly successful Scarsdale Medical Center and in 1979 had published an expanded version of the diet he had long recommended to his overweight patients under the title *The Complete Scarsdale Medical Diet*. The book quickly became a best-seller.

At 69, the doctor was physically active and enjoyed a good life: golfing, fishing, shooting, exotic foreign travel and, above all, women. He had first met Jean Harris in 1966 and the following year gave her a large diamond ring and asked her to marry him. Later, when she asked about setting a date, he told her that he could not go through with it. By then she was so much in love with him that all she cared about was continuing the affair, and the idea of marriage was allowed to lapse. Over the years she was aware that he had casual affairs with other women but she turned a blind eye, confident that they were unimportant. She was content to be the hostess at his intimate dinner parties and his companion on foreign trips. She had helped him with his book and was enjoying her share of his new celebrity status.

Then Lynne Tryforos, the doctor's nurse-secretary at the clinic, came on the scene and things began to change. It became obvious that the doctor was planning to trade in his long-standing mistress for a newer model. He began spending more and more time with Lynne, who was 19 years younger than Jean, and in the year before the killing he took two winter holidays: one at Palm Beach with Jean, the other in Jamaica with Lynne. New Year saw him in Florida with the head-mistress, but the nurse made her feelings clear by putting an advert in the *New York Times* which read: 'Happy New Year, Hi T. Love always, Lynne.'

Jean's love for the doctor was as strong as ever but she feared that she was about to be jilted. An important dinner was to be held at the Westchester Heart Association on 19 April 1980 to honour Dr Herman Tarnower and Jean assumed that she would accompany him – only to find that he was proposing to take Lynne. This came at a time when Jean was facing problems at school. A consultant hired to report on the school had recommended that she should be dismissed and though a second study had supported her it was made clear to her that she was on probation.

The basic facts of what happened on 10 March 1980 were never in dispute. On that stormy evening Jean Harris drove from Virginia to New York, a five-hour journey, arriving at the doctor's home at around 11 pm. She had with her a .32 calibre revolver, bought 18 months earlier, with five of its six chambers loaded and she carried another five rounds. She let herself into the house and went to the doctor's bedroom, where he was already asleep. During the scene that followed several shots were fired and the doctor received four bullet wounds from which he died within the hour.

Suzanne van der Vreken, the doctor's cook, was watching television when she heard the buzzer from his room. When she picked up the intercom phone she could hear shouting and banging, then Jean

Harris's recognizable voice, then a gun shot. Suzanne woke her husband and called the police. Upstairs she found the doctor slumped on the bedroom floor, his pyjamas drenched in blood and his pulse scarcely detectable. Meanwhile Jean had left the house, driving off without attempting to summon help, but when she saw the police car approaching she did a U-turn in the road and returned to the house. She told the police detective that she had driven to the doctor's home with the intention of killing herself. There had been a struggle and the gun had gone off several times, but she did not know who had control of the gun at the time. 'I've been through so much hell with him,' she said. 'I loved him very much, he slept with every woman he could and I had had it.'

At her trial for murder Jean, now 57, pleaded not guilty and the defence counsel pointed out that they were not asking for sympathy because of the defendant's age or sex and that they were not claiming mitigation on the grounds of diminished responsibility. Their contention was that she had intended to shoot herself and that the doctor had died as the result of a 'tragic accident'. There were basic problems with this line of defence: a woman intent on killing herself might well carry a loaded gun but why would she take along extra rounds of ammunition? It was also difficult to explain why the doctor sustained four bullet wounds while the would-be suicide escaped without a single wound.

Complex ballistics evidence referred to ricochet points and bullet trajectories and experts contradicted one another over whether or not the wounds were consistent with Jean Harris's account of a struggle between herself and the doctor. Dr Louis Roh, Deputy Medical Examiner for Westchester County, even produced a life-size plaster model of a man to illustrate where the bullets entered the body.

The case would obviously turn on the jury's opinion of Jean Harris when she gave evidence. The defence portrayed her as a victim: exhausted, lonely, frail, vulnerable. Unfortunately for this line of defence, the defendant came over as a woman with a strong personality and a quick mind. She frequently passed notes of instruction to her counsel, spoke contemptuously to the prosecutor and even once appealed angrily to the judge, who had to remind her that she had a lawyer to make objections on her behalf. It was difficult to picture this woman as a victim.

All the same, the defence mustered a good deal of evidence to show that Jean had been in a suicidal state before the killing. She had been taking antidepressants prescribed by the doctor and shortly before the killing she had made her will and written farewell notes to friends and colleagues. One read 'I wish to be immediately cremated and thrown away', while another said 'There are so many enemies and so few friends . . . I was a person and no one ever knew.' Asked in court what she had meant by this, she said, 'I wasn't sure who I was and it didn't seem to matter. I was a person sitting in an empty chair . . . I can't describe it any more.'

Jean said that she had chosen the spot where she planned to kill herself, near Herman Tarnower's pond, where the daffodils were thick in the spring. She had rung the doctor on the afternoon of 10 March, telling him that she wanted to come to talk to him for a few minutes. She had intended to see him one last time without telling him her intentions. When she arrived, she found the house in darkness and the doctor asleep. When she woke him and tried to talk to him he told her, 'I'm not going to talk to anybody in the middle of the night.' Jean went into the bathroom where she found a satin negligée belonging to Lynne. She threw it on the floor and, angry and frustrated, she then hurled a box of curlers at the window, breaking it. The doctor hit her across the face. She threw another box and he hit her a second time.

She sat on the edge of the spare bed and lifted her face to him, saying, 'Hit me again, Hi. Make it hard enough to kill.' When he walked away without touching her, she took her gun from her handbag and put it to her head, saying, 'Never mind, I'll do it myself.' The doctor grabbed for the gun and it went off, putting a bullet through his hand. 'Jesus Christ, look what you did,' he exclaimed. As he made for the bathroom, she went down on her knees to retrieve the gun. The doctor lunged across the bed and seized the gun in his right hand, pressing the buzzer with the left. In the struggle that followed she had felt what she thought was the muzzle of the gun pressing into her stomach and had pulled the trigger, but it was the doctor who fell back. Another bullet had ricocheted into the cupboard but she did not remember any more shots. She had put the gun to her head again 'and I shot and I shot and I shot' but it just went on clicking. Afterwards she had banged the gun on the edge of the bath until it broke. The doctor was still conscious and she did not realize that he was dying when, discovering that the bedroom phone seemed to be broken, she ran out to get help. She was driving to find a phone box when she saw the police car and turned back. When her defence counsel asked if she had meant the doctor harm she said, 'Never in 14 years and certainly not that night.'

Perhaps the jury might have accepted the picture of a dignified and sensitive woman, so distressed by the doctor's callous behaviour that life no longer seemed worth living, if it had not been for one damning piece of evidence which came to be known as the 'Scarsdale letter', written on the morning of the fateful day. Jean had sent it to the doctor by registered post and it had been recovered from the mail. It was an agonized shriek of a letter, full of anger and violent emotion, railing against the wrongs she had suffered. She wrote 'distraught' because he proposed taking Lynne to the dinner on 19 April. She was determined to be there 'even if the slut comes – indeed, I don't care if she pops naked out of a cake with her tits frosted with chocolate'. Hatred of her rival raged through the letter as she accused Lynne – 'your psychotic whore' – of ripping up her clothes, stealing her jewellery and making obscene phone calls. She had received a copy of the doctor's will with Lynne's name substituted for hers. She had grown poor loving him, she said, while 'a self-serving, ignorant slut has grown very rich'.

The letter, with its ugly language, undermined the 'fine lady' image presented by the defence. It also revealed the jealousy and rage she

A policeman reacts to the pushing and shoving as Jean Harris arrives at court shortly before the jury delivers its murder verdict

was feeling. In cross-examination she had answered 'No' when the prosecution asked if she had ever felt publicly humiliated by the fact that the doctor was seeing Lynne Tryforos in public. Yet, in the letter, she had written: 'I have been publicly humiliated again and again.'

The prosecution described a phone call between the victim and the defendant on the morning of the killing. 'Goddammit, Jean, stop bothering me,' he had said. This, they alleged, was the trigger that had caused Jean to take her revolver and the extra ammunition and head for the doctor's home. She may well have planned to kill herself but she planned to kill the doctor first.

The jury agreed and found her guilty, a verdict carrying a mandatory sentence of 15 years to life. In a final flash of spirit, Jean Harris told the judge: 'I want to say that I did not murder Dr Herman Tarnower, that I loved him very much and did not wish him ill. For you or for Mr Bolen [the prosecutor] to arrange my life so that I will be in a cage for the rest of it . . . is not justice; it is a travesty of justice.'

Mary Pearcey

WHEN A WOMAN'S body was found lying on a pile of rubble in a north London street in 1890, the skull crushed and the head almost severed from the body, rumours said that it was the work of Jack the Ripper, who had left a trail of bloody corpses in the streets of the East End two years earlier. However, police soon linked the body with two other discoveries: a perambulator with bloodstained pillows found a mile or so away and the corpse of an 18-month-old baby, found on waste ground in Finchley. Both mother and baby were the victims of a jealous woman caught in an impossible love triangle from which she could see no other escape.

Frank Hogg, a bearded and jovial furniture remover, had two girl-friends at the same time in his bachelor days. One was the warm-hearted and vivacious Mary Pearcey, but it was the less attractive and meeker Phoebe Styles who became pregnant and expected him to marry her. Frank was tempted to escape the problem by emigrating and leaving both women behind and it was Mary who urged him to stay, even if it meant seeing him married to her rival: 'Do not think of going away, for my heart will break if you do; don't go, dear. I won't ask too much, only to see you for five minutes when you can get away; but if you go quite away, how do you think I can live? I would see you get married 50 times over – yes, I could bear that far better than parting with you for ever . . . you must not go away. My heart throbs with pain only to think about it.' On another occasion she wrote: 'Oh, Frank! I should not like to think I was the cause of all your troubles, and yet you make me think so. What can I do? I love you with all my heart, and I will love her because she will belong to you.'

Frank married Phoebe and the couple lived with Frank's mother and sister Clara in Prince of Wales Drive. Nevertheless, Frank continued his affair with Mary, who lived in nearby Priory Road. He had a key to her house and she would leave a light in the window when it was safe for him to come straight in. Mary continued to write passionate letters, saying that if Frank took away his love 'then I should quite give up in despair, for that is the only thing I care for on earth. I cannot live without it now'. She became a friend of the family, spending a good deal of time with Phoebe and Clara Hogg, and making much of the baby. When Phoebe's second child miscarried it was Mary who nursed her and sat with her.

Frank came to her whenever he could but their time together was brief and Frank spent much of it bemoaning his lot, weeping in frustration and even threatening suicide to escape the misery that his marriage had become. Mary must have become more and more angry and bitter towards the woman who had robbed them of a life of happiness together and, in the end, killing Phoebe seemed the only way out. On 23 October Mary sent Phoebe a note, saying, 'Dearest: come round this afternoon and bring our little darling, don't fail.' That afternoon she drew the blinds at her house, presumably in readiness for the planned murder, but Phoebe failed to respond to the note. The next day Mary wrote again, giving a boy a penny to deliver the message, and this time Phoebe came, pushing the baby in the pram and telling no one where she was going.

Exactly what happened next will never be known, but there was a violent struggle in Mary's kitchen. Phoebe was bludgeoned with a poker and her throat slashed with a carving knife. Neighbours heard screams, breaking crockery and smashing windows, but assumed it was some domestic dispute and decided to mind their own business. Mary may have suffocated the baby as part of her plan to rid Frank of his burdens, or simply to stifle its cries. Another theory is that, when she loaded Phoebe's heavy, ungainly body into the pram, the baby was suffocated accidentally. About two hours after the screams had been heard, when darkness had fallen, Mary was seen pushing a pram, heavily laden and covered with a black shawl, along Priory Road. It was only later that these events assumed a sinister significance.

While Mary was out, Frank called round to find the house empty. He had scribbled a brief note which read, 'Twenty past ten. Cannot stay', and this note went a long way towards convincing the police that Frank was not involved in Mary's murderous plans. When Phoebe did not return home that night Frank and Clara were mystified – but the morning paper carried a report of the discovery of a woman's body, the only pointer to her identity being the initials 'PH' embroidered on her underclothes. Clara asked Mary Pearcey to go to the mortuary with her and it was there that Mary attracted attention, insisting that the dead woman was not Phoebe, crying hysterically and trying to pull Clara away.

Mary was a very inefficient murderer, for when the police searched her house they found plenty of clues: a poker with blood and hairs on it, a bloodstained knife in the dresser drawer and spatters of blood on the kitchen walls and ceiling. While they searched, Mary sat at the piano and played nursery rhymes and when she was asked about the blood she went on playing, chanting 'Killing mice, killing mice' over and over again. Even her underwear still bore the stains of her victim's blood. Though at first she insisted that Phoebe had not visited the house on the day in question, she later admitted that she had arrived with the baby in the pram, but said that she only came to borrow money. 'I did not tell you before because Phoebe asked me not to let anybody know that she had been here,' she explained.

Throughout her trial at the Old Bailey, and even in the face of the 'guilty' verdict, Mary maintained her innocence. She faced her death sentence calmly, though Frank Hogg's refusal to visit her in the condemned cell left her desolate. 'He might have made death easier to bear,' she said sadly. To the prison chaplain who was with her on her way to the scaffold she confided enigmatically that 'the sentence is just; the evidence was false'.

Christiana Edmunds

EVEN unrequited love can become a powerful motive for murder, as the case of Christiana Edmunds proved. Christiana, not content with attempting to poison the woman she saw as her rival, was prepared to poison complete strangers to disguise her crime. She was a spinster of 42, who always claimed to be 10 years younger, living with her widowed mother in Brighton, England. The two women took a walk along the seafront every day and it was there that Christiana first saw Dr Beard, a well-known local physician. Perhaps he cast admiring glances at the tall woman with eye-catching fair hair or perhaps it was all in Christiana's mind, but for her it was love at first sight.

The fact that Dr Beard was a married man with a family did not discourage her for a moment. She began to invent headaches and vague stomach pains as excuses to call in the doctor, who found her reclining gracefully, her hair spread across the pillow. He found little wrong with her, but was quite happy to accept a new patient from a well-off family. In his presence Christiana sparkled and he found her obvious admiration flattering. He introduced her to his wife and Christiana put herself out to be charming, so she was soon accepted as a friend of the family. She began writing long letters to Dr Beard and these were far more than friendly: they began 'Caro Mio', referred dismissively to Mrs Beard as 'La Sposa' and were signed 'Dorothea'. A sensible man would have stamped on the correspondence from the beginning but Dr Beard kept all the letters and even replied to them, in friendly but restrained terms, all without telling his wife.

Mrs Beard, then, had no reason to be wary of Christiana when she made an unexpected visit one afternoon in March 1871, bringing a box of chocolates as a gift. She insisted that Mrs Beard should try one, selecting one she claimed to be her favourite and popping it in her hostess's mouth before she had a chance to refuse. Finding it unpleasantly bitter, Mrs Beard delicately removed most of it into her handkerchief and refused the pressing offer of a second. Later in the afternoon she had sharp stomach pains and accompanying nausea which she traced to the offensive chocolate. Perplexed, she told her husband that she thought she had been poisoned. Dr Beard immediately put two and two together, at last realizing that Christiana's attentions went far beyond harmless flirtation, and he told her in no uncertain terms that he no longer wished to see her, either privately or professionally.

Christiana was beside herself with fury at the disastrous outcome of her plan and she immediately hatched a new one, a way of convincing Dr Beard that his suspicions were unfounded. If he could be made to believe that a maniac poisoner was at work in the town, he would see how wrong he had been to accuse his 'Dorothea'. If other people developed the same symptoms as Mrs Beard after eating chocolates, she reasoned, she herself would be beyond blame.

She stopped a small boy playing in the street and paid him to collect a bag of chocolate creams from the fashionable shop run by John Maynard. When he returned, she said that they were the wrong type of chocolates and sent him back to change them, but the chocolates she sent back had already been laced with strychnine. She did the same thing several times over the next few months, until poisoned chocolates must have been in circulation all over the town. Later, many people complained that the chocolates had made them ill but, surprisingly, no complaints reached the authorities until tragedy struck and four-year-old Sidney Barker died in early June after a kind uncle had given him a bag of chocolates.

Several people came forward to say that they had experienced unpleasant symptoms after buying sweets from the same shop. One of them was Christiana Edmunds, who reported that she had noticed a metallic flavour in chocolates bought from Mr Maynard and that after eating one she had had a violent burning sensation in her throat. The verdict was accidental death but over the next few days the dead boy's father received several anonymous letters, signed only 'seeker after justice' or 'indignant tradesman' – later shown to be in Christiana's handwriting – urging him to start proceedings against Mr Maynard.

To Christiana's disappointment no further action was taken and the whole affair seemed to be dying down. She could no longer target the sweetshop, so she hit on a new scheme and began sending parcels of fruit or cakes to well-known Brighton residents, always with a cryptic note suggesting that they were a surprise gift from a close friend, saying things like: 'You will guess who this is from. I cannot mystify you, I fear.' Though the recipients *were* mystified they would eat the contents of the parcels with pleasure, only to find themselves becoming sick or doubled up with pain. Several children were ill after a stranger gave them chocolates on their way home from school and a shopkeeper who found a bag of sweets on the counter, left by a customer, had tried one and become sick: later, they were all to identify Christiana Edmunds.

It was when Dr Beard at last came forward that attention focused on Christiana. The boys who had run errands to and from the sweetshop were questioned and her writing was analysed. A chemist, Isaac Garrett, remembered selling her strychnine on more than one occasion; she said it was to dispose of some cats that were causing havoc in her garden and had signed the poison register in an assumed name. When she was arrested she protested that it was all a mistake: after all, was she not one of the people who had suffered at the hands of the poisoner?

She was due to be tried at Lewes Assizes but feelings against her ran so high in Sussex that it was obvious that she would not get a fair trial and the case was transferred to the Old Bailey. On 15 January 1872 she was tried for the murder of Sidney Barker. The most surprising witness was her mother, Mrs Ann Edmunds, who told a sad story of insanity on both sides of the family. Her husband had been confined in an asylum for two years before his death in 1847, her father had lost his mind while still a comparatively young man and had died in a fit at the age of 43. Christiana's brother had died after spending six years in an asylum and her sister, who died at the age of 36, had also suffered from mental instability. Mrs Edmunds had always dreaded that Christiana would go the same way. In spite of this testimony, the jury decided that Christiana was in full possession of her faculties, quite sane enough to know what she was doing, and she was sentenced to death. When asked if she had anything to say, Christiana spoke out clearly and rationally. It was because of her treatment by Dr Beard that she found herself in this position, she said: 'I wish the jury had known the intimacy and his affection for me, and the way I have been treated.'

Following the trial the Home Secretary commuted the sentence to life imprisonment and Christiana was confined in Broadmoor, an institution for the criminally insane, where she died in 1907.

Simone Deschamps

It was love that impelled Simone Deschamps to stab and slash to death a helpless woman – albeit a twisted and horrifying form of love. She was a middle-aged woman, not an impressionable young girl, when she met physician Yves Evenou in 1953 but he was to transform her life, filling it with the excitement of sadistic sexual pleasure.

Simone was thin and plain, a dressmaker leading a humdrum existence, but there must have been something about her that attracted the doctor immediately, for they first met when she came to his surgery as a patient. Perhaps he sensed in her a kindred spirit, for though he was a married man and, by all accounts, a devoted father, he needed a woman he could subjugate and use as he pleased. Simone happily became that woman, not protesting when he insulted her in public, treating her like a doormat and calling her lewd names in front of embarrassed waitresses. They indulged in flagellation and in sex orgies involving groups of men Yves recruited on the streets. As their perverted relationship progressed, Yves installed her in an apartment on the ground floor of the Paris block where he lived with his wife and family, so that she would be easily available at all times. Simone was besotted with him, revelling in the unbridled orgies, a willing pupil for the sado-masochistic indulgences he suggested.

When he told her that she was to kill his wife, Simone seems to have accepted it without demur, obediently going out to buy a heavy clasp-knife with a horn handle. On the appointed night, Simone sat alone in her apartment, patiently waiting for her lover's call that would tell her everything was ready. Upstairs, Yves had eaten the meal his wife Marie-Claire had cooked for him then gone out for a stroll while the sleeping pill he had given his wife took effect. Then he summoned Simone.

She put on her fur coat to walk upstairs to the Evenou apartment, for she was naked except for red high-heeled shoes and black gloves. It was what Yves had ordered her to do. When she entered the flat she removed her coat, took the knife from the pocket and advanced on the drugged woman in the bedroom. Yves pulled aside the bedclothes and pointed to his wife's heart. 'Stab, stab!' he commanded.

Simone brought down the knife again and again, stabbing Marie-Claire's defenceless body 11 times. At her trial, the defence was to claim that she was totally bewitched by Yves Evenou so that she was not responsible for her actions, but the prosecution was to point out that after the murder she had washed the blood from her knife and gloves and sewn them neatly into her mattress, indicating that she was fully aware of her guilt and the consequences if she was caught.

When the police came for the lovers each tried to put the blame on the other but Yves, his health destroyed after years of heavy drinking, died in prison while awaiting trial, leaving Simone to answer for both of them. For the most part she listened impassively to the evidence throughout the three-day trial in October 1958, though at one stage she did say that she would always feel remorse for what she had done. Yves had been everything to her: she had loved him, she had obeyed him.

Perhaps it counted in her favour that Yves Evenou was not there to speak for himself for the jury found that, though she was guilty, there were extenuating circumstances, as she had been under the control of a sadistic brute. In spite of her bloody and horrific crime, Simone escaped the guillotine.

Simone Deschamps after her arrest

Denise Labbé

DENISE LABBÉ murdered her two-and-a-half-year-old daughter because her lover ordered it as proof of her love for him. If she killed the child he would marry her; if she refused he would leave her. She called it a 'ritual murder'.

The Labbé family came from a small French village near Rennes. They were always poor and things became even harder after Denise's father committed suicide when she was 14. She worked in a factory to help the family finances but, ambitious and determined to rise in the world, she spent all her spare time studying for a university degree. By the time she was 20 she was working as a secretary with the National Institute of Statistics. By this time she had discovered sex, moving quickly from one affair to another, sometimes taking more than one lover at a time, enjoying the excitement of lies and secret meetings. She had no interest in settling down to marriage and a family, but an affair with a married doctor left an unwelcome legacy: her illegitimate daughter Catherine.

She left Catherine with her mother and sister when she moved to the headquarters of the Institute in Paris but she visited frequently and it was at a May Day dance in Rennes that she met 24-year-old Jacques Algarron, an officer-cadet at the famous Saint-Cyr military school. Jacques had a brilliant but strangely twisted mind. He was a follower of the 19th-century philosopher Nietzsche and thought of himself as a 'superman' in Nietzsche's terms, so that his actions could not be judged by normal moral standards. Women, he considered, existed only to become the slaves of men.

Denise was soon completely under his spell. The perversions he taught her satisfied her strong sexual urges and she took pleasure in

Denise Labbé is taken into custody

grovelling at his feet while he used and humiliated her in every possible way. One of his requirements was that she should bring young men to the flat and seduce them while he watched unseen. Afterwards she would have to spend hours begging his forgiveness for her 'betrayal' on her knees.

Jacques' desire for complete power over his mistress knew no bounds and he required more and more extravagant proofs of her devotion. In the autumn of 1954 the situation came to a head when he demanded that she should kill her daughter. Denise made several abortive attempts at carrying out the murder, but drew back at the last moment. She wrote to Jacques with a keen sense of drama: 'If it were not for our great love, I would give up. Will my love be stronger than fear? Will the devil triumph over God?'

Then, on 8 November, she took the child out into the yard of her mother's house for a wash in the stone basin and pushed her head under water, holding it there, in spite of her struggles, until she drowned. Her mother, returning from the shops, almost caught her in the act but by then all attempts to revive the child failed. Neither her mother nor the police believed Denise's story that Catherine had fallen into the basin by accident and that her mother had passed out from shock, coming round only after her daughter had drowned.

Under prolonged questioning, Denise told the police the whole story and both lovers were arrested. When they appeared before the magistrate Denise was hysterical, accusing Jacques of being a devil who forced her to kill her daughter. He had told her: 'Kill for me. There can be no great love without sacrifice and the price of our love must be your daughter's death.' Jacques was cold and sneering; he had tired of Denise and her 'sacrifice' was a matter of complete indifference to him. 'The woman is mad,' he shrugged.

Denise was tried for murder while her lover was charged with provoking the crime. Her lawyer asked the court to recognize that the young woman had been a puppet in the hands of a cruel and immoral man who had dominated her every action. The jury could hardly avoid

finding her guilty but added that there were extenuating circumstances for the crime, so that instead of the death penalty Denise was
given a sentence of life imprisonment. Jacques Algarron, the architect
of the murder, was sentenced to 20 years' penal servitude.

Chapter Two

POISONOUS WOMEN

Introduction

POISON is one of the oldest weapons in the world and has always been a favourite with women. As the makers of meals and pourers of drinks they have the perfect opportunity to administer the lethal potion and then, when the victim becomes ill, they can turn nurse and top up the dose at will. Poison needs no physical strength, it spatters no blood; it takes only stealthy cunning and steely resolve, yet it is one of the cruellest of weapons, condemning the victim to a lingering and painful death.

Most women poisoners have worked within the family, killing husbands, children and in-laws. Sometimes the whole family went to the grave over 10 years or more – as though once the killer found how easy it was to get away with murder, she could not resist disposing of more and more inconvenient relatives until it was impossible for the authorities to ignore the procession of deaths any longer.

In past centuries, poisoning was easy. Arsenic was easily available and frequently used, and the symptoms were much like those of many other diseases rife at the time. Though the heyday of the poisoner came to an end with advances in medicine and toxicology, that good old stand-by rat poison remained a popular household choice well into modern times.

Amy Archer-Gilligan

In 1907 33-year-old Amy Archer and her husband Jim opened the Archer Home for Elderly People and Chronic Invalids in a small town in Connecticut, USA. Amy had been a nurse at New York's Bellevue Hospital and was a competent professional who saw to it that her patients were fed well and kept comfortable. She was kind and thoughtful, and the home ran like clockwork. Amy was never short of patients but she selected them carefully, always interviewing them and checking on their financial circumstances.

Each new guest was expected to make a substantial initial payment in return for care for life. This meant that the longer the life, the less the profit. Amy made sure there was never any problem on that score, for deaths at the Archer Home were frequent and the neighbours remarked that the hearse always seemed to be at the door. In the first five years there were 48 deaths, about six times higher than the average for the area.

In 1912 Amy took on a handyman, red-haired Michael Gilligan, who was to renovate the house in return for free board and lodging. Jim complained to his drinking companions that Amy was giving Michael far too much attention but Jim died soon afterwards and in 1915 Amy became Mrs Archer-Gilligan. It was soon obvious that her second marriage had not lived up to expectations and within 12 months Michael, too, was dead.

Patients at the home were still dying at such a rate that a reporter on the local newspaper decided to make enquiries. At first he hoped to find that Amy was the beneficiary of insurance policies taken out on her elderly guests but there he drew a blank. Amy did not need to resort to such measures to profit from the deaths of her patients; she

93

was amassing a handsome nestegg from the advance fees they had paid for care they would never need. Undeterred, the reporter toured the pharmacies in neighbouring towns, armed with a picture of Amy, and found that she had made numerous purchases of rat poison, giving a variety of names. He was able to ascertain that several of the more recent purchases had been made shortly before a death occurred at the home.

His discoveries prompted the police to begin their own investigations and the body of the most recent victim, Franklin R. Andrews, was exhumed. Andrews had been taken ill suddenly after supper one evening, complaining of stomach pains, and had died in the night. The doctor had given the cause of death as gastric ulcers, but it was now clear that Mr Andrews had ingested a large dose of arsenic. More bodies were exhumed, including that of Michael Gilligan, with the same result.

In June 1917 Amy Archer-Gilligan was tried at Hartford on an indictment which initially included five charges of murder, though arguments by her counsel eventually reduced the counts to one: the murder of Franklin R. Andrews. In the court, Amy looked the model of sober rectitude: dressed in black and holding a bible, she denied all charges and claimed that her only interests in life were the welfare of her patients and her commitment to the church. None the less the jury found her guilty and she was sentenced to death. Later she won an appeal; the prosecution had been so keen to show that she had murdered a whole string of residents that they had introduced evidence unrelated to the single charge on which she had been indicted.

The second time around Amy pleaded guilty and was sentenced to life imprisonment. Later she was certified insane and transferred from prison to a secure mental institution, where she died in 1928 at the age of 59.

Marie Lafarge

MARIE LAFARGE, sentenced to life imprisonment at the age of 24 for the murder of her husband in 1840, was probably the victim of her own romanticism. In her daydreams she was the adored and petted wife of a rich husband and the centre of an admiring family, presiding over a magnificent French château. The reality was so bitterly different that she could only see one way out of an unbearable situation. A few years earlier a clever defence might have enabled her to hide her crime by exploiting disagreements between doctors over the presence or absence of arsenic in the body, but the new science of toxicology was coming into its own and the foremost chemist in France was able to demonstrate to the satisfaction of the court that Charles Lafarge died from arsenical poisoning.

Though Marie had royal blood her descent was illegitimate, so she was always left on the fringes of aristocratic society; she never had the security and expectations of the well-born girls at the fashionable Paris school she attended. By the time she was 18 both her parents were dead and she went to live with an aunt and uncle who had little genuine affection for her and regarded her as a liability. Though she had various admirers she considered them too far below her socially, so her guardians, anxious to marry her off, applied to the De Foy matrimonial agency. This specialized in advertising for suitable husbands for respectable young ladies with equally respectable dowries, and the candidate who was produced seemed eminently suitable: a wealthy young ironmaster from the south of France with a large and prosperous estate. Though Marie found him boorish and uninteresting at their first meeting she was pressured by her guardians, who insisted of publishing the marriage banns three days later, and tempted by the position she would hold as mistress of the great château of Le Glandier. Charles had brought watercolours showing the house of her dreams, a beautiful converted monastery oozing history and romance from every stone.

If Marie's uncle had taken the trouble to make further enquiries, he would have discovered that Charles was not what he seemed. His iron foundry was bankrupt and he was deeply in debt. He had married before for the sake of a dowry but by the time his first wife died all her money had been used up. As for Le Glandier, Marie arrived to find it filthy, dilapidated and infested with rats, the surrounding estate hopelessly run down. The horrified bride locked herself in her room, issuing a note to Charles, saying that their marriage had been a terrible mistake and begging to be allowed to leave him. Marie gave her imagination full rein and invented a lover who had supposedly followed them and was waiting for her to join him. She then added a paragraph that would be used against her later:

'Get two horses ready. I will ride to Bordeaux and then take a ship to Smyrna. I will leave you all my possessions . . . turn them to your advantage . . . you deserve it. If this does not satisfy you, I will take arsenic – I have some. Spare me, be the guardian angel of a poor orphan girl or, if you choose, slay me and say I have killed myself.'

Eventually Marie was persuaded to leave her room and admit that the lover was a fabrication. Charles made some effort to pacify her, promising that Le Glandier would be thoroughly renovated according to her wishes and that he would be content to live with her like a brother, rather than a husband, until everything met with her approval. At the time, Marie decided to make the best of things, making endless plans for restoring the estate to its former glory and imagining a time when she and Charles could spend six months a year in Paris and the rest at the château. She wrote letters to her Parisian friends that painted a picture of married life as she wished it to be, rather than as it was. She described Charles as hiding a noble heart 'beneath a wild and uncultured exterior' and her new family as 'delightful and kind'. She was, she said, 'admired . . . adored . . . always in the right . . . a spoilt and happy person'. In fact, she met nothing but hostility from her new family, particularly her dour and critical mother-in-law.

Four months after the marriage, in December, Charles made a journey to Paris to raise money for his business and instructed Marie to write letters to all her influential acquaintances asking for their help – a task she found unpleasant and embarrassing. Before he left, husband and wife made wills leaving all their property to one another but Charles, who had years of practice in confidence trickery, secretly made a second will, cancelling the first and leaving everything to his mother.

Marie, having obtained arsenic from the chemist, ostensibly to deal with the rat population of Le Glandier, suggested that Madame Lafarge should make some of Charles's favourite cakes for him to enjoy over Christmas, a reminder of his loved ones at home. In Paris, one of the hotel staff watched Charles open a box containing a single cake: he ate only a small piece then, complaining that the flavour was poor, threw the rest away, thus foiling Marie's plan that he should die hundreds of kilometres from home. As it was, he suffered agonizing stomach cramps and severe vomiting, which went on for days.

It was a fortnight before he was strong enough to travel home. On the day of his return, Marie ordered more arsenic. She was all solicitude, cooking special dishes for her ailing husband and mixing his drinks herself, while Charles grew worse day by day. Several members of the household saw Marie mixing a white powder, taken from a box in her pocket, into his drinks but she reassured them that it was only gum arabic, to soothe his stomach. Once, in front of Madame Lafarge, Marie drank down a whole glass of milk that had been meant for Charles in order to allay her mother-in-law's well-justified suspicions. When Charles died, on the early morning of 14 February 1840, Madame Lafarge accused Marie openly of poisoning her son. At first, when Alfred the groom supported Marie's story that she had given all

Marie Lafarge denounced to her dying husband by his mother

the arsenic to him and that he had made it into paste and laid it down for rats, it seemed as though Madame Lafarge would have to take back her accusation – but when the rat-paste as examined it was found to contain nothing but bicarbonate of soda. However, arsenic was found in the remains of an eggnog prepared by Marie for her husband, in some of his vomit, carefully preserved by his mother, and in the box Marie carried with her.

In spite of an impassioned defence by Charles Lachaud, a young lawyer who was infatuated with her and believed her completely innocent, Marie was sentenced to life imprisonment. For a time she basked in her notoriety as she was showered with letters from thousands of admirers and well-wishers sympathetic to her story; for once in her life, she was getting the attention she had always craved. She wrote her memoirs, portraying herself as little loved and much maligned, but she never confessed her crime.

Mary Ann Cotton

MARY ANN COTTON, Britain's most active mass murderess, must rank among the foremost of the world's poisoners. She seems to have disposed of anything up to 21 people: husbands with tempting life insurance, children who were too expensive or troublesome to keep, relatives or friends who were in the way of her plans. By the time she was arrested in 1872 40-year-old Mary Ann already had many years of killing behind her, but it was the death of her stepson Charlie that aroused the suspicion that led to her downfall.

There had already been several deaths in the Cotton family since they arrived in the village of West Auckland, Co. Durham, less than two years earlier. The first to go was Frederick, Mary Ann's husband (though the marriage was bigamous), who doubled up with stomach pains at work, just a few weeks after Mary Ann had met an old lover, Joseph Nattrass, and reopened her affair with him. At the time she planned to marry Nattrass but that was before she found another lover with more to offer: an excise officer called Quick-Manning. Now she saw Nattrass, her two stepsons and her own baby by Cotton as obstacles to a good marriage and a boost in society. Within three weeks Nattrass and two of the children were dead, supposedly from gastric fever, which was prevalent at the time. Only Charlie was left and Mary Ann tried to put him in the local workhouse. She failed and when he died a few days afterwards tongues began to wag. The keeper of the general store remembered Mary Ann complaining that it was hard on her to keep a boy who was not even her own and adding: 'But I won't be troubled long. Charlie will go like all the Cotton family.' The chemist remembered Mary Ann sending the boy for two-pennyworth of arsenic and soft soap to dispose of bed-bugs.

Dr Kilburn, who had seen Charlie the day before his unexpected death, insisted on a postmortem and an inquest was held at the Rose and Crown, next door to Mary Ann's house. The doctor's examination revealed no poison, though he was still suspicious and took away some of the stomach contents in case of further questions. The inquest returned a verdict of death by natural causes and Mary Ann promptly collected the £4 10s due on Charlie's insurance policy. All the same, the gossip about the doomed Cotton family spread and reporters began enquiring into Mary Ann's past. The result was an article in the *Newcastle Journal*, pointing out that the Cotton deaths were only the latest in a series of suspicious fatalities associated with Mary Ann.

Her first husband had been William Mowbray who died of 'gastric fever', leaving her with the handsome sum of £35 insurance money. Six of her eight children had already succumbed to 'gastric fever' and another died a few months later. The only survivor was Isabella, who was sent to live with her grandmother. This left Mary Ann free to take a job nursing a 32-year-old engineer, George Ward, who became her second husband. George lasted only a short time after he lost his job, leaving the couple poverty-stricken.

Mary Ann then went as housekeeper to James Robinson, a Sunderland widower with five children. She soon became his mistress and looked forward to a third wedding but, just at the wrong moment, her mother fell ill and Mary Ann was summoned to look after her. It was only a temporary inconvenience. Mary Ann was not prepared to test Robinson's affections by staying away too long and within nine days of her arrival her mother was dead. Mary Ann went back to Sunderland with nine-year-old Isabella and very soon Isabella was dead, along with three of the Robinson children. Though the children's aunts were uneasy about their deaths, suspecting that Mary Ann's ministrations had something to do with their violent symptoms, Robinson was besotted with Mary Ann and determined to marry her. At first all went well, but Mary Ann's extravagance soon began to cause problems. When Robinson found that she was keeping back for herself some of the money he gave her to pay the building society as well as trying to take out loans behind his back there was a scene and Mary Ann walked out. When she tried to return later she found that Robinson had gone to live with one of his sisters, who shut the door against her. Robinson was the only one of Mary Ann's husbands to survive; he was the only one who had refused to take out insurance.

As the rumours about Mary Ann's terrible past grew, Dr Kilburn decided to put the contents of Charlie Cotton's stomach through a more rigorous examination. This time he found traces of arsenic; Mary Ann was arrested and the authorities decided to make further enquiries. They exhumed the corpse of Joseph Nattrass, who had died immediately after making a will in Mary Ann's favour and when they found a considerable amount of arsenic in his body they decided to exhume the rest of the Cotton family. At the time paupers were buried in a special section of the churchyard, the graves unmarked and crowded together and though one grave after another was opened the only bodies found of the Cotton family were those of 14-month-old Robert and 10-year-old Frederick. It was enough: examination showed that both had died from arsenical poisoning.

Mary Ann's committal hearing was postponed for several months for she was pregnant with Quick-Manning's child but after the birth she was committed to stand trial at Durham Assizes for the murder of Charles Cotton. If she were acquitted other murder charges would follow but, though Mary Ann pleaded not guilty, there was little chance of acquittal. The defence counsel did his best to demonstrate that Charlie could have ingested arsenic in various ways – from particles dropping from the mixture pasted over the bedstead to get rid of bed-bugs or from the peeling wallpaper, which had arsenic in its green colouring – but evidence about the long string of accidental deaths that attended Mary Ann made nonsense of the idea of accidental poisoning; the jury took only an hour to reach the expected verdict. When the judge donned the black cap to read the death sentence, Mary Ann fell into a faint and was carried out by two wardresses.

Mary Ann maintained her innocence to the end, trying to organize a petition for a reprieve, while the *Newcastle Journal* described her as 'a monster in human shape' and the *Durham County Advertiser* talked about her 'diabolical inhumanity'. Five days before the hanging her baby, Margaret, was taken from her. She had chosen new parents for the child herself but at the last minute she clung to her and wardresses had to tear the baby from her arms. Tears of sympathy were pouring down the wardresses' faces as, for the moment, they forgot that Mary Ann was probably the most dangerous mother in the world. For many years after her death, Durham mothers used to discipline their children with the threat; 'If you're naughty, Mary Ann Cotton will get you.'

Lydia Sherman

AT THE time of her trial Lydia Sherman was called the 'Queen of Poisoners.' In her confession she gave details of 11 killings – her three husbands, six children and two stepchildren – but added carelessly that there could have been a dozen more. No one will ever know the true figure.

She began her career as a poisoner in 1864. At the time she was married to Edward Struck, a patrolman with the New York Police Department, and had borne him six children. When he was dismissed from the police department for showing cowardice when dealing with a dangerous incident he turned from a reliable breadwinner into a liability, unable to find work and drinking too much. Lydia's solution was simple: she bought ten cents' worth of arsenic from the pharmacist, saying that her apartment was 'alive with rats', then mixed it into her husband's warm oatmeal. By the time the doctor arrived Edward Struck was dead and when Lydia suggested consumption as the cause he signed the death certificate.

This murder had been so easy that Lydia proceeded to dispose of all her children over the next two years. One by one they died – Mary Ann, Edward, William, George, Anne and finally the youngest, her namesake Lydia – and each time Lydia called in a different doctor and put on such a convincing display of grief that they all believed the deaths were due to natural causes. Lydia had now collected seven modest sets of insurance money, so that she was now both free and much better off than before.

Two years later she went as housekeeper to a 75-year-old farmer, Dennis Hurlbut of Connecticut. Within a few weeks he had proposed and made a will in her favour. Eleven months later the old man was dead. Next she married Nelson Sherman, a widower with four children and a difficult mother-in-law, Mrs Mary Jones. There were constant rows in the house and Lydia became convinced that it was only the baby, nine-month-old Frank, who was keeping Mrs Jones with the family. 'I was full of trouble and not knowing what to do I put some arsenic in his milk,' she explained later. Mrs Jones called in Dr Beardsley, the family doctor, who diagnosed colic, but Frank died within the day.

Next, Lydia turned her attention to 14-year-old Addie, who was first taken ill while she was helping to decorate the church Christmas tree. She went home to bed, where her stepmother gave her two cups of strong tea with generous helpings of arsenic. Addie died next day. Lydia's wish was now fulfilled, for Mrs Jones moved out, but Nelson Sherman, devastated by the loss of the two children, took to drink. Lydia was unwilling to be burdened with another alcoholic husband, so she began putting arsenic in his hot chocolate. When he became ill, Dr Beardsley put it down to his excessive drinking. Nelson died on 12 May 1871. 'I just wanted to cure him of the liquor habit,' said Lydia.

By now Dr Beardsley was suspicious and he insisted that the dead man's stomach and liver should be analysed. When enough poison was found to kill several people, he called in two other doctors and had the bodies of the two children exhumed and examined, with the same result.

Lydia had a strong sense of self-preservation and at the first signs of trouble she fled to New York. However, the police quickly tracked her down and brought her back to Connecticut under arrest, where she pleaded that she had committed the murders out of compassion, believing that her victims would be better off: 'all these people were sick, after all!' At her trial the 48-year-old widow cut an impressive figure, dressed in a neat alpaca dress trimmed with silk velvet, a mixed black and white woollen shawl and a white straw hat trimmed with black velvet and a brown plume.

Perhaps the jury felt squeamish about the idea of executing a woman, for they brought in a lenient verdict of murder in the second degree. Lydia was sentenced to life imprisonment in Weathersfield Prison, where she died in 1878.

Sarah Jane Robinson

SARAH JANE ROBINSON was another of the '19th-century Borgias' who managed to put most of her family under the ground before anyone suspected that the constant illness and death that surrounded her was anything more than bad luck. In most cases the motive was the insurance money, that mainstay of the hard-up poisoner of the time, but once she had become accustomed to dispensing arsenic-laced drinks this became a convenient way of ridding herself of any family member who was proving a nuisance.

The first murder may well have been committed to cover up a theft, though it only came to light five years later, when Sarah Jane's other crimes were discovered, and there was no proof one way or the other. Sarah Jane was 42 at the time, the mother of five children and a resident of Massachusetts, USA. She had married Moses Robinson at the age of 19 and, since his wage as a factory worker had never been enough to support the family, she worked as a dressmaker, a trade she had learned back home in Ireland. Even then they were forever in debt, with loans taken out on the very chairs they sat on and rent always owing. When the bills added up to more than they could ever hope to pay the Robinsons would organize a 'moonlight flit' and start again in another dismal tenement building, stacking up a whole new set of debts.

It seems that Sarah Jane found a new way out of her financial problems in 1881. Her elderly landlord Oliver Sleeper became ill and she volunteered to nurse him. When his death had been hastened by arsenic she sent a hefty bill to his executors and denied all knowledge of the $3000 missing from the premises since Sleeper had fallen sick. Any money Sarah Jane had acquired from her landlord's death afforded the Robinsons only a temporary respite, for 12 months later they were being threatened with eviction. The rent problem should have been solved in July for Moses Robinson died, his system full of arsenic, leaving life insurance of $2000. Unfortunately there was a dispute over the payment records and no immediate payment could be made, so that left Sarah Jane casting around for another source of funds.

She saw her opportunity when her sister Annie Freeman fell ill. Annie had pneumonia but was mending nicely under the care of a nurse her husband Prince had called in. Then Sarah Jane decided that only her personal care would suffice and immediately Annie took a turn for the worse. Sarah Jane began hinting to Prince that if Annie did not recover he should bring his two children to live with her. Annie died soon afterwards and Prince moved into Sarah Jane's three-bedroomed flat, which was soon bursting at the seams. That didn't worry Sarah Jane, for she knew that the overcrowding would not last for long.

The first to go was 12-month-old Elizabeth Freeman; looking after a baby was far too much trouble for Sarah Jane. She made no secret of her dislike of Prince, either: she told a number of people that he was idle and shiftless and would be better off dead. Those words were to count heavily against her in the future. Prince died in June 1885, but not before Sarah Jane had checked whether his insurance policy was fully paid up and, finding that a premium was still outstanding, had borrowed the money to pay it. When Prince first moved in she had persuaded him to name her as the beneficiary, so that she would have enough money to look after his children.

Most of the $2000 insurance went on paying off her ever-mounting debts, but she kept enough to pay for an insurance policy on her daughter Lizzie. In February 1886 Lizzie died and Prince's seven-year-old son Thomas followed her in July. The next victim was her 23-year-old son William, whose death would bring another healthy $2000 payout. The perfect opportunity presented itself only a few weeks after Thomas's death when William had an accident at work and Sarah Jane was solicitous in making him rest and plying him with tea. When he began vomiting she blamed it on the after-effects of the accident but she confided to a friend that she had had a dream in which Lizzie came back to tell her that William would soon be joining her. The friend remembered that a similar dream had warned her of Prince's death, though that time it had been Moses who thoughtfully warned her of the forthcoming demise.

Before he died, William told the doctor: 'The old woman dosed me.' His words, together with the unusual number of deaths in the family, were enough to launch an enquiry. When arsenic was found in William's system, Sarah Jane was charged with murder. The subsequent trial was a hurried affair with badly presented evidence and the jury were not allowed to hear incriminating facts about the surprising list of deaths in the family, with the result that they were unable to agree on a verdict.

Meanwhile, the insurance company had pressed for a full investigation of the demise of anyone close to Sarah Jane Robinson over the past five years. The superintendent of the local cemetery, who had buried them all, now 'took them pretty much all up', he later told the court. The authorities decided that their best chance of obtaining a conviction was to charge her with murdering Prince Freeman, because in so doing they could also bring evidence about the murder of her sister Annie, who had been removed as part of the plot to dispose of Prince and obtain his insurance money.

At her second trial, Sarah Jane's lawyers maintained that she was a harmless victim of circumstances, an unlucky woman who had lost many of those near and dear to her. They tried to suggest that William had been poisoned, not by arsenic, but by noxious fumes at the ironworks where he was employed. When the scientific evidence made this claim look ridiculous, they tried to find someone else to take the lion's share of the blame, casting suspicion on old Dr Beers, a known admirer of Sarah Jane, who peddled a patent medicine said to cure a whole range of ills. This medicine, it was claimed, could make the recipients so sick that those with weak constitutions could well die, worn out from vomiting. It would be easy enough to add poison to such a concoction.

Dr Beers appeared in the witness box, so doddering and confused that he seemed incapable of such a crime and the jury had no hesitation in putting the full blame where it belonged. When the verdict of guilty was announced and the death penalty given, Sarah Jane remained as self-possessed and unruffled as she had been throughout the trial.

Velma Barfield

VELMA BARFIELD remained on Death Row in North Carolina, USA, for six years before being put to death by lethal injection, the first woman executed in the USA for 22 years. She had confessed to three poisonings, though her motives were confused and her mind befuddled by drugs.

She had married at 17, eloping with Thomas Burke, who was just a year older, to escape a home where she had suffered abuse. They had two children and for the first 15 years of marriage were happy enough, but their luck deserted them when Burke lost his job and, soon afterwards, was injured in a car crash. He took to drink while Velma worked to support the family and began to depend on tranquillizers to get her through the day. In 1969 Burke died from asphyxiation, after falling asleep while smoking and setting light to his bed. Two years later Velma married a retired widower, Jennings Barfield, who was kind to her and gave her some feeling of protection. Barfield was already suffering from heart disease and he died a few months later.

After that, Velma was hospitalized several times after suicide attempts and accidents while under the influence of drugs. She went from one doctor to another to obtain medication, taking large quantities of tranquillizers to calm her nerves and antidepressants to lift her black moods. Her medical bills were larger than her income and her cheques began to bounce; in 1975 she was imprisoned for six months for issuing dud cheques.

The following year she took a job as a live-in maid with Dollie Edwards and her 93-year-old bedridden husband. Velma felt that Dollie was always criticizing and that no matter how hard she worked, she could do nothing right. Mr Edwards died in January 1977 and Velma stayed on with Dollie, but by now she hated her so much that she fed her ant poison. However, she was taking so many pills that when Dollie was convulsed with pain she wondered why she was 'writhing and moaning', no longer able to connect it with anything she had done.

In the spring she moved in with another elderly couple, Mr and Mrs Lee. She was no happier there, for the couple bickered constantly and Velma felt that her nerves were stretched to breaking point. She was in urgent need of money for drugs so she forged a cheque for $50 on John Lee's account then, afraid of discovery, she decided to 'make him sick' to give herself time to replace the money. When he died in June the doctor recorded the cause of death of his 80-year-old patient as a heart attack, so Velma managed to convince herself that he had died of natural causes and she was not responsible.

While working in the Edwards household Velma had met Dollie's nephew, Stuart Taylor, a farmer 10 years her senior, with a serious drink problem. They planned to marry, but Stuart was angry when he found out about her prison record and threw it in her face every time they argued. There was more trouble when he discovered that she had forged a cheque on his account. Though she promised him that it would never happen again, the next time she was desperate for new drug supplies she stole another of his blank cheques and forged his signature. When she was collecting a prescription from the drugstore, she saw the ant poison that she had used before and she began feeding it to Stuart, planning to make him sick enough to stave off discovery – or so she claimed later. At one point, when Stuart was really ill, Velma took him to the hospital emergency room, where the doctor told him it was probably a flu virus and he should go to bed and drink plenty of liquid. Three days later she called a highway patrol rescue unit to take him to hospital, where he died on 4 February, within an hour of admission.

When a postmortem was suggested, Velma readily agreed. As

Velma Barfield

usual, she had managed to convince herself that her ministrations had only caused sickness and that death had been due to something else – in Stuart's case the flu virus. When the presence of arsenic was shown and detectives came to question her, her answers were confused. When they left she collected together all her pills, planning to kill herself, but she fell asleep before she could take them. She woke to find her son Ronnie at her bedside and, on his advice, she gave herself up. When a detective at the station asked, 'Did you poison Stuart Taylor?' she answered simply, 'Yes.' 'There have been others, too?' he asked. Again, her answer was 'Yes.'

In her autobiography, *Woman on Death Row*, Velma described the misery of coming off drugs in prison. As the amounts of medication were decreased, she suffered serious withdrawal symptoms and though she was still unable to think clearly, she had to face up to what she had done. 'I'm the most contemptible person in the world. The world would be better off without me,' she wrote. She hated herself, her whole life and the world she lived in.

In 1978, Velma underwent a religious conversion in prison and over the years she gave valuable support and understanding to other inmates, several of whom said that they would never have survived prison without her help. Her appeals went all the way to the United States Supreme Court but were unsuccessful and a final appeal to the governor of North Carolina to commute her sentence to life imprisonment was denied. On 2 December 1984, when Velma was put to death, a crowd of several hundred kept a vigil with lighted candles outside the prison.

Anjette Lyles

THE ANONYMOUS letter received by Mrs Bagley of the small Georgia town of Cochran, USA, read: 'Please come at once. Little Marcia is getting the same doses as the others. Please come at once.' Marcia was her nine-year-old niece, the daughter of Anjette Lyles, who ran a restaurant in the nearby town of Macon.

The letter was passed to the county sheriff, who had only just begun to make enquiries when little Marcia died. She was the fourth member of Anjette Lyles' close family to die in the past seven years. The first was her husband, Ben F. Lyles Jnr. They had been married for four years, had two daughters, Marcia and Carla, and they had opened a successful restaurant in partnership with Ben's mother. Early in 1951 Ben fell ill with severe stomach pains and was taken to hospital, where he lapsed into a coma and died soon afterwards. Anjette collected more than $12,000 in insurance money.

Four years later, Anjette opened another restaurant and among her regulars was Joseph Gabbart, an airline pilot. Though he was more than 10 years younger than Anjette, he fell in love with the attractive widow and within two months of meeting they were married. Anjette saw to it that her new husband took out more than adequate life insurance, with two policies of around $10,000. Five months after the wedding Joseph went into hospital for a minor operation and everyone noticed how devoted his new wife was, always at his bedside, bringing him fresh fruit juices to build up his strength. However, far from getting better, Joseph got worse, developing intense abdominal pains and a bad case of dermatitis. In spite of all that the puzzled doctors could do, he died on 2 December 1955. Once again, the grieving widow collected the insurance money and promptly changed her name back to Lyles.

In the summer of 1957, Anjette's mother-in-law ate a meal in her restaurant and was taken ill with stomach pains afterwards. Her daughter-in-law visited her frequently in hospital, where she developed the same symptoms as her son. The nurses noticed that Anjette was always convinced that her mother-in-law would die and that, even though she was so attentive to Mrs Lyles, she admitted to the hospital attendants that she hated the woman. After Mrs Lyles died in September, a will was found, leaving two-thirds of her property to Anjette and her daughters, while the remaining third went to her second son. There was talk in the hospital: the will was dated four weeks before Mrs Lyles died, when they were certain that she was incapable of holding a pen, let alone writing a legible signature. There was talk among the restaurant staff, too: while Mrs Lyles was eating in the restaurant Anjette had been seen with a bottle of ant poison in one hand and a glass of buttermilk meant for her mother-in-law in the other.

It was Carrie Jackson, a cook at the restaurant, who wrote the anonymous letter in March 1958. She knew that Anjette kept a bottle of ant poison in her big black handbag and more than once she saw her disappearing into the cloakroom carrying drinks meant for Marcia, with her black handbag over her arm. Anjette had made plenty of unkind comments about her elder daughter, who took after the Lyles family rather than her mother and constantly reminded her of people she would rather forget. She had even made remarks to the effect that she would have done away with her long ago if little Carla had not been so attached to her. When Marcia fell ill in March, Carrie Jackson was convinced that she was being poisoned.

When Marcia was taken to hospital her mother regularly brought her grape juice and more than once she was seen taking it into the cloakroom just before she gave it to Marcia – and, of course, she had her black handbag with her. At one point, when Marcia's doctor told her that the child was getting better, she flatly contradicted him. No, she said, Marcia was sure to take a turn for the worse. She was proved right and Marcia died on 5 April.

By now the authorities were thoroughly alerted and a postmortem was ordered. When a large amount of arsenic was found in Marcia's body, exhumations were ordered on Anjette's two husbands and her mother-in-law. In each case, arsenical poisoning was found to be the cause of death. Anjette was arrested but declared: 'I have committed no crime. I have done nothing wrong.' When her house was searched detectives were amazed to find it a 'witch's lair,' with a wide stock of ingredients for love potions and a strong smell of incense. There were also several bottles of ant poison which contained arsenic as one of its main ingredients.

At the trial a number of people, both from the restaurant and the hospital, reported seeing Anjette carrying drinks into the cloakroom before giving them to her relatives. Several of them knew that she carried ant poison in the handbag that was constantly on her arm. When her maid had queried this Anjette had told her that the restaurant was plagued by ants, but the pest exterminator firm that regularly serviced the restaurant gave evidence that there had never been a problem with ants in the building.

A nurse recalled a conversation with Anjette, who told her that Marcia had swallowed some ant poison while playing doctors and nurses because she liked the sweet taste. After Marcia died, her younger sister Carla had said she wanted the same drink as Marcia, so that she could go and join her in heaven. A neighbour, Mrs Leo Hutchinson, remembered an even more sinister conversation when Anjette had talked seriously about getting rid of Marcia, saying 'I'll kill her if it's the last thing I ever do.'

Handwriting experts gave evidence about the will supposedly signed by Anjette's mother-in-law shortly before her death: the signature had been forged with the aid of tracing paper. A letter received by Joseph Gabbart's insurance company shortly before his death, purporting to come from him and asking questions about his policy, was also a forgery.

Anjette claimed that she was innocent and had never administered arsenic to anyone, but no one believed her and she was sentenced to die in the electric chair. Though her appeals failed, doctors observing her over the months that followed eventually decided that she had lost her reason and she was confined to an asylum.

Charlotte Bryant

THERE WAS nothing at all romantic about the lover for whom Charlotte Bryant poisoned her husband in Dorset, England in 1935; he was a gypsy pedlar, loutish and unkempt, a known womanizer unlikely to entertain deep feelings for any of his bedfellows. To Charlotte, however, he must have offered an escape from her dreary, poverty-striken life.

An illiterate Irish girl, Charlotte met her husband Frederick when he was serving in the army and came to England to marry him in 1923. By 1933 Fred was working as a farm labourer and they had four children and a tiny cottage that was ill-kept, for Charlotte neglected her home just as she neglected her personal hygiene. The main entertainment of her life was drinking in the public houses in the evenings, where she was well-known as an amateur prostitute. Fred seems to have looked the other way and accepted the extras that Charlotte's earnings provided – anything for a quiet life.

It was in the pub that she met the pedlar, Leonard Parsons, and she became totally infatuated with him. She took him home as a lodger, letting him sleep on the sofa overnight and share her bed when Fred was out at work. Once again Fred seems to have accepted the situation without fuss, even when Charlotte became pregnant again and it seemed highly likely that Parsons was the father. Parsons stayed for two years on and off, sharing Fred's razor and his wife's favours, though he would occasionally go back to his wandering gypsy ways. More than once Charlotte followed him, leaving Fred to cope with the cottage and the children as best he could.

It was Parsons, not Fred, who eventually tired of the arrangement and he began talking about leaving. Perhaps Charlotte had already decided that she would tempt him to stay by getting rid of an inconvenient husband and installing Parsons in his place, for in May 1935 Fred had the first of several bouts of pain and sickness. In spite of Charlotte's pleadings Parsons left in the autumn, but she was determined to get him back and trekked from one gipsy camp to another in search of him. She found more than she bargained for at a camp near Weston-super-Mare, where a woman named Priscilla Loveridge told her that she had been Parson's 'wife' for years, and had borne him four children. In spite of that she had nothing good to say about him, describing him as a 'woman's fancy man and a home-breaker'.

No sooner had Charlotte returned home than Fred was taken ill again and he died three days later. The cause of death was found to be arsenical poisoning and it was the evidence of a friend, Lucy Ostler, that led to Charlotte's arrest. The night before Fred died, she said, she had seen Charlotte persuading him to drink a cup of Oxo which had made him very sick. The next day Charlotte had been anxious to get rid of a weedkiller tin, which she had tried to burn and then thrown on the rubbish heap. The tin, which contained traces of arsenic, matched the description of a tin of weedkiller sold by a local chemist to an illiterate woman who had to sign his poison register with a cross instead of a signature. More traces of arsenic were found in several places in the Bryants' cottage.

When Charlotte was charged she said 'I never got poison from anywhere. I don't see how they can say that I poisoned my husband.' At her trial she insisted that her marriage had been happy and the only trouble had been caused by Parsons; far from her chasing him, he was the one who chased her. Parsons, never once looking towards the dock, said that shortly before he left Charlotte had told him she might soon be a widow and free to marry him, but he had replied that he would not marry her, even if Fred was out of the picture.

Charlotte was sentenced to hang and spent six weeks in the condemned cell while an appeal was mounted. The ordeal turned her hair white. As a last attempt to save her life she sent a telegram to the

King: 'Mighty King, have pity on your lowly subject. Don't let them kill me on Wednesday.'

No reply came from the palace, there was no stay of execution and Charlotte Bryant was hanged at Exeter Prison on 15 July 1936.

Mary Elizabeth Wilson

MARY ELIZABETH WILSON, who has gone down in history as the 'widow of Windy Nook', became a murderess in her mid-sixties and managed to rid herself of four unwanted men in a three-year period before she was eventually brought to justice.

A working-class girl from the industrial north of England, Mary went into service with a builder's family at the age of 14 and married the eldest son of the house, John Knowles, in 1914. At the time it must have seemed a good match for her but John never rose any higher than labouring work and though the couple stayed together for more than 40 years, they ceased to share a bed or communicate over anything but the basic necessities of life. They took in a lodger, a chimney sweep named John George Russell, who soon became Mary's lover while her husband looked the other way, not caring where his wife found her pleasures so long as it did not disrupt his comfortable routine. For several years all three of them seemed content with the arrangement but then in July 1955 John Knowles, who had always been strong and fit, was taken ill and within a fortnight was dead.

Mary told her neighbours that it was time for a change – something she had been discussing with her husband before he died, she said – and she made arrangements to move to a larger, more modern house in Windy Nook, taking her lodger with her. Perhaps she had expected him to marry her, only to find that the lack of any ties or responsibilities suited him too well, or perhaps she found that her new life did not provide enough of a change from the past. Whatever the reason, she must have decided that John Russell must go the way of John Knowles. Just before Christmas 1955, the lodger fell ill with stomach cramps and vomiting. Mary made him plenty of hot soup to warm him

Mary Elizabeth Wilson

in the bitter winter weather and his condition deteriorated day by day until his death in January. John left Mary £46 and no sooner had the doctor signed the death certificate than she set about redecorating his room.

In the summer a new lodger moved in. He was retired estate agent Oliver James Leonard, aged 76, and Mary had reason to believe that he had a comfortable nest-egg. On 21 September they were married but either Mary found the marriage a great disappointment or she could not wait to lay her hands on Oliver's savings, for her new husband did not last very long. Thirteen days after the wedding Mary came knocking frantically on the door of a neighbour, Ellen Russell, to say that her husband was ill. Oliver Leonard was lying on the bedroom floor, doubled up in pain. The women helped him into bed and Mary brewed a pot of tea but when Mrs Russell brought him a cup, Oliver knocked it out of her hand. Later this was brought up as evidence that he knew that his wife was poisoning him.

Mary did not call in the doctor – she reckoned there was no point, as he was obviously going to die anyway – but next day she went to report that her husband had died in the night. The doctor recalled that Mr Leonard had been to him a few days before with a bad cold and had seemed very feeble and tottery, so he signed the death certificate without a second thought and Mary collected her late husband's modest savings and the payment on his insurance policy. Everyone in Windy Nook felt for the new bride in her sad loss.

Mary waited just over a year before marrying again, this time a 75-year-old retired engineer, Ernest George Lawrence Wilson, with £100 in savings. This husband, too, lasted only a fortnight. The doctor was called in when the old man had a slight stomach upset then, a few days later, he answered a second call, only to find that his patient had already been dead for several hours. This time there was talk, especially when people remembered that at the wedding reception, when someone mentioned that there was a good deal of cake left over, Mary had laughed, 'Well, we can always keep it for the funeral.'

So far, Mary had escaped detection because it was hard to believe that an elderly woman would suddenly turn to murder and take such risks for such meagre rewards. After all, none of her men were well off, none had much in the way of possessions or property, and she had taken out no new insurance policies for them. However, so many deaths in a single household in such a short time, coupled with stories of Mary's behaviour, which was unsuitable to a grieving widow, led to a police investigation and the exhumation of the four bodies.

All four corpses were found to contain both phosphorus and wheat-germ, ingredients of a popular rat poison called Rodine. John Knowles and John Russell had been in the ground too long for any positive conclusions to be drawn and the inquests returned open verdicts on both of them. The other two bodies still contained lethal quantities of phosphorus and, as a result, Mary found herself standing trial for two murders.

The doctors who had written death certificates for Oliver and Ernest both admitted that they had no experience of phosphorus poisoning and had no reason to suspect that the deaths were due to anything but the natural processes of old age. One had written the death certificate without actually seeing the body; the other had been called only after the patient had died. There was a long discussion about the means by which Rodine could have been administered to the two victims, as it has a strong smell and an extremely unpleasant taste. Tests in previous cases had shown that it could not be disguised in a cup of tea but that the taste could be concealed in strongly flavoured jam – though in this case it was more likely to have been given in the cough mixture which was taken by both men. No container of Rodine was found at Mrs Wilson's home, but this was used by the prosecution as proof that suicide and accident could both be ruled out.

The defence lawyer produced a bottle of pills, freely available from the chemist, which contained phosphorus and were recognized for use as an aphrodisiac. 'What more natural,' she said, 'that these old men, finding a wife in the evening of their lives, should purchase these pills? It was a brave try, but no such pills were found in the house and an expert pointed out that to obtain a lethal dose of phosphorus, it would be necessary to take three whole bottles full. On the advice of her counsel, Mary chose not to give evidence so many questions remained unanswered, but she was found guilty of both murders. Though she was sentenced to death she was reprieved five days later by the Home Secretary, probably because of her age. She died in prison at the age of 70.

Edith Carew

A MYSTERIOUS 'woman in black' flitted in and out of the enquiry into the death by arsenical poisoning of Walter Carew. She was an insubstantial, shadowy figure who could have been a murderess – but was far more likely to have been the figment of a murderess's imagination.

Walter Carew's death, and the events that followed it, shocked the comfortable European community in Yokohama, Japan, where Walter was engaged in the import–export business. He had brought his bride Edith to Japan seven years before, in 1889, and they enjoyed the elegant expatriate lifestyle, with Walter the secretary of the British club and Edith a popular and successful hostess. When Walter fell ill in October 1896 it seemed to Dr Wheeler, who attended the British families, like an ordinary bilious attack. When he suffered another, more serious attack a few days later Dr Wheeler called in a second opinion, but both doctors were mystified. The patient was sent to the naval hospital, where he died within two hours of arrival.

Meanwhile, a strange note had been pushed under Dr Wheeler's door saying: 'Three bottles of arsenic in one week!' It added the name of a local chemist, Maruya, and when the doctor made enquiries he found that three orders of arsenic had been supplied to Edith. She admitted that she had bought the poison, but only at her husband's request. He used it to treat a painful, longstanding complaint which he had never mentioned to the doctor, she said.

At the inquest Edith told a dramatic story about a Miss Annie Luke, with whom her husband had had a brief affair in his bachelor days and who had appeared at the house asking to see him only two weeks before his death. She had been dressed in black and so heavily veiled that Edith did not see her face, but she had left a calling card with the initials 'AL'. Edith produced a letter, also supposedly from Annie Luke, which had been found among Walter's papers:

'I must see you . . . I cannot meet her again. She makes me mad when I think of what I might have done for you. I cannot give you any address. I am living wherever I can find shelter; but you can find me and help me if you will, as I know you will for the sake of old times.'

Another letter, written by the same person, had been sent to the lawyer advising Edith:

'Dead men tell no tales; no, nor dead women either, for I am going to join him. Do you know what it means, waiting for eight long weary years? I have watched and waited. Waited until I knew he would grow tired of that silly little fool, and then I came to him. What is the result? We, between us, electrify Japan. I have never pretended to be a good woman but, for the sake of a few lines, I do not see why I should let a silly, innocent woman be condemned for what she knows nothing about.'

Another witness, a young bank clerk called Henry Dickinson, gave evidence that he had seen a veiled woman in black hanging about the club at the time when Annie Luke was supposed to be asking for Walter. He was the only person apart from Edith to have seen this oddly dressed woman, which was quite remarkable, as any European stranger would have stood out and become an object of speculation. However, it was enough to suggest that Edith was not the only possible suspect and the jury decided that Walter had died from arsenical poisoning but that there was 'no direct evidence to show by whom it had been administered'.

A week later Edith Carew was arrested and charged with murder. There had been another sensational development in the Carew household for the children's nurse-governess, Mary Jacob, who was on poor terms with her employer and suspected that letters addressed to her were being intercepted by Edith, had been checking through the waste-paper basket in search of them when she came across some torn-up love-letters. They had been written to Edith by Henry Dickinson, the only person to substantiate her story about a 'woman in black'.

At the trial the letters were read out and Henry Dickinson confessed to his infatuation for Edith (though there was no evidence that adultery had ever taken place) and that they had discussed the possibility of the Carews' divorce. There were references to Walter's cruelty and Henry revealed that Edith had painted a picture of her husband's ill-treatment, which she claimed made her life a misery. He now knew that this account was false.

A handwriting expert for the prosecution gave evidence that Edith had probably written the Annie Luke letters herself, but this was contradicted by experts on the other side. The defence tried to suggest that it was Mary Jacob who had written the letters and that she had developed a relationship with Walter. At one point the young governess was arrested, but there was no real evidence against her and she was quickly released. Needless to say, no new evidence of the existence of a real Annie Luke was produced, though Edith had publicized a £500 reward for information.

Edith's counsel reasoned that she had no convincing motive for killing Walter: he was a cheerful, kind husband, she was an affectionate wife and mother and their life together was comfortable. The jury did not accept his summation and they found Edith guilty. She was sentenced to death, though this was later commuted to life imprisonment and she was returned to England to serve her sentence.

Mary Blandy

THE POISON Mary Blandy used to kill her father came through the post, in little packets labelled 'powders to clean Scotch pebbles'. These pebbles were fashionable ornaments of the time, but the white powder that accompanied them was destined for a far less innocent purpose – for Mary saw her father as an obstacle to her union with her beloved, the Honourable William Henry Cranstoun, the fifth son of a Scottish peer.

Mr Francis Blandy was a prosperous English lawyer and town clerk of Henley-on-Thames and his daughter Mary was a charming, attractive young woman with a £10,000 fortune of her own and expectations of a respectable inheritance in the future. She was a 'good catch' and could be expected to marry well but, though there was no shortage of suitors, no young man had yet managed to please both Mary and her father.

Mary was 26 when she first met Willy Cranstoun, a captain with the recruitment service, at a ball given by his uncle, Lord Mark Kerr. He was some 20 years her senior and by all accounts a rather unattractive fellow, but his military bearing and city sophistication proved irresistible to Mary. She was soon deeply in love and had no hesitation over accepting his proposal of marriage. Her father, who was less impressed by his prospective son-in-law, was appalled to receive a letter from Lord Mark Kerr which tactfully pointed out that his nephew already had a wife and child in Scotland; he had married a Miss Anne Murray two years before but his father had disapproved of the match and, as he depended on parental generosity for his standard of living, he soon left her behind and returned to London, leaving his wife and child dependent on her family.

Willy, faced with the letter and Mr Blandy's indignation, chose to deny everything. It was all a misunderstanding, he said: he had at one time promised to marry Miss Murray but the marriage had never taken place, though Miss Murray had been posing as his wife, to his considerable embarrassment. Meanwhile, he was persuading Anne Murray that he had no chance of rising in the ranks of the army as a married man with a family but that if she agreed to deny the marriage and say that she had only been his mistress, he would soon achieve promotion which would provide him with sufficient money to support her properly. Eventually Anne gave in and provided him with a letter 'disowning' the marriage, which he used to try to get it anulled. He failed and the marriage was confirmed as legal.

Mary, her heart still set on marriage to Willy Cranstoun, wanted to hear none of it and the more that her father tried to make her understand the realities of the situation, the more she resented his interference. It was then that Willy started sending the powders. Later, she was to claim that he told her that they were potions that would change her father's temper, leaving him well-disposed towards Willy, and that he had obtained them from a fortune-teller called Mrs Morgan, who provided love potions to the best families. At first Mary gave her father a good helping in his tea, but it was so bitter that he refused to drink it, so instead she began mixing it in his food.

Mr Blandy soon took to his bed, weak and in pain, with his devoted daughter ministering to him, his decline perplexing his doctors. When a kitchen maid, Susan Gunnel, became ill after tasting some food destined for the invalid, Mary forbade the servants, on pain of instant dismissal, from touching anything she prepared for her father. They became suspicious, and one even suggested the possibility of poisoning to Mr Blandy, but he could not believe his daughter capable of such a thing. He was even shown a letter in which Mary warned Willy to be careful what he wrote, but all he said was, 'Poor, lovesick girl! What a woman will do for the man she loves.' Susan, remembering how sick she had been after tasting Mr Blandy's gruel, felt less

Mary Blandy

charitable towards her mistress and when she found traces of white scum on a saucepan which had contained the latest batch of gruel, she took a sample which was passed on to the doctor.

It was too late to save the sick man, for Mary, acting on Willy's instructions, had increased the dose and her weakened father had no chance of survival. As he was dying, Mary was suddenly overcome with remorse and flung her arms round him, confessing her guilt and asking for his blessing.

Mary was tried at Oxford Assizes in March 1752 and the servants were able to describe all her suspicious actions during her father's illness. At one point, in a panic that she might be discovered, she had tried to burn Willy's letters and a packet of 'pebble powder'. The packet had been rescued from the fire by the cook and was produced in evidence, identified by several doctors as arsenic. The jury took only five minutes to find her guilty of poisoning her father. Mary went to the gallows in a smart black dress with a prayerbook in her hand, and requested that she should not be hung too high 'for the sake of decency'. William Cranstoun escaped justice by taking refuge in France, where he died six months later, still maintaining that the poisoning was entirely Mary's idea.

Daisy de Melker

IN 1932, 20-year-old Rhodes Cowle was living with his mother Daisy, an ex-nurse, and her third husband, rugby player Clarence de Melker, in Johannesburg, South Africa. The atmosphere in the house was highly charged, for Rhodes was a bad-tempered young man with a grievance. His father had died nine years earlier and Rhodes, who was unable to find a job, thought that when he reached the age of 21 he should inherit his father's estate. His mother, with the financial reins firmly in her hands, was not willing to concede and they had many bitter arguments, with Rhodes alternately threatening to commit suicide and resorting to violence.

In March, Rhodes died suddenly after a four-day illness diagnosed as malaria and the house became peaceful again – but there were those who could not believe that yet another of Daisy's relatives had died of natural causes. Daisy had had five children by her first husband, William Cowle, and none had lived to attain their majority. William himself had died in 1923 after 14 years of marriage, apparently of a cerebral haemorrhage, leaving her with an insurance policy worth £1700.

When Daisy married her second husband, Robert Sproat, three years later he had already drawn up a will leaving his £4000 savings to his mother, but Daisy had soon convinced him that it was only proper to leave it to his new wife. In November 1926, Robert died, just as unexpectedly as his predecessor. Robert's brother, Albert Sproat, was worried about the circumstances of his death but was never able to find any proof of wrongdoing. He had not spoken to Daisy for years and it was the news of the death of Daisy's last remaining child, a fit young man, that prompted him to contact the authorities.

Preliminary enquiries showed that the number of surprise deaths in Daisy's family went far beyond the bounds of coincidence or ill-fortune. Rhodes's body was exhumed and found to contain arsenic. The bodies of Daisy's first and second husbands were also examined and both contained traces of strychnine. Their doctors, when contacted, admitted that their symptoms could have indicated poison, though they had no cause to look for it at the time.

Daisy was arrested and the police began enquiries among the local chemists but at first they drew a blank: there was no evidence that she had ever purchased poison. However, widespread newspaper publicity eventually produced a chemist from the other side of the city who remembered Daisy buying arsenic a few days before Rhodes Cowle became sick. She had told him that she wanted to get rid of stray cats that were ruining her garden.

The trial of Daisy de Melker lasted 30 days; at that time it was the longest-ever trial of a white person in South Africa. In the witness box the defendant was an unsympathetic figure, giving the impression that she was a cold and emotionless woman who might well be capable of causing a painful death in an unwanted family member.

On the day the verdict was to be announced, police officers from Rhodesia stood ready to take Daisy into custody if she was acquitted on the current charges; they had reason to believe that she had been involved in several deaths there before coming to South Africa. Their presence was unnecessary. Daisy was convicted and hanged at Pretoria Central Prison on 30 September 1932. She never admitted her guilt.

Mary Bateman

MARY BATEMAN was well-known as a witch in the Leeds area of northern England in the late 18th century but her success owed more to trickery, a lying tongue and a grasping nature than to the supernatural. As a child she was hired out as a servant but in every household she joined small items went missing and were soon traced to Mary, so she never kept a job for long. Later she turned to dressmaking and managed to make extra money on the side by fortune-telling for her customers.

She married a wheelwright, John Bateman, who was to stick to her through thick and thin, even when her thieving meant that they were turned out of their lodgings, and when she made up a story to get him out of the way for a couple of days and sold off every stick of furniture they owned.

Over the years, Mary managed to build up a thriving little business in charms and love potions and a stream of gullible clients came to her for marriage predictions or to have a fancied curse lifted. She invented two 'wise women', Mrs Moore and Mrs Blythe, who gave her messages from the world of the supernatural, so that when her prophecies proved wrong, she could put the blame on them. It also protected her from direct accusations of witchcraft, for she could always claim to be merely a go-between. Even so, most of her clients were too frightened of her powers to attempt to denounce her.

She became more and more daring in her trickery. She told one of her customers that her husband had been kidnapped and that unless she produced several gold coins to be melted down by Mary as part of a spell to ensure his release he would certainly be killed. Sure enough, the husband returned home safe and sound a few days later –

hardly surprising, as he had never been in the hands of kidnappers. Another woman was told that her husband was having an affair and the only way to stop it was to pay Mary three half-crowns for a special spell to restore her husband's affections. Later she was told that this had been successful and that she had nothing more to worry about. She only began to doubt Mary's honesty when her husband, a soldier, came home on leave and convinced her that infidelity had never crossed his mind.

In 1806 Rebecca Perigo came to consult her, complaining of pains in the chest, which she attributed to the curse of a neighbour. Mary, after apparently consulting the reclusive Mrs Blythe, confirmed that it was a strong curse and that strong measures must be taken to counter it. She told Rebecca and her husband William to bring her four guinea notes which she sewed into a pillowcase, keeping the money and secretly substituting four sheets of blank paper. She then told them to take the pillowcase home and sleep on it. This was only the beginning; over the following months she invented one essential charm after another, charging so much that the Perigos had to part with their life savings and became so impoverished that they were going without food to meet Mary's demands. Eventually, when they had nothing more to offer and she felt that William was becoming critical of her methods, Mary decided that it would be simpler to dispose of them than to risk repercussions.

She produced a letter, supposedly written by Mrs Blythe, which predicted that they would both fall seriously ill in May 1808 and that they would 'seem dead but live'. Mary said that she would provide them with a special potion which they must add to a pudding which would last them for six days and they must start eating it on 15 May. They did as they were told and, after the first serving of pudding, they both started vomiting. William, who already had his doubts about Mary's potions, refused to eat any more but Rebecca, who had complete faith in the witch's brew, continued to follow her instructions. She died on 24 May.

Though Mary had told the couple that all her work would be in vain if they consulted a doctor, William called in his physician, who confirmed that both he and Rebecca had been poisoned. William immediately told his story to the authorities but when they went to arrest her Mary, in anticipation of their arrival, was vomiting and complaining of stomach pain, accusing William of giving her poison and attempting to hold him responsible for his wife's death.

It was soon obvious who was telling the truth for a variety of poisons were found at Mary's home, including mercuric chloride and arsenic, and several of the servants who had worked for her in the past gave evidence that she had included poison in her potions, especially when a client wanted to harm his enemies. Mary Bateman was sentenced to hang on 20 March 1809 but the large crowd that assembled to see sentence carried out was strangely silent, still afraid that Mary might use her witch's power to avenge herself.

Henrietta Robinson

HENRIETTA ROBINSON was a mystery woman from the moment she arrived in the town of Troy, New York, in 1852. She obviously had a wealthy lover, for a luxurious carriage appeared at her door from time to time and a richly dressed gentleman dismounted to spend an evening in Henrietta's cottage. He was said to be an important politician. Then, one night, neighbours heard raised voices and slammed doors as the top-hatted gentleman left in a hurry and for the last time.

The townsfolk were naturally curious about the newcomer and the tales told by Henrietta herself fed the rumours. She told a number of different tales about her background – she was descended from European royalty and had been brought up in a French château; she was the daughter of an Irish lord and had been turned out of his castle because she married a working man; she was the illegitimate child of an aristocrat and had been brought up in an English convent. She told her Irish gardener an involved story about being turned out by her father, an Irish admiral, when she became pregnant by a worker on his estate. Her lover had taken her to America, where he had deserted her; later she had become the mistress of an influential New York official who had installed her in the cottage in Troy but now had deserted her too.

After this last desertion her behaviour became stranger and stranger: sometimes, while talking to people, she would burst into tears, sometimes she would start laughing uncontrollably and sometimes she would break into a strange, jerky dance. She did make some attempts to join in the social life of the town but these attempts came to an abrupt end after an unpleasant incident at a dance, where a young man named Smith apparently made an improper suggestion to

139

her. A few days later she cornered Smith in the grocery store and held a pistol to his head until he apologized. She went on to threaten him with death if he dared to insult her again but by this time the owners of the shop, Timothy Lanagan and his wife, had recovered from their initial shock and they hustled Henrietta out, scolding her vigorously for her unwarranted behaviour and threatening her with arrest if she produced the gun again.

For the next two months Henrietta was at daggers drawn with the Lanagans and it seemed that she could hardly bring herself to speak to anyone in the town. Then, one day in May, she arrived at the shop, all smiles and apologies. She hoped that they would forget the past and make friends after all and as a mark of the new beginning, she would like to buy them a beer. The Lanagans were astonished at her sudden change of heart but they knew that it was good business to encourage a well-heeled customer, so they agreed to drink a beer with her and invited her into the kitchen where one of their relatives, Catherine Lubee, was preparing a meal.

Mrs Lanagan brought beer and glasses and also powdered sugar, which Henrietta had requested, as she liked her beer sweetened. When Catherine Lubee went out into the yard for some potatoes, and Mrs Lanagan had left for a moment to attend to a customer, Henrietta announced that she was hungry and asked Mr Lanagan for one of the boiled eggs he kept in the shop. When the three returned, they found that Henrietta had poured the beer and added sugar to all four glasses. She proposed a toast and Mr Lanagan and Mrs Lubee drank with her, surprised to find how bitter the beer tasted. Mrs Lanagan had been called into the shop again and by the time she returned, Henrietta was leaving. Mrs Lanagan, who disliked sugared beer, was glad that she did not have to drink out of politeness and she poured the contents of her glass down the sink.

During the afternoon both Timothy Lanagan and Catherine Lubee were taken ill. By 5 pm Mr Lanagan was dead and Catherine Lubee died next day. From the moment her husband started vomiting

Mrs Lanagan was sure that he had been poisoned by something that Henrietta had put in his beer so she summoned the police immediately and Henrietta was arrested. Arsenic was found in both bodies and a packet of arsenic was found concealed beneath a rug in the cottage. Henrietta had bought it from the local pharmacist 10 days before.

Reporters covering her trial called her 'The Veiled Murderess', for her face was shrouded by several blue lace veils which she only lifted briefly when it was essential for a witness to identify her. The defence counsel did his best to prove her insane and doctors who interviewed her in prison testified that they thought that she was irrational and incoherent, but she was judged legally sane and sentenced to death. The sentence was commuted to life imprisonment on the day set for her execution – 3 August 1853. It was only 37 years later when she set fire to her cell in a vain suicide attempt that she was finally transferred to a hospital for the criminally insane, where she died in 1905 at the age of 89.

Louisa Merrifield

LOUISA MERRIFIELD was a plump, smiling 46-year-old, a homely and reassuring presence even as she stood in the dock, accused of poisoning her employer, Mrs Sarah Ricketts. Louisa had recently married for the third time when she answered 80-year-old Mrs Ricketts' newspaper advert for a housekeeper and, with her 71-year-old husband Alfred, moved into the old lady's bungalow in Blackpool, England.

Louisa had been running a lodging house when Alfred moved in as one of her boarders but the business was doing poorly and Louisa never had enough money to meet the bills. She borrowed money from anyone who would lend it and seldom paid them back. When she married Alfred he was shocked to find that she had not even paid the bill for her second husband's funeral. She was finally forced to leave the lodging house to keep a step ahead of her creditors.

At first, all went well in her new life. Louisa put herself out to look after her employer's every need. Mrs Ricketts thought herself very fortunate and, as an incentive to the couple to stay on as long as she might need them, she changed the will that left her house to the Salvation Army and left it to the Merrifields instead. The honeymoon period was soon over. Louisa found Mrs Ricketts bad-tempered and demanding and Mrs Ricketts found that her new housekeeper's devotion to her duties was shortlived. She considered that Louisa was extravagant with the housekeeping and rather too fond of her tot of rum. She began to think seriously about sacking her and, of course, a rethink of the will would follow.

On the night of 14 April 1953 Mrs Ricketts died, but Mrs Merrifield did not call the doctor until the next morning. She had been busy looking after the old lady, she explained, trying to make her comfortable and giving her an occasional sip of rum. She didn't want to leave her at that time of night to go in search of a doctor. At the end Mrs Ricketts had got out of bed on her own; Louisa had found her lying in the hall and had picked her up to get her back to bed. Her last words had been thanks for all that Louisa and Alfred had done for her.

Louisa hoped to arrange a quick cremation for her employer and, though the death came as no great shock, the unseemly haste made Mrs Ricketts' doctor wonder if all was in order. A postmortem was arranged and this found that Mrs Ricketts had been poisoned by yellow phosphorus, an ingredient of rat poison. Though Louisa had recently bought a rat poison containing phosphorus, none could be found at the bungalow; however, a spoon coated with a gooey substance which experts thought was probably a mixture of rat poison and rum was found in Louisa's otherwise tidy handbag. The suggestion was that she had hidden it there after feeding the deadly mixture to Mrs Ricketts and then forgotten about it.

The evidence might have been insufficient to convict but for Louisa's garrulous nature, for her chattering tongue had already betrayed her. Three weeks before Mrs Ricketts died, Louisa met a friend in the street and exclaimed: 'Oh, David, I've had a bit of real luck. Where I'm living an old lady has died and left me a bungalow worth £3000.' When visiting another friend she told her: 'I can't stay. I've got to go home and lay out an old woman,' adding quickly 'Actually she's not dead yet but she soon will be.' She confided in an astonished stranger at a bus stop that she had come home one day to find Alfred and Mrs Ricketts in bed together. If it happened again, she said angrily, 'I'll poison the old bitch and my husband as well.'

When Louisa and Alfred were both put on trial for murder in July 1953 Louisa denied that any of the incriminating conversations had ever taken place, saying that the witnesses were jealous of her legacy because they were all 'up to their necks in mortgages'. There was no question that rat poison had been fed to Mrs Ricketts, but there was some doubt whether the amount she had consumed was enough to kill

*The crowd waiting outside Strangeways Prison, Manchester examines the
bulletin posted after Louisa Merrifield's execution, 18 September 1953*

her. If she had died of natural causes, then the defendants would only have been guilty of attempted murder and not subject to the death penalty.

Louisa was found guilty and was hanged at Strangeways Prison on 18 September. On the matter of Alfred's guilt, the jury was unable to agree a verdict and it was decided not to proceed with a second trial. As nothing had been proved against him, Alfred was able to inherit a half share in the bungalow his wife had been so determined to own and with the proceeds of the sale he bought several caravans, living in one and renting the rest. He died at the age of 80.

Gesina Gottfried

WHEN Gesina Gottfried finally appeared in the dock in 1828 she had 10 years of killing behind her and admitted to murdering at least 30 people by mixing white arsenic in their food and drink.

The first was the young man she married in her home town of Bremen, Germany, in 1815. Everyone had warned her that he was a hopeless alcoholic who could never keep a penny in his pocket but Gesina was too spoilt and wilful to listen and she married him for his good looks. She soon found that it was a mistake, for her husband was so often in a drunken stupor that he could not satisfy her sexually. Once she found a lover she decided to dispose of her husband by lacing his wine with arsenic. No one wondered at his death; they only wondered how anyone who drank so much could have lived so long.

Now Gesina was free to marry her lover, Gottfried, but he was reluctant to tie the knot. At first he said that the stumbling block was Gesina's two children, fathered by another man. This obstacle was soon removed by Gesina, who simply poisoned them. Her next problem was her parents, who were shocked at the idea that she should contemplate marriage so soon after the death of her husband and children. She asked them to lunch and fed them poisoned stew. Their painful deaths were attributed to gastric inflammation.

Though there now seemed to be nothing in the way of an immediate marriage, Gottfried still prevaricated. Soon he was ill in bed with Gesina nursing him devotedly. Realizing that he was dying and overcome with gratitude for her selfless care, he summoned a priest to conduct a bedside marriage ceremony and a lawyer to change his will, leaving everything to his new bride.

In the years that followed, Gesina managed to poison anyone she disliked or anyone she fancied had done her a bad turn. By 1825 she had overreached herself in buying a large house on which she could not afford to keep up the mortgage. When the bank foreclosed the house was sold to a wheelwright named Rumf and his family. When she lamented that she had nowhere else to go, Herr Rumf invited her to stay on as a housekeeper. It seemed like an excellent arrangement on both sides and Gesina excelled in preparing delicious meals for the family. Herr Rumf relied on her more when his wife died soon after giving birth to her latest child. When the children of the family fell ill, one after another, Gesina looked after them just as she would her own – and one by one, they died.

Perhaps, by the time only Herr Rumf was left, Gesina had grown careless, for the wheelwright began noticing a film of white powder on his meals. He took a white-speckled piece of meat to the police, who soon confirmed that the meat had been sprinkled with white arsenic. In due course Gesina was arrested and charged with the murder of Frau Rumf.

Far from trying to deny her crimes or excuse herself, Gesina openly admitted that she had killed the Rumf family and boasted of killing some 30 people, as though it was a pleasure to be able to parade her cleverness before an audience at last. Committing a murder, she said, had given her an all-enveloping rush of excitement, like a sexual climax. Only a woman with a very strong personality, she announced proudly, could accomplish what she had accomplished. When it was time to face the executioner's axe she stood just as tall and proud, apparently convinced that she had performed some feat to be admired.

Caroline Grills

CAROLINE GRILLS was a kindly little woman of 63, affectionately known as 'Aunt Carrie' around her suburban neighbourhood in Sydney, Australia, where she was always ready with tea and sympathy. But neither her age nor her harmless exterior could save her from a life sentence after she was charged with four counts of murder and two of attempted murder in the 'Aunt Thallie' poisoning case.

In 1947 Caroline called in the pest control officer to deal with an infestation of rats. The poison that he used, based on thallium, did the job in no time and he left an extra supply in case the problem recurred. Later that year Caroline's stepmother, Mrs Christiana Mickelson, died. She was 87, so no one was unduly surprised and no one expected Caroline to shed many tears; she had never liked her father's second wife.

Caroline's husband inherited a cottage when 84-year-old Mrs Angeline Thomas died. She had been fond of him since he was a boy and Caroline was jealous of their affection for one another. The following year Caroline's brother-in-law, 60-year-old John Lundberg, died. The Grills and the Lundbergs had been spending a holiday together and when he became ill he blamed the seafood he had been eating. When his hair began to fall out he could no longer blame it on a simple case of food poisoning. Nothing that his doctor could do seemed to help and he died in October, followed soon afterwards by Mary Ann Mickelson, widow of Caroline's brother, who suffered the same symptoms.

John Lundburg's widow, Eveline, had been feeling off-colour since her husband's death and Caroline was a frequent visitor. When Eveline and her daughter Christine began losing their hair and felt a

148

spreading numbness in their limbs, Caroline was full of concern; she was round every afternoon, making pots of tea and serving it with her own home-made cake. One afternoon Christine's husband, John Downey, wandered into the kitchen just as Caroline was making tea, ready to carry it out to the verandah, where the two women were sitting, comparing symptoms. John saw 'Aunt Carrie' take something from her pocket and add it to one of the cups – the one she handed to Eveline a few seconds later. That evening Eveline was feeling much worse and John Downey was sure that he knew why. The next day he made a point of being at home during Caroline's visit. This time, when he saw her drop something into Eveline's tea he snatched the cup from her and took it straight to the police station. An analysis by the police chemist showed that it contained thallium, a deadly poison without taste or smell, so that it was easy to administer without the knowledge of the victim.

At Caroline's trial Eveline Lundberg was a star witness for the prosecution. She was a pitiful figure suffering from the permanent effects of thallium poisoning, completely blind and walking with the aid of sticks. Though there was a possible motive for the first two murders, there seemed no good reason for the rest. According to the prosecutor Caroline enjoyed the sense of power she gained from controlling the life and death of her victims. She had found murder easy, he said, and 'continued her career of poisoning out of habit'.

Martha Rendall

IT WAS a sad day for Thomas Morris's children when he took Martha Rendall into his home in Fremantle, Western Australia. Thomas, a railway worker, had turned his wife out of their home because of her slovenly ways and when Martha took over he was delighted by her careful housekeeping and high standard of cleanliness.

His five children were less delighted for though she insisted that they called her 'Mother' she had no affection for them, disciplining them harshly and beating them frequently. The neighbours noticed that the children, once healthy and happy, were now pale and listless and losing weight fast. They muttered among themselves but no one had the courage to take any action.

The children frequently caught cold and by summer 1907 Anne and Clive, both under 10, were suffering so badly from coughs and sore throats that the doctor was called in. He prescribed throat swabs and these were administered by Martha, ignoring the screaming and crying of the children, who found the process agonizing. The children grew steadily worse and in July Anne died, followed soon afterwards by Clive. The doctor who examined them noted the inflamed mucous membrane of the throat in each case and certified that the cause of death was the dreaded disease diphtheria.

Twelve months later 14-year-old Arthur also developed a severe sore throat and Martha once again produced the throat swabs and took no notice of Arthur's cries of agony. The neighbours listened to his shrieks in astonishment: surely no medicine could be effective if it caused so much pain? Still they were reluctant to report Martha's strange behaviour. Arthur died on 6 October 1908 and this time the doctor decided on an autopsy. This revealed nothing untoward and once again the death was attributed to diphtheria.

In April 1909 young George, one of the two remaining Thomas children, took a cup of tea from Martha and found that it was so hot it scalded his throat. Martha announced that throat swabs would be the perfect remedy but George had listened to the screams of his brothers and sister and he had watched them die. He was determined that he was not going to suffer the same fate, so while Martha was preparing the swabs he bolted out of the door and did not return.

His disappearance was reported to the police, who on making enquiries in the neighbourhood, soon heard from the neighbours about the ill-treated Morris children and Martha's strange idea of nursing. When George was found he said that he was afraid that 'Mother' was going to kill him, like the others.

Further enquiries revealed that over the past three years Martha had bought large quantities of hydrochloric acid from the chemist. The bodies of the three Morris children were exhumed and this time a more thorough postmortem was carried out, showing that their throats had been washed with large amounts of hydrochloric acid, producing inflammation hardly distinguishable from that caused by diphtheria.

Martha and Thomas were both charged with murder, but there was no evidence to convict Thomas. Martha, it was shown, was a sadistic murderer who had given the children acid in their tea to make their throats sore, then had used copious amounts in the swabbing procedure. She was, apparently, jealous of the attention Thomas gave to the children and wanted to have him to herself. Martha Rendall became the last woman to be hanged in Western Australia, on 6 October 1909.

Susan Barber

MICHAEL BARBER was a reliable, hard-working family man, well-liked in the English seaside town where he lived with his wife and three children. He was captain of the local darts team, keen on sea fishing and car mechanics. No one liked to tell him that his wife Susan was having an affair with his friend and partner in the darts team, Richard Collins.

One Saturday morning in May 1981, Michael set off early for a sea-fishing expedition but, finding that a strong wind was whipping up the waves, he decided to abandon the trip and return home. This was unlucky for Susan who, not expecting her husband back before dusk, was enjoying herself with her lover in the marital bed. Michael flew into a rage, punched Richard and slapped Susan hard across the side of the head. This seemed to bring Susan to her senses and, when she visited the doctor with an ear problem caused by the slap, she asked Michael to go with her, so that they could consult him about counselling for their marital problems.

Michael was not in need of counselling for long. About 10 days later he complained of a severe headache, then a sore throat and stomach pains. He collapsed at work and was taken to the local hospital, then transferred to an intensive care unit at a major London hospital where his condition deteriorated. On 27 June, three weeks after his first symptoms, he died.

For the doctors, it had been a puzzling case. When he was first admitted his illness had been diagnosed as pneumonia, then later it had looked like a case of the little-known and usually fatal Goodpastures Syndrome. But his symptoms did not exactly fit the usual progress of the disease and one member of the medical team thought that it looked more like paraquat poisoning. The consultant ordered specimens of blood and urine to be sent away to be tested for poison. Later he was told – mistakenly, as it turned out – that the results were negative.

The pathologist performing the postmortem noted signs that would normally indicate paraquat poisoning but, as this seemed to contradict the test results, no action was taken. It was only several months later, when the notes on this unusual case were being prepared for use at a medical conference, that the doctors discovered that samples had not, in fact, been sent to the National Poisons Unit. Michael Barber's internal organs and a sample of his blood which had been stored in the research department were then dispatched and both tested positive for paraquat.

It was nine months after Michael Barber's death that the case was turned over to the Essex Constabulary and they were faced with two initial problems. The type of paraquat used was Gramoxone, a deadly weedkiller only available to professionals who could be assumed to use it for its legitimate purpose, so how did it come to be in the Barber household in the first place? Moreover, Gramoxone had an extremely strong and unpleasant smell, so that it would be almost impossible to take it unknowingly and its formula was such that the stomach would reject it immediately and anyone drinking it would become violently sick. The first problem was solved when it was discovered that Michael had worked as a landscape gardener in the late 1960s. He had been familiar with Gramoxone and might well have kept some for his own use in the garden and never finished it. The makers of Gramoxone were then contacted and it was found that both the smell and the emetic that would cause vomiting had been added in 1977 to guard against accidents and misuse. If, as seemed likely, Michael Barber had obtained his supply in 1970 or earlier, it would have been possible for him to take the poison without knowing it.

After Michael's death Susan had collected £15,000 from his pension fund and Richard Collins had moved in with her. However, their affair did not last long and since then she had had a number of lovers. She had spent part of the insurance money on a CB radio and had used the call sign 'Nympho' to contact new men. She had met her latest lover this way. There were local rumours about sex parties and even black magic rituals taking place in the house.

When the police arrived to question Richard Collins he was so taken aback that he was soon confirming that Michael had been poisoned, but he denied any involvement, pointing the finger firmly at his ex-lover. Susan Barber was also taken by surprise by the rigorous police questioning and before long, she found herself admitting to putting poison in her husband's food. She had not meant to kill him, she protested, only to make him ill, so that he would be forced to leave her alone.

It was after the discovery of her affair with Richard, she said, that he had become unbearable, dogging her footsteps, insisting on knowing where she was at every minute of the day and constantly taunting her with her infidelity. All she wanted to do was to see him suffer as much as he had made her suffer. She knew about the poison in the shed and had added it to the gravy she made to go with a steak and kidney pie, knowing that Michael was the only member of the family to add gravy to his meal. When the first dose did not have a dramatic enough effect, she had repeated the process. The police believed that she had given Michael a third dose, adding it to his medicine, but this was never proved beyond doubt.

Throughout her trial, Susan insisted that she had only meant to make her husband ill and pleaded not guilty to murder – but the jury did not believe her and the judge told her: 'I cannot think of a more evil way to dispose of a human being.' She was gaoled for life, though in July 1983 she was allowed to marry her lover, the CB enthusiast. Richard Collins was tried for conspiracy to murder and gaoled for two years.

Christa Lehmann

CHRISTA LEHMANN had an unhappy youth and made a miserable marriage. She grew up in Worms, Germany, in the 1920s and 1930s, a time of deep economic depression. Her mother was committed to an asylum when she was in her teens and her father drowned his sorrows in drink. Christa was caught in a number of petty thefts and put on probation.

She hoped to turn over a new leaf when she married Karl Franz Lehmann in 1944 but her happiness was short-lived when she realized that, like her father, he was a drunkard. No one expected her to be grief-striken when a ruptured stomach ulcer led to his death in 1952. After that, Christa was free to take lovers and to spend a good deal of her spare time with her closest friend, Anni Hamann.

On 12 February 1954, Christa generously offered several of her neighbours cream-filled chocolate truffles. Most of them ate and enjoyed them right away but 75-year-old Eva Ruh, Anni's mother, put hers in the fridge for later. When Anni came home from work she saw the tempting sweet and took a bite, only to grimace and spit most of it out on to the floor, where the family dog wolfed it down eagerly. Shortly afterwards Anni was doubled up with stomach pains and only minutes later she was dead. The dog, too, went into convulsions and died.

At first the police were at a loss: Anni had obviously been poisoned but the forensic examination failed to detect any of the usual poisons. It was only when a university scientist was brought in to help that the cause of death was identified as a new and lethal phosphorus compound known as E–605, developed as a chemical insecticide.

Eva Ruh had witnessed the effect of the chocolate truffle, yet it was hard for her, or the police, to believe that Christa would poison her best friend. However, they soon discovered that her husband had died suddenly, and in great pain, and that the following year her father-in-law, with whom she had been living since Karl's death, had fallen off his bicycle soon after leaving home and died in the street after several agonizing convulsions. It was obvious that Christa had some explaining to do and she was taken into custody.

Within a few days, Christa had confessed all. She admitted that she had given a poisoned sweet to Eva Ruh – she, not her daughter Anni, had been the intended victim. Christa had a grudge against her because she fancied that the old lady was trying to break up her friendship with Anni. Obviously thinking that she no longer had anything to lose, she also admitted to murdering her husband and her father-in-law. She had seen the new insecticide on the shelf at the local chemist's shop. It had been labelled 'poison', so she assumed that it would do the job.

At her trial, Christa's lawyer tried to argue that she should not be held responsible for her actions as she was a 'moral primitive' who had grown up without developing the standards by which normal people measured their actions. It was an unconvincing defence and Christa was sentenced to life imprisonment on 20 September 1954. Even then, she seemed quite cheerful about her crimes, telling newspaper reporters that she had always enjoyed a good funeral. 'I suppose I shouldn't have done it,' she was quoted as saying, 'but except for Anni, they were all nasty people.'

Christa's discovery of E–605 as an effective poison started a new fashion, with a couple of dozen murderers following her lead and more than 70 suicides using it to escape the hopelessness of the current recession.

Ann Bilansky

THE CASE of Ann Bilansky was always puzzling: if it was never certain why she should have murdered her husband, why she should have married him in the first place was even more of a mystery. Ann, a personable 35-year-old widow, came from North Carolina, USA, and had been in Minnesota for six months when she married Stanislaus Bilansky, a notoriously bad-tempered, violent man. Three wives had already walked out on him, tired of his petulance, his sulks and his heavy drinking. He had not worked for some time and his savings had been eaten up, so that by the time he met Ann he was already in debt and throughout their marriage the situation worsened.

After the first few months there was clearly no love lost between them and Stanislaus told friends that his wife was sleeping with her young nephew, John Walker, who lived with them. In February 1859, he told them that she was going back to North Carolina with Walker and asked if they knew anyone who could come and keep house for him. On 2 March there was a full-scale row when Stanislaus, after wolfing down the huge meal that Ann had cooked for him, wanted to make love to her and she refused. Later that evening he fell ill and when the doctor was called in he diagnosed a bad case of indigestion. He probably did not take his patient's illness too seriously, for not only was Stanislaus a confirmed hypochondriac but he had a morbid fear that he was destined to die in March and always complained of feeling bad at this time of year. With hindsight his fear seems like a premonition for a little over a week later he was dead.

After the funeral the rumours began to grow. Rose Sharf, a girl who had been employed to nurse Stanislaus, spread the word that Ann and her nephew were sharing a bedroom. Lucinda Kilpatrick, a friend, remembered seeing Ann buying rat poison to get rid of vermin and saying that she wouldn't mind giving her husband 'a pill'. It was enough to start an enquiry and though the postmortem was inconclusive and failed to prove that Stanislaus died from arsenical poisoning, both Ann and John Walker were arrested and charged. John was later released but Ann stood trial in May.

According to the prosecution, Ann had disposed of her unloved husband in order to pursue her affair with John Walker. She had been seen to buy arsenic, and none remained in the house. She had had every opportunity to administer it to the luckless Stanislaus, for she was the only person to prepare his meals. Since the initial postmortem, the organs of the deceased had been analysed by experts in Chicago and they decided that arsenical poisoning was the cause of death.

Ann denied that she felt anything more than family affection for John Walker and said that nothing improper had occurred between them. If Stanislaus had died from arsenical poisoning, then he must have taken the poison himself. After all, he was known to be deeply depressed about his debts. In spite of her protestations, she was found guilty of first-degree murder and sentenced to death by hanging.

She had every reason to hope that the sentence would not be carried out, for no woman – nor, come to that, any white person – had ever been hung in Minnesota. While her lawyers fought, unsuccessfully, for a new trial on the basis of a legal technicality she escaped from gaol and joined up with John Walker, attempting to leave the state dressed as a man, but she was soon recaptured. Appeals to the governor for clemency were rejected: he saw the murder of a husband by a wife, who instead of cherishing him laced his food with poison, as a particularly heinous crime.

Before the sentence was carried out on 23 March 1860, Ann Bilansky said: 'I am a guilty woman, I know, but not of this murder . . . I die a sacrifice to the law. I hope you all may be better judged than I have been and by a more righteous judge. I die prepared to meet my God.'

Chapter Three

METHODS OF MURDER

Introduction

AMONG THE ladykillers whose stories are told on these pages, the gun probably comes next to poison as the favoured choice of murder methods. In the USA firearms have always been freely available and in farming communities all over the world women are used to handling guns. They kill quickly without physical contact, a big advantage for a woman. There's a useful line of defence, too – the killer can claim that she did not understand firearms, that the gun went off by accident, that it was only used in self-defence.

Few women use a knife as a weapon, but when they do there is usually a vast amount of pent-up fury behind the blows. This does not mean that women need to keep at arm's length from their victims and many a murder is committed with any handy household object – a heavy ornament, an ashplate, a hammer. From the 19th century comes a whole list of servant killers who used the strength developed from a lifetime of manual work to batter or strangle their employers. These fearsome women were usually also desperate women; threatened with dismissal and an uncertain future with no home or job, they hit back in the only way open to them, even though they had little hope of evading justice.

Sharon Kinne

IN THE USA, where gun licences are easy to obtain and many ordinary families keep a revolver beside the bed or in the glove compartment of the car, deaths by the bullet are frequent and it is much easier to claim that the shooting was an accident. Police called to investigate the death of James Kinne at his home near Kansas City found James lying dead on his bed, shot in the back of the head, and a sobbing young wife, Sharon. Through her tears she told how her two-and-a-half-year-old daughter had been playing a game of cops and robbers with her father's gun, with fatal results. James was always leaving the gun around the house, she said, and the little girl often played with it.

There were those who had their suspicions, knowing that after four years of marriage the Kinnes quarrelled frequently and that Sharon wanted a divorce, but the child was obviously accustomed to handling the gun and Sharon's story was accepted. As soon as she received the money from her husband's insurance policy she bought a flashy new car from an attractive salesman, and in the weeks that followed they became more than friends. Only two months after James Kinne's death the body of Patricia Jones, the salesman's wife, was found in an area well-known as a haunt for courting couples. She had been shot four times with a .22 calibre revolver and it was Sharon Kinne and a boyfriend who discovered the body. Sharon said they had been out looking for Patricia because they thought she was seeing another man and did not want to tell her husband before they had concrete proof.

A witness came forward to say that she had seen Patricia getting into Sharon's car early on the evening of her death and a friend described buying a .22 pistol for her, which she did not want registered in her name. Sharon admitted having such a pistol but said that she had lost it some time before. Though she was charged with murder, all the evidence was circumstantial and not strong enough to convict her. The previous owner of the pistol was traced and he remembered firing bullets from it into a tree. These were dug out and examined, but they did not match the bullets in Patricia's body. Though the witness said that he had owned several guns and could well have been mistaken about the pistol used on the tree-shooting day, his mistake helped in Sharon's acquittal.

Her troubles were not yet over; she was arrested again, this time on the charge of murdering her husband. A review of the evidence, in the light of subsequent events, had revealed holes in her story and a witness gave evidence that she had once offered him $1000 to kill her husband. The court decided that a toddler would have been unable to pull the trigger and found her guilty, but a clever lawyer managed to have the verdict set aside on a technicality and the replacement jury could not reach agreement. Once again, Sharon was free.

She dropped out of sight for four years until the night of 18 April 1964 when a motel owner in Mexico City heard gunshots and, hurrying to investigate, found Sharon Kinne still with the pistol in her hand and a man lying dead on the floor. This time Sharon could not deny the shooting but said that the man, a Mexican radio presenter called Francisco Ordonez, had invited her back to his motel room because she was feeling ill. Once there, he had attacked her and tried to rape her, so she had been forced to defend herself.

It was one story too many and this time, no one believed her, especially when it was found that bullets fired from her .22 gun matched those found in the body of Patricia Jones. She was sentenced to 13 years in gaol.

Kathryn England

KATHRYN ENGLAND, living in a Tennessee farming community, had the choice of two guns: with one she practised her husband's murder, lining up her shot, so that with the other she could shoot him as he lay on his bed. The couple had been married for 25 years and, as far as those who worked with them in the tobacco fields knew, their marriage seemed happy enough – but in reality they had both begun to look outside for fulfilment.

Early one Saturday morning in March 1982, a neighbour of the Englands' scrambled into his clothes to answer the hammering on his door. Kathryn England, shaking and tearful, gasped: 'Please come. Something's happened to my husband.' At the Englands' house, he found 45-year-old Franklin lying in his own blood in the bathroom. He assumed that Franklin had committed suicide but the police had other ideas. There was a large bloodstain on the bed, which seemed to be where Franklin had been shot. Though the bullet had missed his heart, a fragment had opened an artery in his arm as he staggered from the bedroom to the bathroom. It looked far more like murder than suicide.

Above the bloody patch there was a hole in the bedroom ceiling and closer examination showed another, smaller hole which had been stopped up. Below it, a .22 bullet was found buried deep in the mattress. In the attic, near the hole in the ceiling, were two guns: a .22 rifle and a .270 weapon. Kathryn's first explanation was that she had been in the attic shooting at the blackbirds that were damaging her garden when the gun had jammed; as she tried to free the bullet it had fired while the gun was pointed at the floor, penetrating the ceiling and accidentally hitting her husband.

Her story left many questions unanswered and she told several others over the weeks that followed, including one in which she fired a shot at her husband just to wake him up. When she came to trial the prosecutor maintained that she had planned the murder carefully, testing out the angle of the shot with the lighter gun, plugging up the hole so that her husband would not notice, then using the heavier rifle to fire on Franklin.

Kathryn now told a different tale, painting a graphic picture of a violent marriage and herself as a victim, a battered wife who lived in fear of her husband. He had forced her into perverted sex acts, assaulted and ill-treated her, once causing a miscarriage. He threatened to kill her if she told anyone of his brutal treatment, which explained why no doctor could testify to the bruises she had sustained from his fists. She had considered killing herself many times but had never quite had the courage.

She had to admit, under cross-examination, that she had a male friend who had taken her away for weekends and that she had once consulted a lawyer about her financial status as a widow. All the same, she protested that she had never intended to kill Franklin, whom she had once loved, but only to stop the beatings. It was a good performance but the jury remained unconvinced: she was sentenced to life imprisonment.

Ruth Ellis

RUTH ELLIS has gone down in history as the last woman to be hanged in Britain. Ruth, a peroxide blonde who worked as a club manageress, had gunned down the lover who had tired of her, racing car driver David Blakely, in full view of passers-by in a suburban London street. She made contradictory statements about where she got the gun and it still remains something of a mystery. If someone else was involved, giving her the gun when she was obviously full of drink and jealousy, then he would have been implicated in the murder and Ruth might never have hanged.

Ruth, who was 28 when she committed murder, had led a chequered life. She left school at 14 to work as a waitress and at 18 she had an affair with a French-Canadian soldier which resulted in an illegitimate baby. In her ambitious search for a more affluent lifestyle she became a night club hostess and at the Court Club she met dentist George Ellis, a big spender who bought her champagne, clothes and expensive presents. They married and she bore him a daughter, but George was a violent drunkard and they soon separated. Ruth moved on to work as a call-girl and nude model, then as manageress of the Little Club, an upstairs drinking room in Knightsbridge. It was at this time that she met David Blakely, who came from a far more affluent background. Born in 1929, the son of a Sheffield doctor, he was educated at a leading public school but, in spite of his upper-crust accent and suave charm, he was temperamentally incapable of holding down a steady job. He had a passion for racing cars which he could indulge on the legacy left by his father but, though he raced at well-known venues like Silverton and Le Mans, mixing with the stars of the racing circuit, he was never successful. When Ruth first met

Ruth Ellis with her lover David Blakely

him he was drunk and insulting and she thought him a 'pompous ass'. Unfortunately for her, she later succumbed to his boyish charm and easy, cultivated manner.

Though David was engaged to another girl, he and Ruth became lovers and late in 1953 she found she was pregnant. She later said that David had offered to marry her but at the time she was not really in love with him and thought that she could 'get out of the mess quite easily' by having an abortion. Perhaps in an attempt to distance herself from David, Ruth began a new affair, this time choosing a more dependable lover, 33-year-old company director Desmond Cussen, who fell deeply in love with her. Predictably, this sharpened David's interest. He became jealous and began hanging around the club all the time, telling her that he had broken off his engagement.

When Ruth took a flat in Egerton Gardens, Kensington, Cussen lent her money to pay the rent but it was David who moved in with her. They lived there as Mr and Mrs Ellis but there was nothing harmonious about their relationship. David was drinking heavily at Ruth's expense – he had by now frittered away his inheritance – and had fits of violent jealousy about her continued liaison with Cussen during which he would beat her so badly that she had to use camouflage make-up to cover the bruises. Ruth was also jealous of David's growing friendship with a married couple, Carole and Anthony Findlater, and suspected him of having an affair with Carole.

Things came to a head at Easter 1955 when Ruth and David had had a bitter row, with Ruth receiving a black eye and David a superficial cut from a knife. On Friday 8 April, David told the Findlaters that he was becoming worried about what Ruth might do and that he wanted to get away from her. They invited him to spend the weekend with them in Tanza Road, Hampstead, and though he was expected home that evening he accepted. Ruth, who had had a miscarriage 10 days earlier and was feeling ill and depressed, waited all evening for David to arrive, then phoned the Findlaters at about 10.30 pm. She spoke to Anthony, who denied that David was with him. Ruth phoned several times after that but found that as soon as she spoke, the receiver was replaced. In the early hours of the morning Ruth went to Tanza Road, where she saw David's green Vanguard parked outside the Findlaters' flat. No one answered when she rang the bell, so she banged on the windows of the van until they fell in, trying to make as much noise as possible. Anthony Findlater appeared at the door in his pyjamas, still insisting that David was not there, while Ruth shouted to her lover to come down and talk to her. The police were called and though Ruth insisted that 'I shall stay here all night until he has the guts to show his face', they eventually persuaded her to go home. Too upset to sleep she paced about smoking until morning, when she went back to Tanza Road and hid in a doorway, watching David and Findlater come out of the house and drive off in the Vanguard.

On the Saturday night Ruth was back in Tanza Road, watching the flat from the road while the Findlaters held a party. She could hear David's voice and a woman she thought to be the Findlaters' nanny giggling in response. Later, when the blinds in the nanny's room went down, David's voice was no longer audible and Ruth concluded that he was 'up to his tricks' again and that the nanny was the new attraction. She spent another night sleepless, fuming and drinking. By the evening of Easter Sunday, she admitted at her trial, 'I was very upset. I had a peculiar feeling I wanted to kill him.'

Once more she went back to Hampstead but this time the Vanguard was not in Tanza Road, so she made her way to the Magdala pub at the foot of South Hill Park. When she arrived, David and a friend, car salesman Clive Gunnell, were just leaving, carrying three quarts of light ale. At first, neither of them noticed Ruth. Gunnell went round to the passenger side of the Vanguard while David, juggling the flagon of beer, fumbled for his keys. Ruth called his name, but he did not seem to hear. Again she called him, pulling a heavy Smith and Wesson .38 revolver from her handbag. As David ran for the back of the van, two shots rang out in quick succession. He slammed against the side of

the vehicle, then staggered towards the motionless Gunnell, screaming to him for help.

'Get out of the way, Clive,' shouted Ruth, firing a third shot at David
as he tried to run for safety. As David fell to the ground, Ruth stepped
up to his body and fired three more shots. The sixth bullet ricocheted
off the road and hit the hand of a woman who was on her way to the
Magdala to join her husband for a drink. Ruth stood still, unmoved by
the blood and the cries of the gathering spectators. As a customer
from the saloon bar approached her, she told him, 'Phone the police.'
PC Thompson, who had been enjoying an off-duty drink, replied, 'I am
a police officer', and took the gun gently from her.

From then onwards, Ruth remained cool and composed. Before
her trial one of her main concerns was that her hair was showing its
dark roots and arrangements were made for the right dye to be sent
into Holloway Prison. Though she pleaded not guilty, Ruth did not put
up a spirited defence. She was unwilling that too much of her past
should be revealed in court and she refused to invite the sympathy of
the jury. When answering her counsel's questions about the times
David had beaten her she made light of them, saying, 'He only used to
hit me with his fists and hands, but I bruise very easily.'

When Mr Christmas Humphreys, for the Crown, rose for cross-
questioning he asked only one question: 'Mrs Ellis, when you fired
that revolver at close range into the body of David Blakely, what did
you intend to do?'

'It is obvious', replied Ruth simply 'that when I shot him I intended
to kill him.'

With that reply, she sealed her fate. In his summing up, the judge
pointed out that it was no defence to show that the accused was
jealous, unwell and badly treated by her lover and that she was overcome with an uncontrollable urge to kill him. If the jury was satisfied
that Ruth Ellis fired the shots that killed David Blakely, the only other
question to decide was 'that at the same time she fired those shots she

had an intention to kill or do grievous bodily harm'. It was obvious that the only possible verdict was 'guilty'.

From the death cell, Ruth wrote to David's mother, saying, 'I shall die loving your son and you should feel content that his death has been repaid.' When she heard that there was to be no reprieve, she wrote to a friend about her coming execution: 'Don't worry, it's like having a tooth out and they'll give me a glass of brandy beforehand.' She was calm to the end – 'the bravest woman I ever hanged' said the official hangman, Albert Pierrepoint.

As for the gun, Ruth originally claimed that it had been given to her about three years before by a man in a club, but she did not know his name. The police did not believe the story at the time and after the trial she made a statement saying that Cussen, with whom she had been drinking, had given her the gun, ready loaded, and had even driven her to Hampstead. This was never proved and Cussen flatly denied all knowledge of the gun. 'She was a dreadful liar, you know,' he said.

Pauline Dubuisson

FOUR YEARS before Ruth Ellis's crime, Pauline Dubuisson shot her ex-lover dead in his Paris flat. In her case the jury brought in a verdict of murder without premeditation so that she was sentenced to imprisonment rather than execution. It was a surprising decision which seemed to fly in the face of all the facts.

In 1946 Pauline had enrolled as a medical student at the University of Lille, where her first report described her as very intelligent but 'not a steady worker. She is well-balanced but haughty, provoking and a flirt. Her conduct is mediocre'. At university she plunged into a stormy three-year-long affair with another student, Felix Bailly, but Pauline never managed to remain faithful to one man; she continued to sleep around and even kept a notebook recording details of the comparative performance of her various lovers. Though Felix wanted to marry her, she was enjoying herself too much to settle down and eventually Felix decided to end the relationship and continue his studies in Paris.

For 18 months there was no contact between them. Pauline had a number of lovers and it was not until she heard from a friend that Felix was engaged to be married that she decided to visit him in Paris and attempt to start up their affair again. When she found that Felix was no longer interested Pauline was furious and spent her cash birthday present from her father on a .25 calibre automatic. She left a note for her landlady in Lille to say that she planned to kill Felix and herself, so by the time she arrived in Paris in March 1951 Felix had been warned and was on his guard. He refused to let her into his flat and would only agree to meet her in a public place, with one of his friends present.

Pauline did not go to the arranged meeting-place; instead, she sat in a café opposite Felix's Left Bank flat, calmly sipping coffee as she watched the two men leave and return an hour or so later. She waited until the friend had left then made her way up to Felix's seventh-floor flat. Felix was expecting the arrival of a second friend, Bernard Mougeot, who was taking over the role of protector, so when Pauline knocked he may have opened the door expecting to find Bernard standing there. Instead it was Pauline, with pistol at the ready. She shot him three times. Any one of the three shots could have killed him but Pauline was taking no chances: the final bullet entered her ex-lover's head behind the right ear.

Pauline then turned the gun on herself but it jammed on the fourth bullet, so she disconnected the pipe leading to the gas cooker in the kitchen, put the free end in her mouth and lay down, preparing to die. Bernard Mougeot, whose taxi had been stuck in a traffic jam, arrived to find the smell of gas seeping into the corridor. Inside the flat, his friend was lying in a pool of blood on the living-room floor and Pauline was unconscious in the kitchen. He quickly removed the pipe from her mouth and called the fire brigade, who revived her to stand trial for murder.

When he heard the news Pauline's father, overcome with shame, killed himself, first taking a dose of poison and then gassing himself. On the day fixed for her trial Pauline was found unconscious in her cell, bleeding profusely from a cut wrist. Her suicide note said: 'I think my family is accursed and myself also. I only hurt those whom I love most in the world.' Once more she was revived and the trial began a month later.

It was difficult for the defence to represent Pauline's act as a 'crime of passion' when she had been separated from Felix for 18 months – and when her acid remarks about her various lovers were read out in court she could not claim to be deserted and lovelorn. Far more pitiful was Felix's fiancée, robbed of her happiness by Pauline's jealousy. Pauline's background was also against her: she had been in her early teens when the German occupation of France began but by the age of

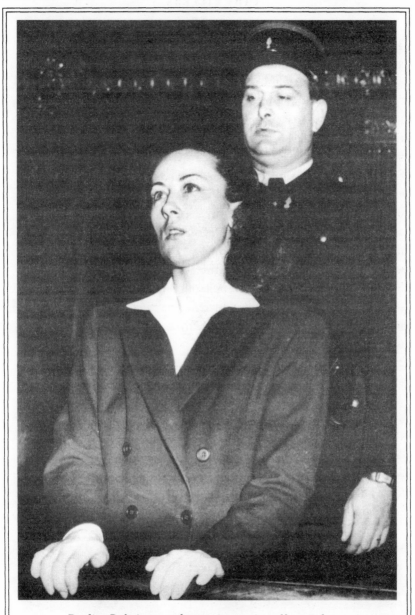

Pauline Dubuisson at the opening session of her trial

17 she was the mistress of a 55-year-old German colonel, so that after the Allied landings she suffered the punishment reserved for collaborators and had her head publicly shaved.

The prosecutor even mocked Pauline's suicide attempt, suggesting that it was just too convenient that the gun had jammed. Perhaps she had only turned on the gas tap when she heard steps approaching the flat door. Then again, she had managed to fail when cutting her wrist. She had managed murder far more efficiently than she had managed suicide, he suggested. However, it may have been the suicide attempts that caught the sympathy of the jury, for the evidence showed that her story of the gun jamming on the fourth shot was correct, and that by the time the firemen arrived she had second-degree asphyxiation and was foaming at the mouth. By the time she was discovered bleeding in her cell, she had lost a litre (2 pints) of blood. Whatever the reason, the verdict resulted in a more lenient sentence than Pauline might have expected.

Leone Bouvier

LEONE BOUVIER was far more deserving of sympathy than Pauline Dubuisson, though she too killed her lover with a bullet. However, the French court handed down the same verdict, ignoring the extenuating circumstances of her miserable background and blighted love affair. Leone had been a victim all her life, growing up in an unloving household with a violent, alcoholic father and a bitter, hard-drinking mother. She was a plain girl of limited intelligence but with a generous nature and need for love that made her an easy prey for the local lads who laughed at her behind her back.

Her luck seemed to be changing when she met Emile Clenet, a 22-year-old garage mechanic in Nantes. They first met at a dance and made a date for the next afternoon, but on the way to the rendezvous Leone's bicycle had a puncture and by the time she got there Emile had gone. It was six months before they met again at the local Lent carnival. 'You're six months late', joked Emile. 'Never mind, we've found each other again.' After the fair Emile took her to a hotel where they made love, and Leone felt valued for the first time in her life.

Sunday was Emile's only free day and it soon became the one highspot in Leone's dreary life. The couple would ride on Emile's motorbike, go dancing sometimes, and end the day in a cheap hotel. They talked about marrying and Emile took her home to meet his parents, who were welcoming and kindly. Everything seemed to be going well but Leone seemed dogged by misfortune. A minor accident with the motorbike resulted in a bang on the head and after that she suffered from headaches and depression which got on Emile's nerves. A few months later Leone became pregnant, only to lose the baby and find her bouts of depression getting more frequent and less manageable.

In January 1952 she was sacked from her factory job, resulting in a violent row at home with her mother screaming and her father raining blows on her. Leone took off on her bicycle, riding all night to reach the garage where Emile worked. She was exhausted and tearful, he was irritable and unconcerned: she had no business bothering him at work, he had no time to listen to her and at the moment he was too busy even to meet for their regular Sundays. Leone was devastated. She had no money and nowhere to go, so she spent days wandering the streets and nights sleeping rough before drifting into prostitution to buy food and shelter. She found herself standing outside gun shops, mesmerized by the gleaming weapons in the window. She could not explain later what was going through her head – perhaps suicide, perhaps murder – but one day she had a hallucination, seeing a young man standing at her side saying: 'Don't. He is too young. He has a right to live.' Subconsciously she must have been thinking of killing Emile, even if she had not admitted it to herself yet.

Over the next few weeks she saw little of Emile but she pinned her hopes on her birthday on 15 February. Last year they had been close and happy and Emile had bought her a bicycle lamp, the only present she had received since childhood. She was thrilled when he agreed to meet her but he did not acknowledge her birthday and he stayed with her only long enough to use her body, just like the men she picked up on the docks. The next day she bought a gun. Even for an illiterate girl like Leone, there was no problem; the .22 automatic had recently been designated a 'sporting weapon' and was available to anyone.

When Emile asked her to meet him at the Lent carnival, Leone hoped that the carnival, with all its memories, would be a new beginning for them – but she must have had her secret doubts, for she carried her gun in her handbag.

At first all went well; they wandered through the gaily decked stalls and Emile spent some time at the shooting range. Then he casually told her that he was leaving for a job in North Africa and did not plan to return. When Leone asked what had happened to their marriage plans, he merely shrugged and told her to find someone else. He drove her back to where she had left her bicycle and, deaf to her entreaties, prepared to ride away. Leone asked him to kiss her one last time, drew him towards her with her left arm and kissed his cheek. At the same time she placed the barrel of the gun against his neck and fired a single bullet. Afterwards she fled to the convent where her sister was a nun, and where she was arrested the following day.

The judge at her trial was hostile, unwilling to concede that Leone's circumstances made any difference to the case. If her sister could rise above her home background and become a nun, then why should Leone have gone wrong? He found it outrageous that she should have shot her lover while she kissed him and demanded to know why she killed him.

'I loved him,' Leone answered simply, tears streaming down her face.

Middle-class women had walked free from French courts on the excuse that they had committed a 'crime of passion' but poor, dim Leone Bouvier was sentenced to penal servitude for life – a minimum of 20 years.

Dr Alice Wynekoop

DR ALICE WYNEKOOP, a frail 62-year-old widow who was highly respected in her neighbourhood of Chicago, seemed an unlikely murderer, hardly the type to shoot a young woman in cold blood. Yet not only did she commit the crime but she left the body in her basement surgery while she cooked an evening meal of pork chops and mashed potatoes for herself and Enid Hennessy, her lodger. Then the two women sat and chatted about the book Miss Hennessy had recently been reading, a volume of Galsworthy's *Forsyte Saga*.

It was late in the evening of 21 November 1933 when Alice's daughter Catherine, a doctor specializing in paediatrics, took a distraught phone call from her mother. 'It's Rheta,' she gasped. 'She's dead . . . she's been shot.' When the police arrived Dr Alice let them in, saying, 'Something terrible has happened here.' She led them down to the surgery, where they found a naked girl lying face downwards on the operating table. A revolver lay near her head and her clothes were heaped on the floor. When the police pulled away the blanket they found that she had been shot in the chest and there were burns on her face, thought to be the result of chloroform.

The dead girl was Alice's daughter-in-law Rheta, the daughter of one of the leading merchants of Indianapolis, Burdine H. Gardner. She had recently married Alice's favourite son Earle. As Earle had proved incapable of holding a steady job, the young couple had moved in with Alice but the marriage had been a disaster from the start. Earle saw no reason to curtail any of his pleasures – which mainly revolved round liquor and girls – for the sake of his young wife. Rheta, left for weeks on end in the forbidding three-storey house with only Alice and her elderly lodgers for company, soon turned into a nagging neurotic, forever complaining about her health and haunted by the fear of developing tuberculosis.

When Earle, forced to cut short his latest trip by news of Rheta's death, arrived back in Chicago, he made no pretence of grief. He told waiting reporters that his wife was 'sickly and mentally deranged', so much so that she had once tried to poison his whole family by drugging their food. The marriage, he said, was an utter failure. He supported his mother's story that Rheta was killed by a burglar who had broken into the surgery in search of drugs. Rheta, as part of her hypochondria, was in the habit of weighing herself naked in the surgery and the burglar, expecting to find the room empty, must have panicked and shot her.

To the experienced eyes of the detectives, it was obvious that this was not the work of a burglar and they subjected Alice to days of questioning. At first they trod carefully – after all, she was a doctor of some standing, known for her dedicated work among the poor. After her husband, Dr Frank Wynekoop, died she had supported her three children, enabling her daughter to study medicine and her elder son to enter the business world on a good footing. There was nothing in her life to suggest that she was anything but a fine, upstanding citizen, but as the questioning continued her interrogators became convinced that she had committed the crime. Her utter devotion to Earle was obvious and it was equally obvious that she had little time for Rheta. To the rest of the world Earle might be a wastrel who neglected his wife and refused to shoulder his obligations, but in his mother's eyes he could do no wrong. She would do anything for him – even, perhaps, taking action to rid him of a cumbersome wife.

Eventually Alice confessed that no burglar was involved, but she insisted that Rheta's death had been an accident and the gunshot had been an attempt to make it seem like the work of an outsider. The doctor said that Rheta was suffering from a recurrent pain in her side and she had offered to examine her. The pain was so bad that Rheta had asked for an anaesthetic, so the doctor had given her chloroform on a sponge. She took several deep breaths but then stopped breathing and did not revive even after 20 minutes of artificial respiration. The doctor's description of what followed was worded like a medical report, as though she were distancing herself from any possible emotion: 'wondering what method would ease the situation best of all and with the suggestion offered by the presence of a loaded revolver, further injury being impossible, with great difficulty one cartridge was exploded at a distance of some half dozen inches from the patient.' She concluded by trying to explain why she then left the body lying in the surgery while she went about her ordinary household tasks: 'The scene was so overwhelming that no action was possible for a period of several hours'.

Later Alice retracted even this guarded confession, saying that she was not in her right mind after prolonged questioning. Earle never accepted it and, in an attempt to save his mother, he confessed to the murder himself. He was arrested, but released when it was proved that he was on a train to Arizona with his latest girlfriend at the time the shot was fired.

At her trial the defence advanced the burglar theory once more, while the prosecution suggested that Alice had murdered her daughter-in-law for her insurance. Though insurance money has been sufficient motive for many murders, Alice's known character and past life suggests that it was far more likely that she saw this as the best way to liberate her beloved son from a bad marriage. Whatever her motive, she was found guilty of first-degree murder and gaoled for life. She was paroled at the age of 78 and died two years later.

Addie Mae Lemoine

THERE WAS always a gun in the Lemoine household in Louisiana, for Louis Lemoine's greatest pleasure in life was hunting in the swamps and woods he had known since boyhood. Sometimes he was gone for days at a time, usually returning with a deer slung across his shoulders to provide extra meat for the table. But when he went off on 23 April 1962 without letting anyone know where he was going, his brothers were surprised. According to his wife, Addie Mae, he had taken his .410 calibre shotgun, which would point to a regular hunting trip – but Louis always told one of his brothers where he was heading so that if he did not return they could come to his aid. It was a sensible precaution for a man who had been deaf and dumb since birth.

As the days lengthened into weeks, the sheriff began to take an interest in Louis's disappearance. Louis had a reputation as a thoroughly reliable workman, yet he had let down a logging contractor who had engaged him for a job, leaving him short-handed. It was also discovered that he had left his box of .410 shells behind in the boot of his car, where he kept them safely from the children. At this point Addie Mae arrived at the sheriff's office with a letter, supposedly written to her son by his aunt in Baton Rouge. It said that Louis had visited her a few days before and sent his love to his children. It was a bad mistake: the sheriff only had to compare the letter with an example of Addie Mae's handwriting to know that she had written it herself and put it into an envelope posted in Baton Rouge.

Addie Mae's fate was sealed when the local shopkeeper remembered selling her two .410 shotgun shells the day before her husband's disappearance. It had stuck in his mind because no one had ever bought two shells rather than a box-full. Addie Mae pretended no longer. Louis was buried under the washhouse, she said, where she had hidden his body after shooting him.

Addie Mae had married Louis 20 years before when she was only 15 years old. He was eight years older and, strong and silent, he seemed very attractive to the unsophisticated girl who had known nothing but poverty and hardship. They had seven children, so looking after them kept Addie Mae busy, but as time went on she found her marriage unsatisfying. Her husband could make himself understood at work and at home but communication was necessarily limited. Louis was a self-sufficient man, unwilling to mix with people more than necessary; he was given to dark moods and would respond to a disagreement by taking himself to the woods for a couple of days. Addie Mae was still young enough to crave company and fun and the silence weighed heavily on her.

Husband and wife grew apart and after 13 years of marriage Addie Mae obtained a divorce, only to find that living apart from Louis did not bring the freedom and happiness she wished for. The children missed their father and she insisted that it was for their sake that she decided to move back in with Louis. The resentment and anger she felt about her life did not go away: it grew and festered until she could say in her statement that she had watched her sleeping husband on the night of 22 April and 'the more I looked at him the more I hated him'.

They had had an argument the day before and the frustrating, one-sided conversation, with no relief to be had from screaming at one another like most couples, had been the last straw. Now, with the children in bed and her husband sleeping, she loaded one of her two shells into the gun, held it near his head and fired. She had bought the second shell for herself but when the moment came to kill herself she lost her nerve. Instead she rolled the bloodstained bedclothes around her husband's body and pulled it into the washhouse, where she knew it would remain undiscovered until the next day. In the morning, after the children had gone to school, she took up some boards from the washhouse floor and buried Louis in a shallow grave.

Addie Mae pleaded guilty and was sentenced to life imprisonment – an imprisonment that would probably be no more miserable than the prison of her life with Louis. She had tried living with him, she had tried living without him and neither way filled her needs. In the end she saw the only way out as death for both of them, but had lacked the courage to fulfil her intentions.

Winnie Judd

In 1932 Winnie Judd, the wife of a doctor, was committed to a hospital for the insane in Arizona, USA. She had shot her two best friends, Helwig 'Sammy' Samuelson and Agnes Ann LeRoi, then packed their bodies into two trunks and taken them by train from Phoenix, Arizona, to Los Angeles. Her crimes became known as the 'Phoenix Trunk Murders'.

In 1924, at the age of 26, Winnie had married William Judd, 32 years her senior. His work meant frequent moves and by 1931 they were living in an apartment in North 2nd Street, Phoenix, and Winnie was employed as a doctor's secretary at the Grunow Clinic. One of their neighbours in the building, Ann LeRoi, also worked at the clinic and Winnie became firm friends with Ann and her room-mate Sammy, who was ill with tuberculosis. When William Judd moved again, this time to Los Angeles, Winnie stayed behind, living with her two friends for a time before moving to an apartment at 1130 East Brill Street.

On 17 October she rang to say that she would be late getting to work. Shortly afterwards a call came in from someone who said that she was Ann LeRoi and that she was unable to come to work that day; Sammy's brother had arrived on a visit and she had to take him to Tucson. Later the receptionist who answered the phone said that she thought that it was Winnie Judd's voice, disguised in the hope of sounding like Ann. About 15 minutes later, Winnie arrived at the clinic, looking 'as white as a sheet'.

That evening, Winnie called a delivery company and asked them to pick up a trunk from North 2nd Street. When the delivery men arrived there were no lights in the apartment and Winnie told them that the power was cut off because she was leaving and they would have to

Winnie Judd

work with the aid of matches. The men told her that the trunk was too heavy to go as baggage and suggested that they should keep it overnight and send it by express in the morning. Winnie said that she would take it to her sister's home instead and asked them to deliver it to East Brill Street.

The next day Winnie arrived at the railway station with two trunks, which were loaded on to the Los Angeles express. The porter who handled them noticed a dark liquid dripping from the larger trunk and suspected that it might contain a butchered deer. Winnie's brother Jason accompanied her on the journey and at the other end the trunks were stored in the left luggage office. When Winnie and Jason returned to collect them later in the day they were asked to open them, because station staff had noticed an unpleasant smell coming from the larger trunk. Winnie said that she would get the keys from her car and left the station hastily with her brother, but she failed to return. The police were called to the station where they broke open the trunks to find the body of Ann LeRoi in the larger one and the remains of Sammy Samuelson, cut into pieces to fit into the smaller one. Winnie's brother was quickly apprehended and admitted that Winnie had told him about the contents of the trunks and that they had planned to throw them into the sea. He said that his sister was subject to 'insane fits of anger'.

Dr Judd put out a public plea to his wife through the newspapers: 'I earnestly beg and implore her to come to me . . . If she has committed the crime with which she is charged, it means that it was done in a period of irresponsibility and an irrational state or condition. I want to assure her that if this comes to her attention, she will have every support and assistance I am able to give her.' It was several days before Winnie responded and gave herself up at a Los Angeles funeral parlour. At the time her hand was roughly bandaged and later a .25 calibre bullet was extracted from between her middle and index fingers. At her trial, it was shown that the bullets from the victims' bodies and that from the prisoner's hand all came from the same gun and that this gun, together with a set of surgical instruments, was in a hat-box carried by Winnie on her train journey.

A long, semi-incoherent letter from Winnie to her husband was found, in which she gave an account of the murders. According to her she had quarrelled with the two girls over breakfast, while they were all still in their pyjamas. Sammy had threatened her with a gun, whereupon Winnie put her hand over the muzzle and grabbed the breadknife. The gun went off, wounding Winnie in the hand but she managed to knock Sammy down and take the gun from her then, maddened by pain, she had shot both girls. Then she had panicked and packed the bodies in the trunks. 'It was horrible to pack things as I did,' she wrote. 'I kept saying "I've got to, I've got to or I'll be hung." '

For the next 39 years, until she was finally paroled in 1971, Winnie managed to remain in the news. Insane or not, she was clever enough to escape from custody seven times. The first six escapes all lasted only a few days and sometimes she gave herself up voluntarily but the seventh time she remained at liberty for over six years, making a life for herself in a California town where she worked as a housekeeper and was liked and trusted.

Claire Reymond

CLAIRE REYMOND arrived at the apartment her husband shared with his mistress, took out a revolver and shot the woman dead. In England she might well have hanged but she committed her crime in France, which had always accepted the idea that a 'crime of passion' was excusable, and a sympathetic jury discounted the apparent premedi-tation and the fact that she tricked her husband into leaving the apartment so that her rival was unprotected and helpless in the face of a firearm. Consequently, she was allowed to walk free.

She was 25 and had been married for four years to a prosperous businessman, her senior by 15 years. The marriage was happy enough, though the couple were disappointed that Claire had not become pregnant. After a year abroad, they returned to live in Paris in 1890. There Claire met up with a close friend from her schooldays, Yvonne Lassimone, a pretty blonde from a moneyed family who, to her great delight, asked her to become godmother to her baby daughter. Unfortunately Yvonne, a self-willed young woman who was used to getting her own way, was discontented with her own marriage, finding her young husband weak and uninteresting, and was immediately attracted to the older, more sophisticated Paul Reynard.

The two couples spent a good deal of time together but it was months before Claire began to wonder if there was more than friend-ship between her husband and Yvonne. One night they were returning from the theatre when their cab passed under a street lamp and, as the light came through the window, she thought for the moment that she saw Yvonne and Paul holding hands. Assuring herself that she had been mistaken, she put the incident out of her head until she found a bill for the purchase of an expensive ring. She had received no such present, but she had noticed a ring matching the description on Yvonne's finger.

In the scene that followed, with Claire in floods of tears, Paul admitted to being tempted into a brief affair but promised to put an end to it immediately. Yvonne, too, was penitent: she could not bear to lose Claire's friendship or have her daughter lose the attentions of her godmother, she said. It was just as important that she did not have to explain an estrangement between the two couples to her husband. However, despite all the promises, the affair continued and when Lassimone's work took him away from Paris Yvonne remained behind, giving the excuse that she was not well enough to face moving at the time. Lassimone had already received anonymous letters about his wife's behaviour – which might or might not have been written by Claire – and soon discovered that the couple had been meeting secretly at his mother-in-law's home. Still in love with his beautiful wife, he hung back, reluctant to risk precipitating a split, but in April 1892 there was a confrontation during which Lassimone struck Yvonne, with the result that she began divorce proceedings.

Things came to a head on 21 May, when Paul broke a lunch date with his wife. Claire, certain that he was visiting his mistress, took the opportunity to summon a locksmith to open his locked portmanteau. Inside she found several dozen love letters from Yvonne and the lease of an apartment, recently rented by Paul Reymond. For Claire it was the last straw; she took her husband's revolver, went to the address she had found on the lease and climbed up to the third-floor apartment. At first her alarmed husband refused to open the door but she slipped a note under the door saying that she had only come to warn them that Yvonne's husband had discovered their love-nest and was on his way, intent on making trouble. Paul opened the door and hurried downstairs to tell the concierge not to admit any strange men, leaving the two women alone.

Yvonne was sitting on the edge of the bed, putting on her stockings, and Claire claimed that she was 'strangled with emotion' at seeing her rival half-naked after making love with her husband. 'How could you be so shameless? It was I who was so good to you, who forgave you,' she cried. When Yvonne only replied mockingly, Claire said she lost her head. She fired five times and, though four of the bullets went wide, the fifth hit Yvonne in the stomach. Some sort of brief struggle followed, with Claire receiving scratches and Yvonne superficial cuts from a knife, then as Yvonne slumped to the floor Claire hastened from the apartment, passing her husband on the stairs.

Later in the day, Claire gave herself up at the police station. She maintained that she had gone to the apartment to catch the two lovers and confirm her suspicions. She had not intended to hurt Yvonne, much less kill her. When questioned about the gun and the knife, she insisted that she was in the habit of carrying them for protection when, as a young woman, she lived with her family in Haiti, and she had carried them ever since.

At her trial, extracts from Yvonne's letters, in which she always signed herself 'your wife', were read to the jury and were powerful tools in swinging the mood of the court Claire's way. In them the woman who professed to be her friend had told Paul that she viewed any affection shown by him to Claire as a 'profanation of my property' and ordered him: 'Stop sleeping in her bed, she disgusts me.' The jury, full of sympathy, ignored the obvious premeditation in Claire's acts – the fact that she had substituted her husband's revolver for her own tiny pistol and the way in which she had bluffed her way into the apartment – and found her not guilty. It was more a comment on the mood of the times than the merits of the case: in the early 1890s in France, more than half the women tried for crimes of passion were acquitted.

Lofie Louise Preslar

LOFIE LOUISE PRESLAR, later Peete, later still Judson, along with a handful of pseudonyms, was imprisoned for one murder and executed in the gas chamber for another. Her method was a quick bullet in the back of the neck, probably while she was chatting pleasantly to her unsuspecting victim, for Louise was an accomplished confidence trickster. She was a good-looking woman, rounded in her middle years, with luxuriant chestnut hair and a refined, ladylike manner. She gave the impression of being trustworthy and reliable but instead she was a cheat, a liar and a thief, as well as a killer. All those who came too close to her were in danger of their lives, for she was responsible for a number of deaths besides the murders she committed with her own hands.

She grew up in Louisiana, USA, and as a young teenager married Henry Bosley. The marriage lasted only two years and after their separation Bosley, still enamoured of Louise, killed himself. In 1913 she was involved in the death of a hotel desk clerk named Harry Faurote. The clerk and Louise, a guest in the hotel, were suspected of stealing a valuable diamond ring and Faurote apparently shot himself rather than face the disgrace of conviction. Louise, the only person left to give evidence, told a plausible tale and was believed. In 1915 she married a car dealer, Richard Peete, who was a steady, loving man and for a time she seemed to settle down happily, giving birth to a daughter, Betty. Five years later she was on the move again. Her husband's business was going badly and his health was declining, so she left him and went to Los Angeles. There she leased a house belonging to a wealthy mining engineer, Charles Denton, who had recently lost his wife and was planning a long trip. The arrangement was that Louise would move in immediately and Denton would stay on in the house for a short time while he made arrangements for his journey.

A few weeks later Denton disappeared and shortly afterwards Louise was displaying fine new jewellery to her admiring friends. When Denton's daughter and friends began to make more pressing enquiries, Louise came up with a colourful story: Denton had lost an arm after an infection turned septic and he had gone away for a time, too embarrassed to see anyone until he had adjusted to his disability. It was such an unlikely explanation that it was accepted for a while, but more questions were asked when it transpired that various business dealings had been left in mid-air and that no record could be found of payments made for the medical care needed by an amputee. Several months after Denton's disappearance a search was made at his house and his body was found buried in the cellar, wrapped in a quilt. Both his arms were intact but there was a bullet-hole in the back of his neck.

By this time Louise Peete had rejoined her husband in Denver, but when it was shown that she had forged Denton's name on cheques, pawned some of his property and charged clothes and jewellery to his late wife's account she was summoned back to Los Angeles for questioning. In 1921 she stood trial for murder and was sentenced to life imprisonment. Richard Peete stood by her during the trial, bringing their four-year-old daughter to court and earnestly telling reporters that Louise could never have committed such a crime. Her conviction was such a blow that he never fully recovered from it and three years later he committed suicide.

Louise was paroled in 1939, when she took the name of Anna Lee, and a few years later she went to live with two old friends, Margaret and Arthur Logan. Arthur was over 70 and fast lapsing into senility and Margaret was glad to have a friend to help with his care. It was not, of course, in Louise's nature to care for anyone. There were heated arguments as she pressed to have him sent to a sanatorium. At the beginning of May Louise married for the third time; her husband, Lee Judson, was a trusting widower, who knew nothing of her past. She invented reasons why he could not move in with her immediately and kept the marriage secret from the Logans. At the end of the month Margaret Logan disappeared and in June Arthur Logan was committed to an asylum where he died a few months later. Judson moved in with Louise, who was once more forging cheques and making free with other people's property.

It was in December that Margaret Logan's body was found, buried in her own garden. She had been shot in the back of the neck and the job had been finished by smashing the butt of the revolver into her skull. Both Judsons were promptly arrested, though the bewildered Lee was quickly cleared and released. Shortly afterwards he jumped to his death from a high-rise building, becoming yet another of Louise's victims.

In court, Louise told the mainly female jury that she had done nothing to harm Margaret Logan. Her husband had killed her in a fit of insanity and Louise had feared that she would be blamed because of her past record, so she had buried the body. The jury was unimpressed and took only a short time to decide on her guilt. She was sentenced to execution in San Quentin. Louise had remained calm and composed throughout both her trials and her demeanour did not change when she was led from the condemned cell and strapped into a chair in the gas chamber, under the gaze of several reporters.

Styllou Christofi

STYLLOU CHRISTOFI was a mother-in-law straight out of a nightmare who killed her son's wife with her own hands. She had come to England from Cyprus to live with her son Stavros, who worked as a waiter at the famous Café de Paris in London's West End. Stavros had been in England for 12 years and had married a German girl, Hella; they lived in a ground-floor flat in Hampstead with their three young children and did their best to welcome Styllou into their home. Unfortunately Styllou was a bitter, bad-tempered woman, overbearing and possessive, and from the day she arrived life in the Christofi household was thoroughly miserable. Nothing that Hella did was right for her; according to her mother-in-law she dressed like a woman of the street, she wasted money on make-up, she knew nothing about bringing up children. Styllou carped and criticized, argued and shouted and it was impossible to reason with her.

Twice Stavros found other lodgings for his mother but no landlady would tolerate her for long and she was soon back with his family. Eventually Hella put her foot down. She decided to take the children to Germany for a holiday and made it clear that, by the time she returned, Styllou must be back in Cyprus. Hella never had the chance to put her plans into effect. When the two women were alone in the kitchen Styllou set about Hella with the ashplate from the stove and battered her into insensibility, then she followed up by throttling her. She then dragged Hella's body out into the yard, soaked it with paraffin and set fire to it, stoking the blaze with newspaper, apparently hoping to make her daughter-in-law's death look like an accident. A neighbour, John Young, had taken his dog into the garden and saw the whole back of the next-door house aglow. When he saw Styllou

Styllou Christofi

tending the fire he assumed that everything was in order and as far as he could tell, as she stoked the flames, she was burning a tailor's dummy. Once she was satisfied that the fire had done its work, Styllou ran into the road, crying that her kitchen was on fire and her grandchildren were in danger.

Police found bloodstains in the kitchen and burned paper and wood soaked in paraffin surrounding the charred body. Styllou told them: 'I wake up, I smell burning, go downstairs. Hella burning. Throw water, touch her face. Not move. Run out, get help.' Later, when the house was searched, they found Hella's wedding ring wrapped in paper and hidden behind an ornament in Styllou's bedroom, though Stavros said that his wife never took it off her finger. Styllou's explanation was: 'I find it on stairs. I wrap it up. I think it is a curtain ring.' In the dustbin were pieces of charred material, part of a scarf that belonged to one of the children, tied in a noose. Styllou had used it to strangle Hella, then cut it from her neck.

At her trial, her previous history was her downfall. It was revealed that as a young woman she had been accused of killing her own mother-in-law by ramming a burning torch down her throat, though for some unaccountable reason she had been acquitted. This time the jury recognized her for the vengeful, uncontrolled creature that she was and brought in a verdict of guilty. They dismissed her feeble story that she had gone to bed that evening leaving Hella doing some washing but had woken to the smell of smoke. Finding that Hella was not in her room, she said she had rushed into the kitchen to find that the back door was open and her daughter-in-law's body was lying in the yard in flames. She had thrown water on her face in an attempt to revive her but when this was unsuccessful she had run into the street for help.

If she had pleaded insanity she might well have escaped execution but she refused, saying 'I am a poor woman with no education but I am not a mad woman – never never, never'. She was hanged in 1954, a year before Ruth Ellis, who killed her lover in the same street – but while the Ellis hanging provoked a storm of protest, Styllou Christofi's execution passed with no lament. To the end she showed no feelings of sorrow or shame; her overwhelming emotion seemed to be anger that her son Stavros had found no way to protect her from her fate.

Julia Ransom

THE GARDEN of a pretty English cottage in Matfield, Kent, was the scene of a triple murder on a summer afternoon in 1940. The body of Mrs Dorothy Fisher was found in one corner of the orchard and her 19-year-old daughter Freda lay dead on the other side of the orchard. Both had been shot in the back. The third member of the household, a middle-aged maid named Charlotte Saunders, lay on the path at the side of the cottage, shot in the head. Inside, the contents of drawers and cupboards had been strewn across the floor.

Mrs Fisher was separated from her husband Walter, who lived at Piddington, Oxfordshire. The Kent police had called in the Flying Squad and Detective Chief Inspector Peter Beveridge went to interview Walter Fisher and search his farm. The most interesting thing he found was an auburn-haired woman asleep in Fisher's bedroom. Though Fisher explained that she was a friend who had been visiting when she felt ill and went to lie down, it was obvious to the detective that the two were lovers.

A little later, when she was up and dressed in blue slacks and a multi-coloured jumper, the woman was introduced as Mrs Florence Iris Ouida Ransom, for some reason known as Julia. Fisher said that his marriage to Dorothy had been over in all but name before the war started. He had begun an affair with Julia, a young widow, while Dorothy had taken a Danish lover. When the elder Fisher daughter married the family finally broke up, with Dorothy moving to Matfield and Walter to Piddington, though he claimed to have a warm regard for his wife, whom he visited frequently.

Beveridge had already checked out Dorothy's Danish friend, who lived in London. She had recently applied to the police for permission to entertain him at her home in Kent but this part of England was a sensitive area at this stage of the war, when preparations were under way to counter the expected invasion by German forces, and permission had been refused. Beveridge had satisfied himself that it would have been impossible for Dorothy's lover to have travelled down to her home and committed murder. Meanwhile, at the two Fisher homes, he was making some interesting discoveries. Among the servants at Walter's farm there was obvious resentment of Julia Ransom, who seemed to be taking over control and acting in a bossy and high-handed manner. She had engaged extra staff, a Mrs Guildford and her son Fred, but no one, including Walter, had known that these two were in reality her mother and brother. Beveridge learned that over the past fortnight, Fred had been teaching Julia to use a shotgun and to ride a bicycle. Julia acknowledged that she sometimes visited Dorothy and Freda but claimed that on the day in question she had not left home. She said that Mrs Guildford could confirm this, but under questioning Mrs Guildford wavered and seemed far from certain.

At Matfield, Dorothy Fisher's bicycle had been found lying in a ditch near the cottage, slightly damaged. In the orchard, between the two bodies, was a woman's white pigskin glove. All the victims had been shot at close range, which led Beveridge to conclude that the murderer was well-known to the Fishers. He guessed that Dorothy and her daughter, who had both been wearing gumboots, had taken their visitor into the orchard, perhaps with the idea of shooting rabbits. The maid had been preparing tea in the kitchen and had dropped the tray, smashing four cups, saucers and plates when she heard cries from the orchard and hurried out to see what was wrong.

A teenage boy from the village remembered seeing a woman with a bicycle circling the cottage on the day of the killings and stopping several times to peer through the hedge. His description of the auburn-haired woman, who wore blue slacks and a multi-coloured jumper, matched Julia Ransom exactly. The ticket collector at

Tonbridge station remembered the same woman arriving on the train from London a few minutes past midday, carrying a long thin parcel that might well have been a shotgun. A taxi-driver who drove her to Matfield agreed with the description. Four and a half hours later the woman had returned to the station and boarded the London train.

Julia Ransom was arrested and several witnesses picked her out at an identity parade as the woman seen in Matfield on the fateful day. One or two said that she had been wearing white gloves and the glove at the scene fitted her hand perfectly, though its mate was never found. A routine medical examination, performed when she was arrested, recorded abrasions on her knees that were consistent with a fall from a bicycle and detectives believed that she had taken Dorothy's bike to check out what was happening at the cottage, but had fallen off and left the bike in the ditch.

The prosecution case was that she had arrived in Matfield with the shotgun she had borrowed from her brother Fred. He admitted that he had been teaching her to use the gun and that on 8 July, the day before the murders, she had borrowed it. On 10 July she had returned it, saying that it needed cleaning. At the scene of the shooting she had reloaded the gun at least six times and had fired extra shots into the backs of both Dorothy and Freda as they lay dying. Her motive was jealousy over Walter's continued attachment to his wife and daughter.

At her trial Julia claimed that her mind was a blank, that she had no memory of what she did on 9 July. She was found guilty and sentenced to death, but was later certified insane and confined to an asylum.

Bridget Durgan

BRIDGET DURGAN was one of a number of notorious servant killers who turned to brutal murder after dismissal by their employers, using the nearest household implements to commit, or attempt to conceal, their crimes. Bridget was a 22-year-old Irish girl who had spent several years in America working for one family after another. She was quiet and unremarkable and most of her employers remembered little about her; there was certainly no hint of the horror to come when she joined the household of Dr and Mrs Coriell in New Jersey in 1866.

Bridget was very happy with her new employers. Mary Ellen Coriell, a frail little woman whose body had suffered from a number of miscarriages, was kind to her, she was well paid and the work was not too hard. Unfortunately the Coriells were not so happy with Bridget. She suffered from a type of epilepsy and had frequent fits, and she was incapacitated for several days every month with 'women's sickness'. This, combined with some unpleasant personal habits that offended Mary Ellen, made the couple decide to dispense with her services. Bridget was devastated: she had nowhere to go and knew she would never find such an agreeable household again.

The night before she was due to leave, the Reverend Little and his wife were roused from bed by a hammering on the door. There stood Bridget, thoroughly dishevelled and in her stockinged feet in the snow, holding two-year-old Mamie Coriell in her arms and babbling that two men were ransacking the house and that Mrs Coriell could be in danger of her life. Mr Little armed himself as a precaution against violent burglars, enlisted the help of neighbours and went to investigate. The first thing he saw was signs of a struggle downstairs and smoke issuing from the bedroom. Upstairs an oil lamp had been thrown at the bed, perhaps in an attempt to set fire to the house and destroy evidence, for on the floor lay Mary Ellen's dead body, soaked in blood. She had obviously fought long and hard, for her face and limbs were a mass of bruises, handfuls of her hair had been ripped out by the roots and there were several dozen knife slashes on both the back and front of the body.

Bridget's version of events was as follows: at 7.30 pm two men, complete strangers, had arrived at the house asking for the doctor, only to be told that he was out, attending a woman in labour. Three hours later they had returned and Mrs Coriell had opened the back door to them, assuming that it was her husband coming home. As the strangers pushed their way in and began menacing Mrs Coriell, Bridget had snatched up Mamie and escaped to summon help. The inconsistencies in her tale were soon apparent. She had claimed that Mrs Coriell thought that she was letting in her husband by the back door, while he pointed out that he always let himself in at the front. The only footprints found in the fresh snow outside the house were those of Bridget and the rescue party. A next-door neighbour had heard thumping and crashing coming from the Coriell house but not at the time that Bridget had described. The Reverend Little had seen a patch of blood on Bridget's skirt when she arrived at his house and she had later tried to change the clothing surreptitiously. When she was seen sneaking out to the garden shed she was followed and the household meat knife was found hidden there.

As the net closed around her, Bridget suddenly decided that she knew the two murderers after all and named two local men. When they could both prove their alibis beyond all doubt, she changed her mind and blamed another maid in the town. The maid, too, was able to show that she had been in bed at the time.

No one had the least sympathy for Bridget, least of all the judge at her trial, who was not even willing to consider the possibility that a previously quiet and inoffensive young woman who suddenly carried out such a frenzied attack, apparently without provocation, might not be responsible for her actions. No convincing motive was ever established, though it is just conceivable that Bridget thought that, with Mary Ellen out of the way, the doctor might need her services and keep her on. Alternatively, perhaps Bridget might have made a last plea to keep her position and, as a row developed and she finally faced the reality of being thrown out into the cold world, Bridget suddenly flew into a rage and attacked.

With or without a motive, she was found guilty and sentenced to death, to the delight of the courtroom spectators. On 30 August 1867 she was hanged in front of an enthusiastic crowd, all jostling for a better view.

Mary Flora Bell

MARY FLORA BELL, aged 11, was a pretty dark-haired child with intelligent blue eyes and a quick mind. She could scarcely have had less in common with such gruesome women as Kate Webster or Styllou Christofi yet she, too, strangled her victims and exhibited no remorse.

She was born to an unmarried mother of 17 in 1957. A year later her parents married and moved to the slums of Newcastle, where William Bell was seldom in work and Betty Bell was hospitalized several times because of psychiatric problems. Mary had an unsatisfactory upbringing; she could never count on affection from her mother, who frequently farmed her out to relatives or friends and once even took three-year-old Mary along to an adoption agency and tried to give her away to a woman who was leaving as she arrived. At school Mary was known for clever lying, showing-off and fighting at the least excuse.

On 25 May 1968, two boys exploring a derelict house in the Newcastle slums found the body of four-year-old Martin Brown lying in an upstairs room. Nearby lay an empty pill-bottle. At first it seemed that Martin had taken a lethal dose of pills, but later it was established that he had been asphyxiated. The following day there was a break-in at a nursery school nearby and several notes were found, obviously written by children, all referring to murder. One read: 'We did murder Martin Brown fuck off you bastard!' and another 'I murder so that I may come back.' A few days later the school's new alarm went off and police found two girls in the building: Mary Bell and 13-year-old-old Norma Bell. The girls were not related but lived next door to one another and, in spite of the difference in their ages, had been inseparable for some time. Both girls insisted that they had never

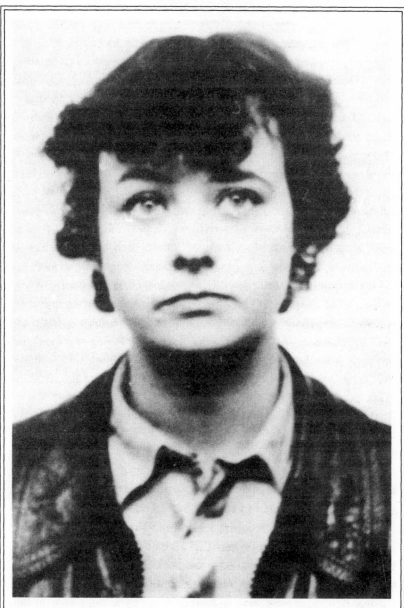

Mary Bell

been inside the school before and no action was taken against them. However, it was obvious that they had developed a morbid fascination with death. Mary called at the Brown's house, asking to see Martin, and when Mrs Brown told her that he was dead she replied cheerfully: 'Yes, I know he's dead. I wanted to see him in his coffin.' Horrified, Mrs Brown slammed the door in her face. Both girls went several times to see Martin's aunt, asking strange questions about how much she missed him and giggling at her answers.

On 31 July the body of three-year-old Brian Howe was found on a patch of waste ground in the same area of Newcastle. He had been strangled and there were cuts on his stomach and small puncture wounds on his legs. Police circulated hundreds of questionnaires to families with children, asking which of them were known to play on the waste ground where the body was found, what they were doing on the day of the murder and whether they had seen any strangers in the area. A number of children were questioned further about their answers, including Mary and Norma. Following their interviews, the two girls were asked for samples of their handwriting. Comparisons with the notes left at the nursery showed that they were the authors. When some of their clothes were sent for forensic examination, fibres from one of Mary's dresses matched with those found on both Martin Brown and Brian Howe. Fibres from Norma's skirt linked her with the second boy.

The children were taken to the police station, where Mary coolly enquired whether the interview room was bugged, demanded to see a solicitor and complained of being brainwashed. As the questioning intensified, the girls both talked about Brian Howe's murder, but each blamed the killing on the other. According to Norma, Mary had pulled the little boy down on the ground and gone 'all funny', squeezing his throat with her hands while he struggled and gasped. Mary had told her that her hands were 'getting thick' and asked her to take over but Norma had run away. Later they had gone back to the body, when Mary had punctured the boy's legs with scissors and tried to carve her initials on his stomach with a razor. Mary, in her turn, said that it was Norma who had strangled Brian while Mary tried to stop her. She had told him to lie down and then started squeezing his neck: 'She squeezed it hard, you could tell it was hard because her fingers were going white. Brian was struggling and I was pulling her shoulders but she went mad. . . . His face was all white and bluey and his eyes were open. His lips were purplish and had all like slaver on, it turned into something like fluff.' It was also Norma, she said, who had collected scissors and razor and marked the little boy's body.

On 5 December 1968 the two girls stood trial at Newcastle Assizes charged with the murders of Martin George Brown and Brian Edward Howe. The prosecuting counsel said that the girls had committed the murders entirely 'for the pleasure and excitement afforded by killing' and that Mary, though two years younger than Norma, was the dominant personality. As the trial progressed it became obvious that Mary was far more intelligent and dangerous. Norma, on the other hand, had a mental age of less than nine years and was immature and insecure.

The girls continued to blame one another for Brian Howe's death. As far as Martin Brown was concerned, Norma claimed that Mary had talked about murdering him on two occasions and had suggested writing the notes found in the nursery school though Mary, of course, said that the notes were Norma's idea. A 12-year-old-old boy testified that he had been playing with them in the nursery sandpit a week after Martin Brown's death when Mary had tripped Norma up and jumped on top of her, crying, 'I am a murderer.' She had showed him the house where Martin's body was found and told him that was where she had killed him. He hadn't believed her at the time, thinking she was just showing off. Norma's mother told the court that shortly after the first murder she had found Mary apparently trying to strangle her 11-year-old daughter Susan. Her husband had had to slap Mary to make her let go. In his summing up, the prosecutor described Norma as 'a simple, backward girl of sub-normal intelligence' and Mary as 'aggressive, vicious, cruel and incapable of remorse'.

The jury found Mary not guilty of murder, by reason of diminished responsibility, but guilty of manslaughter. They accepted the argument that Norma was completely under Mary's influence and found her not guilty. Mary was sentenced to detention for life but there seemed no suitable institution for housing a girl so young and yet so dangerous. When plans were announced to send her to a remand centre in south-east London worried local parents petitioned the authorities saying that their own children would be in danger should she escape. Shortly afterwards she was transferred to a secure unit established especially for her in an approved school for boys in Lancashire. There were protests from local people here, too, but they were reassured that she would be under strict individual supervision. Mary Bell was in the headlines again in 1977 when, with another girl, she escaped from an open prison. They were at large for three days, long enough to find men to have sex with. Mary told the tabloids that her aim was to stay out in the world long enough to prove that she was a normal young woman.

Magdalena Solis

MAGDALENA SOLIS was a prostitute in the Mexican city of Monterey, with her brother Eleazor acting as her pimp, until they were recruited as gods in a weird cult run by the Hernandez brothers in the farming village of Yerba Buena.

Santos and Cayetano Hernandez had managed to convince the simple villagers that the mountain gods would shower them with wealth if they worshipped fully, and this worship involved constant sacrifices of money, which the farmers could ill afford, and also frequent sexual rites, when the homosexual Cayetano and the heterosexual Santos could satisfy all their fantasies. The brothers were having a splendid time but the farmers' faith was flagging, so they decided that a pretty blonde goddess and a good-looking god would liven up the affairs of the cult.

For a time this worked well, and Magdalena and Eleazor, both homosexuals, could scarcely believe their good fortune. But inevitably discontent spread as the months went by and the promised wealth failed to shower down from the mountain. It was Magdalena who came up with the answer: the gods were not satisfied with the sacrifice of chickens and calves, and to avert their wrath the villagers must sacrifice the unbelievers among them. The two farmers who had led the movement of discontent were stoned and beaten to death, then the whole gathering drank their blood in an unholy ritual that Magdalena had dreamed up. She was able to whip the cult followers into such a frenzy of sadistic excitement that eight more of those who had been murmuring against the leaders were 'sacrificed' over the next few weeks.

Magdalena had appropriated a young teenager, Celina Salvana, as her lover but Celina was not a lesbian and she was tempted from Magdalena's bed by the 'high priest', Santos. Magdalena was beside herself with fury and saw to it that Celina was offered as the next sacrifice. As the girl lay bound and helpless Magdalena beat her until she lost consciousness, then the other cult members joined in and clubbed her to death.

By chance, a 14-year-old village lad, Sebastian Gurrero, was passing the cave where the 'ceremonies' were carried out on his way home from school and, hearing the screams and shouts, he peeped in. Horrified, he witnessed the girl's last moments, then watched as the villagers set light to the body to conceal the evidence. Sebastian ran all the way to the nearest town to report what he had seen to the police. They were very doubtful about his story but his distress was obviously genuine, so a patrolman, Luis Martinez, was sent back with the boy to investigate.

Neither the policeman nor Sebastian returned. At last the police were convinced that something was badly wrong and they enlisted help from the military to storm the village. There was a pitched battle around the cave; three policemen were injured and Santos Hernandez was killed. The bodies of Martinez and Gurrero were found; both had been hacked to death and the patrolman's heart had been cut out. Some of the faithful cult members confidently expected to see their two gods in human shape vanquish the police and rise to the mountain top, but instead they saw them marched off to prison.

On 13 June 1963 Magdalena and her brother, with 12 cult followers, were tried for murder and given 30-year prison sentences. Cayetano, like his brother, did not live to face trial. He was dead before the police arrived, killed by one of the cult members who had never believed the stories of gods and treasure but had gone along with the sex and killing for the excitement it offered. Now that his lust for killing had been fed, he had decided to get rid of Cayetano and take his place.

Margaret Allen

IN THE early morning of 28 August 1948, a bus driver saw what looked like a bulky sack lying in Bacup Road in the town of Rawtenstall, England. When he opened the sack he found the body of a 68-year-old eccentric, Mrs Nancy Chadwick. Her head had been smashed to a bloody pulp with what was eventually shown to be the pointed side of a hammer. She was well-known in the neighbourhood, where she wandered about with a knitted shopping bag on her arm, and local rumour said that she carried a large amount of money around with her. She was last seen alive walking along Bacup Road the previous morning and her shopping bag was found floating in the nearby river Irwell 24 hours later.

Among those questioned on the first morning was Margaret Allen, usually known as 'Bill'. She was a thickset 42-year-old lesbian who wore men's clothes and had her hair cut short. From the moment the investigation began Margaret followed the investigating officers around, peering over their shoulders and pointing out 'clues' they might have missed. Margaret was an odd character who, even from childhood, when she was the twentieth of 22 children, always preferred masculine clothes and pastimes. She told people that she had a sex-change operation, but in view of the state of medical knowledge in the 1930s this was unlikely. She spent most of her spare time drinking in pubs and playing darts and she could curse and swear with the best. The men tolerated her because she often bought the drinks but she had only one woman friend, Mrs Annie Cook, who accepted her peculiar ways but had had to turn down her amorous advances when they took a holiday in Brighton together.

Margaret drew attention to herself both by dogging the policemen's footsteps and by claiming in the pub that she had been the last person to see Nancy Chadwick alive, sitting on a bench outside counting her money. She also talked about a secret pocket the elderly recluse had sewn into her clothing. The police, who had been suspicious of Margaret from the beginning, paid her another visit. This time they made a preliminary search of the house and found traces of blood on the walls of the kitchen. They also found rags that Margaret used as floor cloths, which also seemed to be stained with blood. Margaret was unperturbed: 'I'll tell you all about it,' she said and, pointing towards the cellar door: 'That's where I put her.'

She was arrested and charged and had no hesitation in confessing to the murder. She said that she had been leaving her house that morning when Mrs Chadwick came down the road and had asked if she could come in. 'I was in a funny mood and she seemed to insist on coming in. I just happened to look around and saw a hammer in the kitchen. On the spur of the moment I hit her with the hammer. She gave a shout and that seemed to start me off more. I hit her a few times. I don't know how many. I put the body in my coalhouse.'

The ashes found in Nancy Chadwick's hair came from Margaret's cellar and fibres from her clothes were found on Margaret's jacket and trousers. The only defence was one of insanity, but this was rejected and Margaret was sentenced to death by hanging. No motive for the crime was ever discovered. Though there were suggestions that Margaret, finding herself deep in debt, had murdered the old lady for money, there was never any proof that Mrs Chadwick had been carrying cash with her. Margaret herself volunteered no information.

There was no appeal and though Mrs Cook tried to raise a petition for clemency, she only managed to collect a little over 150 signatures. Margaret was executed on 12 January 1949, the first woman to be hanged in Britain for 12 years. On Mrs Cook's last visit, Margaret told her: 'It would help if I could cry but my manhood stops my tears.'

Jeanne Weber

THE 'Ogress of the Goutte d'Or' used no weapon other than her bare hands to kill over and over again. Her victims were all children and her crimes so horrifying, and so pointless, that those involved in the judicial process were unwilling to believe that she could possibly be guilty. The result was that Jeanne Weber evaded justice twice and was set free to kill again.

Jeanne was the daughter of a Breton fisherman, married at the age of 18 and living in a poor district of Paris known as the Goutte d'Or. She had three children but two died in infancy – an everyday occurrence in the slums of the 1890s – and following the deaths she became deeply depressed and turned to drink for solace. After that, strange things began happening to the children in her care. The first was when Jeanne was babysitting for her sister-in-law Mme Pierre Weber while the latter took the laundry to the public wash-house. Mme Weber was only beginning her wash when a neighbour arrived to say that 18-month-old Georgette was having a choking fit. The mother hurried home to find her baby blue in the face and gasping for air, while Jeanne was apparently massaging her chest. Georgette was revived and her mother went back to her washing, only to be summoned again an hour later to find that Georgette had died. The neighbour, Mme Pouche, tried to draw attention to marks on the baby's neck but no one took any notice and the doctor certified the death as due to convulsions. Only nine days later Mme Weber left Jeanne babysitting for her other daughter, Suzanne, and came back to find that this child too had died, again apparently of convulsions. Once again, Mme Pouche noticed marks on the child's throat; once again she was ignored.

So far, the Weber family seem to have accepted Jeanne's version of events without question and they had every sympathy when her only remaining child, seven-year-old Marcel, died in similar circumstances. They even failed to suspect her when another child from the family, seven-month-old Germaine, died in her care. However, when Mme Charles Weber, another sister-in-law, left her little son Maurice with Jeanne for a few minutes while she did some shopping, only to find Maurice choking in Jeanne's arms, it was one coincidence too many. This time the red marks on the body's throat led to a police investigation. Jeanne Weber was tried, and acquitted, in 1906. The eminent medical expert who examined Maurice and the exhumed bodies of the other children, Professor Thoinot, found no evidence of strangulation.

Jeanne Weber moved on and was not heard of again until 1907, when she had changed her name and was working as a housekeeper for the Bavouzet family in central France. When one of the Bavouzet children died, the local doctor reported the red marks found on the child's neck to the police. Meanwhile one of the older children found newspaper cuttings about the 'Ogress of the Goutte d'Or' in the housekeeper's room and put two and two together. Jeanne was arrested again. The same clever counsel defended her for a second time, insisting that an innocent woman was being hounded for no good reason. Professor Thoinot was involved once more and the medical evidence was so contradictory and inconclusive that the case was thrown out.

Once more, Jeanne changed her name. For a while she worked in a nursing home for sick children but she was sent away hastily after being caught pressing her thumbs into the throat of one of the patients. The event was not reported and so yet another family was exposed to tragedy. In May 1908 an innkeeper and his wife named Poirot were charmed by the woman guest who seemed so fond of their young son. Little Marcel seemed equally fond of his new friend, so when she pleaded loneliness and asked if he could share her bed, his

Jeanne Weber

parents agreed. In the night the guest in the room next door heard screams and rushed in to see the woman bending over Marcel. The child's face was blue and blood poured from his bitten tongue. This time there was no doubt about the cause of death and the guest's true identity was soon revealed. Jeanne Weber had committed her last murder.

Public feelings ran high against the fiend who strangled children and crowds in the streets outside the courtroom cried 'death for the ogress'. Before her first trial, when the Weber family was urging that she should be confined to an asylum, Jeanne had been examined by medical experts but though they reported that she was subject to 'nervous upsets', they had found her completely sane. This time the findings were quite different. She was declared guilty but insane and sent to a secure mental hospital. Her counsel argued that she had only committed one murder, that of Marcel Poirot, and that she had been driven out of her mind by the unjust harassment and constant accusations. Once locked away, Jeanne quickly sank into more obvious madness, suffering fits where she grasped her own throat and foamed at the mouth. She died two years later, her fingers locked tightly around her neck.

Kitty Byron

WHEN Kitty Byron's love affair turned sour and she saw herself about to be cast aside by the only man she had ever loved, she went out and bought a knife. It was this deliberate action that was to result in a verdict of murder rather than manslaughter after she stabbed her lover to death in broad daylight in front of a dozen witnesses, for everyone in court was sympathetic to her plight.

Kitty was a pretty 23-year-old who had been living for several months with stockbroker Arthur Reginald Baker in a flat in the West End, where they represented themselves as Mr and Mrs Baker. At first Kitty was happy; she was deeply in love and Reg declared that she was the only woman for him. However, as the novelty of the relationship wore off, Reg began to tire of his 'adorable Kitty'. He spent a good deal of time away from the flat, he drank heavily and often knocked Kitty about. All the same, Kitty remained loyal, telling no one of his behaviour. Then, one Friday night in November 1902, raised voices from the Baker flat could be heard all over the house. When the landlady went up to investigate she found the flat in chaos, the bedclothes flung all over the floor and, in one corner, a hat ripped to shreds. 'Oh there's nothing the matter,' Kitty told her, laughing it off before she could confront the drunken Reg. 'We've been playing milliner.' Later in the evening the quarrel broke out again and at 1.15 am the landlady went back again in an attempt to stop the noise. This time she found Kitty crouching terrified on the landing in her nightdress. Even then, Kitty insisted that nothing was wrong.

The next morning the landlady, mindful of the peace of her other tenants, gave the couple notice. Over the weekend all was quiet and by Monday morning domestic harmony seemed to have been restored.

Reg took Kitty a cup of tea before leaving for work and Kitty kissed him goodbye as usual. But on his way out Reg spoke to the landlady, asking her to reconsider and allow them to keep the flat. When she was adamant, he revealed that Kitty was not his wife and blamed all the trouble on her. She had 'no class' and he would see that she was gone by tomorrow. A maid overheard the conversation and repeated it to Kitty, who was furious. 'I'll kill him before the day is out,' she exclaimed. The landlady, surprised that any woman would stay with a man who treated her badly when not bound by matrimony, asked why she did not leave him. 'I can't because I love him so,' replied Kitty simply.

Kitty went straight to Oxford Street and bought a large knife with a spring blade that fitted into the hasp. Concealing it in her muff she made her way towards the City, where the streets were crowded with spectators waiting to see the Lord Mayor's Day parade. She arrived at Lombard Street post office at about 1 pm and sent an express letter by messenger to Reg at the Stock Exchange. It read: 'Dear Reg. Want you immediate importantly. Kitty.' The boy had to make two journeys before he found Reg and returned with him, and this meant an extra charge of twopence. Post office staff remembered that Reg flatly refused to pay and Kitty offered Reg a florin to settle up.

The couple were already arguing heatedly when they left the post office. Suddenly the knife flashed and Kitty stabbed her lover twice, once through the back and once through the breast. Though at first the witnesses saw no blood, and thought that she was hitting him with her muff, Reg died almost instantly. A workman grabbed Kitty, sending the knife clattering to the ground, but she broke free and collapsed over her lover's body, sobbing: 'Let me kiss my Reggie . . . Let me kiss my husband.'

Kitty made two separate statements to the police just after her arrest. In one she said: 'I killed him wilfully and he deserved it, and the sooner I am killed the better.' A little later she stated: 'I bought the knife to hit him; I didn't know I was killing him.' She pleaded not guilty at her trial and looked dazed and pitiful as she listened to the 20 or so witnesses called by the prosecution. When a surgeon described the stab wounds on her lover's body she broke down and sobbed. There were no defence witnesses and Kitty did not go into the witness box. Her counsel, Harry Dickens, son of the great Victorian novelist Charles Dickens, tried to show that Kitty had bought the knife to kill herself rather than Reginald Baker, but the idea was given little credence. Far more telling was his description of the prisoner's character and her ill-treatment at the hands of the murdered man.

In his summing up, even the judge admitted that 'if I had consulted my own feelings I should probably have stopped this case at the outset'. All the same, he ruled out manslaughter as a proper verdict and the jury, after deliberating for only 10 minutes, found her guilty, but with a strong recommendation for mercy. The formalities were observed and the death sentence was read out, but there was little likelihood of it being carried out. The Home Secretary quickly granted a reprieve and her sentence was commuted to penal servitude for life. Even that was later held to be too harsh a sentence and she was released in 1908.

Kate Webster

KATE WEBSTER'S victim, the twittery old lady who employed her, stood little chance against the anger and brutality of her tough, square-jawed servant. Julia Thomas, a retired schoolteacher living in Richmond, England, never managed to keep servants for long – she was far too finicky and fault-finding, never satisfied unless every corner of the house shone with cleanliness. Since Kate's standards were not that high, the two women had a number of heated arguments and Kate was soon given notice. However, she had no intention of giving up a comfortable home so easily. Though Kate had no known history of violence she had a criminal past, specializing in lodging-house robberies where she took a room for a few days then robbed the other tenants and disappeared. In 1875 she was sentenced to 18 months in prison for 36 different robberies and by this time she had a young son, whose father had deserted her.

When Mrs Thomas returned from church on the evening of 2 March 1879 Kate was lying in wait for her at the top of the stairs. She struck the side of her employer's head with some heavy household object, then hurled her down the stairs. Leaving nothing to chance, she finished the job with her hands round the old lady's throat. Then she hauled the body into the kitchen, spread it over the table and began to saw through the neck with a meat saw. Once the head was detached she sliced out the entrails with the carving knife, then set to work with the chopper on the shoulder and thigh joints. Her plan was to boil up the dismembered sections of the body so that they would be unrecognizable and then dispose of them. When morning came she lit the fire and filled the copper, loading in the first hunks of flesh. It was hard, thirsty work and by mid-morning Kate decided that she needed to fortify herself with gin, so she left her mistress boiling in the copper while she went to the Hole in the Wall public house two doors away, where she chatted calmly with the landlady over her drink before returning to her gruesome task. The neighbours remarked on an unpleasant smell hanging over the street that morning and later they turned queasy at the thought that Kate had been peddling pots of fresh dripping around the town the following day.

When Kate visited her old friends Ann and Henry Porter for the first time in six years they admired her jewellery and her smart silk dress, believing her story that she was now Mrs Thomas, married and widowed since they last met. An aunt had died, leaving her all her belongings, she told them, and she needed help to dispose of them. She asked 16-year-old Robert Porter to go back with her to help with a heavy box that had to be taken to Richmond Bridge, where a friend would take charge of it. Robert politely carried her black carpet bag but when they called in at a tavern on the way she took the bag and left him for 20 minutes, returning without it. Kate never admitted what she did with the bag, and Mrs Thomas's head was never found. The wooden box bound with cord, which Robert helped her carry to the bridge, was another story. A coal porter driving his cart over Barnes Bridge spotted it the next day, lying half out of the water. At first he thought it contained butcher's meat but police investigation showed that it was human flesh.

Though Kate read the story in the newspaper she was untroubled, and went ahead with her plans to dispose of her victim's furniture. The Porters had introduced her to a possible purchaser, John Church, who kept a beer shop near their home. He spent several pleasant nights with Kate and finally agreed a price of £68. On 18 March Church and his assistant arrived with a van and started loading the furniture. However, the next-door neighbour, Miss Ives, from whom Mrs Thomas rented her semi-detached villa, saw what was happening and asked Kate for an explanation. Kate told her that Mrs Thomas was away for a few days but had asked her to look after the sale of some furniture.

However, Miss Ives wanted to know where she could contact Mrs Thomas and when Kate could not provide an address, she became suspicious and threatened to make further enquiries. Church, seeing an argument in progress, began to suspect that Kate was trying to cheat her landlady out of the rent and refused to have anything to do with the furniture.

Only then, as his van disappeared down the street, did Kate panic and she hastened to collect her child and catch a train to Liverpool. There she boarded a coal boat to Ireland and made her way back to her home town. Back in Richmond, Church, who had advanced her £18 for the furniture and wanted his money returned, was asking friends and neighbours about her whereabouts and suspicions grew. When the police were brought in, they soon heard the story of the heavy box, last seen on Richmond Bridge. Robert Porter could easily identify the box pulled out of the river; the handle on one side was missing and he had skinned his knuckles carrying it by the cord. The Richmond house was searched with sombre results: though Kate thought she had done a thorough cleaning job, there were the remains of bloodstains in the hall and kitchen, some charred bones under the copper and a fatty substance clinging to its sides.

Kate, arrested at her uncle's house in Ireland, made a statement blaming the murder on Church. She claimed that she knew nothing about it until she saw Mrs Thomas's body and that Church had threatened to kill her if she did not keep quiet. She was so plausible that the police arrested Church, only to find that he had a cast-iron alibi for the day in question. Undeterred, Kate made another statement, changing the date of the murder to 4 March and this time claiming that Henry Porter was also involved. At her trial, counsel for the defence did his best with this feeble story, saying that the two men were 'living on Kate Webster like harpies, having her completely under their thumb'. In spite of all his efforts, the jury found her guilty and the judge pronounced the death sentence. Asked if she had anything to say in stay of execution she confidently announced that she was with child. If this had been true she would have escaped execution, but the judge ordered an immediate medical examination which showed that it was yet another lie.

Kate was to make one more desperate attempt to save herself, making a statement from her prison cell saying that it was her child's father who had planned the crime and told her to put the blame on Church. No one believed her but it was only on the night before her execution, when at last she was certain that she had nothing to lose, that she finally confessed. She was reported to have said: 'I am perfectly resigned to my fate and am full of confidence in a happy eternity. If I had a choice I would almost sooner die than return to a life full of misery, deception and wickedness.' After that she slept well and, next morning, walked calmly to the execution yard with no sign of distress.

The next day Mrs Thomas's possessions, including the carving knife and chopper, were sold off in Richmond. Miss Ives had the copper removed from the murder scene but the house remained empty for some time before she could find a tenant willing to use a kitchen where the flagged floor once ran with human blood.

Marguerite Diblanc

THE CASE of Marguerite Diblanc, seven years earlier, had much in common with that of Kate Webster. She too was a servant who killed her employer in a rage after being dismissed from service but her crime took place in London's fashionable Park Lane and set society tongues wagging, as her victim was the mistress of the rich and aristocratic Earl of Lucan, notorious as the man who had instigated the disastrous Charge of the Light Brigade 18 years earlier. Lord Lucan was already in his seventies when he installed his 46-year-old French mistress in Park Lane, where she lived with her actress daughter Julie.

Marie Riel was a difficult, ill-tempered woman guaranteed to make life unpleasant for any servant unfortunate enough to be in her employ. It was inevitable that there would be trouble between Mme Riel and her strong-minded Belgian cook Marguerite, a large-boned 28-year-old with a distinctly mannish look about her. Only a year before Marie had been fighting at the barricades in France, along with the Parisian revolutionaries. She had been forced to flee to England after their defeat but she was not the type of woman to submit to bullying. There were many angry exchanges and in March 1872 she was dismissed with a week's wages. Marguerite refused to go: she was paid monthly and so, she insisted, she was entitled to a month's wages. Mme Riel refused to pay her a penny more in cash but said that she could work out a month's notice instead.

On 31 March, when Julie Riel left for a short holiday before beginning a season of French comedies at St James's Theatre, she left the stage in Park Lane set for murder. The continuing rows between the two obdurate women came to a head on Sunday 7 April, when

224

Mme Riel was expecting a visitor and was concerned that everything should be properly prepared. In the middle of the morning she went down to the kitchen to check on preparations, only to find that Marguerite was still working upstairs. The altercation that followed soon turned violent and Mme Riel ordered Marguerite out of the house immediately. If she wanted money she could go on the streets, which were the right place for her, she said. Marguerite retorted that Mme Riel had been on the streets far longer than she was ever likely to be. For both women, these insults were too much to bear and they set about one another. At one point Marguerite tried to throttle her mistress, at another she caught her such a blow that Mme Riel fell to the floor.

As Marguerite stood over Mme Riel she heard the only other servant in the household, Eliza Watts, coming down the stairs. She hastily pushed and pulled the body into the coal cellar, then she made an excuse to get Eliza out of the house while she found a way to dispose of her mistress. Once Eliza had left, on a quickly invented errand, Marguerite slung a rope round her victim's neck and hauled the body across the kitchen and up the steps that led to the pantry. This was probably the safest hiding place in the house as it contained the safe and was always kept locked, only opened when necessary with the mistress's key. Later Marguerite was to claim that Mme Riel was already dead, killed by accident when she struck an unlucky blow, but it is probably more likely that she made sure of finishing the job with the rope. Once the body was safely in the pantry, Marguerite opened the safe, pocketed a pack of banknotes and carefully locked the pantry door.

Meanwhile Eliza had returned and, finding herself locked out, was knocking vigorously on the outside door. All through the unusual events of that day, Eliza remained unsuspecting. This was, perhaps, not surprising, for she was a slow-witted girl and, as Marguerite and Mme Riel always spoke French, she was accustomed to understanding very little of what went on in the house. Later in the day Mme Riel's expected visitor arrived but, after waiting most of the afternoon for her friend, she finally left. Marguerite then changed into her best satin dress and told Eliza she was going to church. Instead she took the boat train to Dover and travelled to Paris.

The following day Julie Riel returned and discovered her mother's body. The search for Marguerite began immediately. Her parsimonious nature and poor English had left a clear trail: a cab driver remembered an argument about the fare to Victoria and a station clerk who spoke a little French recalled the woman who had wanted an economy fare but had been forced to buy a first-class ticket in order to join the overnight boat train. Marguerite was arrested in Paris and eventually, after much reluctance on the part of the French police, was extradited to stand trial in Britain.

The main defence was that the killing had not been intentional and that Marguerite had suffered great provocation from her unpleasant mistress. The jury found her guilty, adding a recommendation for mercy. Marguerite was sentenced to hang but, eight days after the date initially set for her execution, she was reprieved.

Jeannie Ewan Donald

THE TRIAL of Jeannie Ewan Donald in Edinburgh, Scotland, in 1934 was unusual. Jeannie was charged with the murder of eight-year-old Helen Priestly but no one had seen the child with her and there was no apparent motive: the most important testimony came from pathologists and chemists and Jeannie was convicted on the evidence of fluff, cinders and fibres.

Helen, who lived with her parents on the first floor of a crowded tenement building in Aberdeen, went missing on 20 April. She had come home from school for lunch and her mother, 33-year-old Agnes Priestly, sent her for a loaf of bread. Helen never came home again. Mrs Priestly was worried as the time for afternoon school approached, for Helen was a well-behaved child who would never willingly be late. First she checked at the bakery and found that Helen had been there to buy the loaf. A friend had seen her soon afterwards, carrying something wrapped in brown paper under her arm, but after that she had vanished. None of her friends knew where she was and though neighbours and friends searched the neighbourhood, there was no sign of Helen.

The police were called and they questioned the neighbours and instituted a more thorough search of cellars and storerooms, anywhere a child might be shut in by mistake. One of Helen's schoolmates seemed to provide an important clue when he said that he had seen Helen being pulled along the road and on to a bus by a stranger, and gave a full description of the man, but he later admitted that he had made it all up for a laugh.

It rained heavily that night and the search was called off at around midnight. At 5.15 am a friend of the family, Alexander Porter, came to collect John Priestly to restart the search and as he walked into the building he saw a bulging sack lying behind the staircase. To his horror, he saw a child's feet sticking out of the top. The news of the discovery spread fast and people poured out of their flats, talking and shouting and crying. The only neighbours who ignored the hubbub were the Donalds, who lived below the Priestlys. Jeannie Donald later told how she had been woken by the sounds of knocking and yelling and had asked her husband to go and see what was happening. He had simply turned over and buried his head in the pillow. They were still searching for the lost child, he said, and there was nothing he could do about it. A couple of hours later, when he opened the door to collect the milk, the body was being carried out. Jeannie insisted that she heard a woman cry out: 'She's been used.'

Helen's body had been identified. She was still wearing her serge dress, blue woolly jumper, black stockings and shoes; only her beret and navy blue knickers were missing. The postmortem showed that she had been strangled, dying within an hour of eating her lunch, not later than 2 pm. Though there was no evidence of rape, her genitals and rectum had been ripped, perhaps in an attempt to give the impression that the motive for the attack was sexual. Surprisingly, a small cinder was found between her front teeth and several more in her hair.

The police had decided that the sack had probably been deposited in the hallway by one of the tenants of the building as, in spite of the heavy rain, it was completely dry. Once more they visited all the neighbours and intensified their questioning. The Priestlys had been on friendly terms with all the other families in the building apart from the Donalds. Though Helen and the Donalds' young daughter were the same age and played together at school, their mothers disliked one another and made a point of not speaking. Helen nicknamed Mrs Donald 'Coconut' and often complained that the woman 'followed her with her eyes'.

Detectives noticed a suspicious patch on the Donalds' carpet which

Jeannie Ewan Donald

could have been blood. Though it was later shown to be nothing of the kind it focused interest on the household, and the more time detectives spent with Jeannie Donald the more suspicious they became. She said that on 20 April she had left the house at about 1 pm to go to the weekly market, where she bought eggs and oranges. Then she had called at Raggy Morrison's shop to buy some material for a new dress for her daughter, though she could not find what she wanted among his stock. She had returned home at about 2.15 and had met one of the neighbours, Mrs Mary Topp, outside. Mrs Topp remembered the meeting, though she thought it had taken place at 2.30. She said that Jeannie had gone out of her way to stress that she had come back from shopping early so that she could iron a dress that her daughter wanted to wear to dance in a concert that evening, but she was unable to confirm whether Jeannie had been coming into the house or leaving it at the time they met. When Jeannie was asked about the prices she had paid for her eggs and oranges, she gave the prices charged at the market the week before. Also, it was found that Raggy Morrison's shop had been closed that afternoon.

Under the sink, the detectives noticed ridges of dust where some type of box had been standing and it was Jeannie's daughter who told them that a cinder box usually stood there. When asked what had happened to it, Jeannie simply shrugged and said she didn't know. When the flat was searched a number of articles were taken away for examination, as well as hairs from Jeannie's hairbrush, fibres from the carpet and various samples of household fluff. The results of the laboratory examination that followed led to Jeannie Donald's arrest. When charged she said simply: 'I didn't do that.'

Jeannie did not take the witness stand at her trial but the defence case was that she had had nothing to do with the murder; that the attacker had been a man who had raped the little girl. Jeannie's lawyers produced a young woman who gave evidence that she had seen a girl matching Helen's description, carrying a brown paper parcel, being pulled along by a rough-looking man.

The prosecution version was that Jeannie Donald had lost her temper with the child and choked her to death. She had then used some type of metal instrument, which was never found, to tear her genitals in an attempt to make the attack look like rape. Her statement that she had heard someone crying 'She's been used' as the body was removed was an attempt to reinforce this idea, for all the women present at the time had been interviewed and none of them had uttered those words. The prosecution theory was that Jeannie had hidden the body in the cinder box then, in the early hours of the morning, when her husband and daughter were fast asleep, she had put the body in a sack and dumped it in the hall.

There was a whole battery of technical evidence to show that hairs found on the body matched those taken from Jeannie's hairbrush and that woollen fibres and household fluff in the sack was identical with that found in the Donald home. Bacteria from vomit on the child's clothing and from a flannel found in Jeannie's bathroom showed striking similarities and the prosecution suggested that she had used the cloth to clean up vomit from the kitchen floor. The sack in which the body was found had a hole in the corner, apparently where it had hung from a hook, and several black marks caused by pots. Five sacks with holes in the same place, three of them with similar black marks, were found in Jeannie's flat. No such sacks were found in any of the other apartments.

Though the defence protested that all the evidence was circumstantial and should be dismissed, the judge instructed the jury: 'You must dismiss from your mind any idea that evidence is unreliable merely because it is circumstantial ... circumstantial evidence is just the evidence of proved facts.' The jury took only 16 minutes to reach their decision. Jeannie was sentenced to hang but this was later commuted to life imprisonment and 10 years later, when her husband was terminally ill, she was released on parole.

Louise Masset

ON 27 OCTOBER 1899 the body of a three-year-old boy was found lying on the floor of the women's lavatory on Dalston Junction station, London, naked except for a black shawl and still warm. Nearby lay a stone and the doctor who examined the body thought that it had been used to stun the boy, who had then been suffocated, dying less than an hour before the body was discovered.

When a description was published the police were contacted by Miss Helen Gentle from Tottenham, who later identified the boy as Manfred Masset; he had been boarded with her since he was a few weeks old. He was the child of an unmarried woman of 36, Louise Masset, who lived with her sister in Stoke Newington and worked as a governess. Ten days before, Louise had written to her saying that she was taking him to live with his father in France. She had collected him the previous Friday, much to the distress of both Manfred and Miss Gentle.

When Louise read about the identification of the body in the newspaper she knew that the police would soon be knocking at the door and fled to the home of another sister. 'I am hunted for murder,' she told her, 'but I didn't do it.' Later, when the police caught up with her, she told a strange tale. Early in October she had taken Manfred to the park, where she had sat down next to a woman who had a little girl with her. She had got into conversation with the woman, a widow named Mrs Browning, and had confided that she was worried that Manfred was learning a slovenly way of speaking with his present nurse. Mrs Browning, who spoke beautifully, had explained that she and her sister-in-law were taking a house in Kings Road, Chelsea, where they planned to care for several children. The little girl was her first boarder and she would be glad to take Manfred for the sum of £18 a year. This was less than Louise was paying Miss Gentle and she was sure that Manfred would be happy with Mrs Browning, so she accepted. She had told Miss Gentle that Manfred was going to France so that she would not be offended.

She had arranged to meet Mrs Browning and her sister-in-law at London Bridge station on 27 October, planning to go with them to the house to see Manfred settled in. Unfortunately they were very late in arriving and, as she was catching a train to Brighton, she had to part with Manfred then and there. She had given Mrs Browning £12 as a first payment and the widow said that she would write out a receipt but needed to borrow pen and paper in the refreshment room. She would take Manfred with her and buy him a cake, she said. The two women had taken Manfred in the direction of the refreshment room while Louise waited on the platform but, realizing that her train was about to leave, she had departed without her receipt or a final goodbye to her son.

This was the time when baby-farmers flourished and it was not impossible that an unmarried mother like Louise would pay complete strangers a sum of money to take a child off her hands. Some mothers, only too glad to get rid of the unwanted burden, never enquired about their children again and the unfortunate youngsters were often sold off as cheap servants or even killed.

In Louise's case, the police were more inclined to think that she had disposed of her problem in another way. For some time she had been carrying on an affair with a 19-year-old Frenchman who lived next door to her sister in Stoke Newington, stealing away with him to cheap hotels as often as possible. To Eudore, still only a bank clerk on a salary of a few pounds a month, any idea of marriage was out of the question and he probably viewed his relationship with Louise as an amorous adventure with an attractive older woman, an interesting way of passing the time before he returned to France. To Louise, it may have been much more and she looked ahead to the time when she might be the wife of a respected bank official in Paris. Though she had told Eudore about Manfred and he said that it made no difference to him, she saw the illegitimate child as an encumbrance to any permanent liaison.

When this was suggested at the trial, Louise tried to laugh it off: marriage to a 19-year-old earning £3 a month was an absurd idea, she said. But there was a good deal of evidence against her. Several people remembered Louise on her journey to London Bridge with the crying child who was protesting 'I don't want to go!' His mother told them that he was going to France to join his father – a pointless story, if he was only going to Chelsea. Mrs Rees, the ladies' waiting room attendant at London Bridge, remembered Louise well and could pick her out at an identity parade. She had thought her manner strange and was certain that she had seen her back on the station in the early evening, this time without her son.

Manfred's clothes had been found two days after the murder in the ladies' waiting room at Brighton station and Louise had spent the weekend in a Brighton hotel with her lover. Manfred's favourite toy, which Miss Gentle said he would never willingly have left behind, was found in Louise's bedroom. Needless to say, Mrs Browning and her sister-in-law were never traced and, as a final, damning piece of evidence, the brick found beside the body matched those found in the garden at Stoke Newington.

Louise fainted away when she heard the guilty verdict, followed by the sentence of death. French women working in London teamed up to present a petition to Queen Victoria, imploring mercy – but Louise Masset had not only killed a child, she had outraged Victorian morality into the bargain and for her there was no reprieve. The sentence was carried out at Newgate on 9 January 1900.

Marybeth Tinning

IN JANUARY 1972 Marybeth Tinning gave birth to her third child, Jennifer, at Schenectady, New York. The baby was born with meningitis and was never well enough to leave St Clare's Hospital, where she died nine days later. Perhaps the shock of her new-born baby's death upset some delicate mental balance within the mother – if so, it might explain the tragedy that followed, for over the next 13 years, eight more Tinning children were to die and the police came to believe that she had killed them all.

Only a fortnight after Jennifer died, Marybeth arrived at the emergency room of Ellis Hospital with two-year-old Joseph, saying that he had suffered a seizure and stopped breathing. Doctors admitted him and kept him for 10 days, diagnosing a probable viral infection. He seemed well when he was discharged but later in the day Marybeth brought him back again and this time he was dead on arrival. Two months later Marybeth was back with four-year-old Barbara, who died soon after arrival. A postmortem showed no obvious cause of death but there seemed no reason for suspicion.

Marybeth was to give birth to several more children but none lived longer than a few months. Timothy, born in November 1973, lived less than three weeks, his unexpected demise being ascribed to cot death. Nathan was five months old when he died in September 1975. He had earlier spent a month in hospital after experiencing breathing difficulties and bleeding from the nose. He was thought to have died from pulmonary oedema. Little Mary was admitted for emergency treatment at the age of four months, then a few weeks later she died, apparently another victim of cot death.

When Marybeth and her husband Joseph applied to adopt a child, the adoption agency was sympathetic about their run of bad luck and wanted to help them. In 1979, when baby Michael joined the family, Marybeth was pregnant again and Jonathan was born in the following January. Jonathan died at the age of three months. In August 1981, Michael was rushed to St Clare's Hospital with 'breathing difficulties' but the doctors could not save him. Though they had some reservations, they certified the death as due to bronchial pneumonia.

Marybeth's last child, Tami Lynne, was born in September 1985 and at three months she was found dead in her cot, with blood staining the pillow. This time the doctors were not prepared to write this off as yet another death due to natural causes. Careful consideration of all aspects of the case led them to believe that the child had been suffocated.

Under questioning, Marybeth broke down and confessed that she had held a pillow over her daughter's face because she would not stop crying. After her arrest she admitted that she had also killed Timothy and Nathan, but she always denied doing anything to harm any of the others.

Eventually she was charged with the murder of Tami Lynne and convicted of second-degree homicide. The jury did not find her guilty of planning to kill the children but said that she had a 'depraved indifference to human life'. No motive was ever put forward; Marybeth had told the police that she had smothered the children 'Because I'm not a good mother'.

Chapter Four

GUILTY OR INNOCENT?

Introduction

SOME FAMOUS murder trials pose more questions than they answer, leaving a fascinating puzzle for generations to come as evidence is sifted again and the character of the accused re-examined.

Juries have always been reluctant to convict a woman; they are often ready to believe that if a woman commits such a terrible crime as murder she must have been provoked beyond endurance, that the fatal wound must have been inflicted in a frantic moment, without murderous intent. In past centuries, however, a woman's chance of acquittal depended upon her place in society. Slim circumstantial evidence was enough to send a servant girl to the gallows, while the court found it much harder to believe that a reputable middle-class woman, a wife and mother, could possibly be a killer.

Not all cases are clear-cut: there have been women who walked free because no one could decide how the murder was committed and some women have been convicted mainly because their sex lives outraged public opinion. It is left for today's true crime enthusiasts to decide whether or not justice was done.

Florence Maybrick

FLORENCE MAYBRICK was convicted of poisoning her husband in 1889 at Liverpool Assizes but there was little hard evidence against her and in a different age she would undoubtedly have been acquitted. As it was, she had flown in the face of strict Victorian morality and found herself on trial as much for adultery as for murder. The press had branded her guilty in advance and the judge, his mental powers already in a decline that led to insanity a year later, was obsessed with his view of Florence as an immoral and degraded woman. Her trial left so many question marks that it was to lead to major changes in the British judicial system.

The Maybrick marriage had begun on a romantic note. Florence Elizabeth Chandler was a vivacious 17-year-old, the daughter of an Alabama banker, when she met James Maybrick on the Atlantic liner *Baltic*, on which she was sailing with her mother for a tour of Europe. She was quite a beauty, with curly golden hair, violet eyes and a curvaceous figure. He was the picture of a prosperous British businessman, tall, blond, sophisticated and self-assured – and still a bachelor at the age of 42. They walked together on deck beneath the stars, they played cards and danced and by the end of the voyage they had fallen in love.

Eventually the Maybricks settled in England, in a 20-room mansion in Aigburth, Liverpool. They had two children and five servants and entertained lavishly, but James's business did not flourish and their lifestyle was soon outstripping their means. James tried to keep up outward appearances by budgeting strictly at home but Florence was not the budgeting type and there were daily quarrels over money. Florence was always on tenterhooks in case the ring at the doorbell meant someone else asking for payment of an account and dreaded her husband's return from the office in case he had heard of another of her debts. She wrote to her mother: 'I am . . . in such a state of overstrained nervousness I am hardly fit for anything . . . my life is a continual state of fear of something or somebody.'

There were problems besides money in the Maybrick household. James was a thorough-going hypochondriac who took endless pills and potions for imaginary ills. After being successfully treated for malaria with strychnine and arsenic he took to dosing himself with both drugs and became addicted to daily pinches of arsenic, which he found particularly palatable in beef tea. It was easily available from the chemist and many a Victorian gentleman had acquired the dangerous habit. Florence worried about the strange powders her husband took so frequently, but after the birth of her second child she made a discovery that upset her even more: James was supporting another household, a long-established mistress who had several children by him. In one bitter row, James tore up his will making Florence sole legatee and settled everything on the children instead.

Undoubtedly Florence was hurt and angry and it was at this vulnerable moment that she met one of her husband's younger friends, a handsome, bearded bachelor called Alfred Brierley. They were charmed by each other and he came more and more frequently to the house – especially when James was absent. Throwing caution to the winds, Florence agreed to spend a weekend in London with him. The ill-fated weekend may well have been her idea for she made the arrangements, foolishly reserving a room at a central London hotel in the name of 'Mr and Mrs Thomas Maybrick of Manchester'. It was their first and last passionate rendezvous and, for whatever reason, they resolved to end their short affair. However, a few days later the Maybricks met Brierley at Aintree, where race-goers had gathered for the Grand National and Brierley took Florence to meet the Prince of Wales, leaving James to hear the rumours of his wife's indiscretion from 'well-wishers'. When they got home there was a furious row.

James blacked her eye and the servants heard him shouting: 'Such a scandal will be all over town tomorrow.'

About a month later, in late April, Florence bought a dozen fly-papers from the chemist, saying that 'flies were beginning to be troublesome in the kitchen'. Shortly afterwards she bought two dozen more at another shop. The servants were amazed to see them soaking in a bowl on her bedroom washstand, covered by a plate and a folded towel. Florence was later to explain that she was extracting the arsenic from the flypaper for use in a face-wash mixed with lavender and elder water, and applied with a handkerchief – a recipe used by many of her friends in Germany. Though this may sound ridiculous today, it was not beyond the bounds of probability; in the 19th century many women used small amounts of arsenic to lighten their complexions.

At about the same time James had a bout of vomiting and com-plained of numbness in his legs. He recovered and went back to work, only to be taken ill again after eating a patent food called Du Barry's Revaleta Arabica, made up by Florence. His legs were now very painful and the doctor prescribed morphine. When his sickness increased, Fowler's solution (a mixture of arsenic and carbonate of potash) was prescribed but James's condition did not improve. Another doctor was called in and Florence engaged a nurse.

It was while her husband lay ill that Florence, with a disastrous sense of timing, began writing to Brierley. She gave her letter – written at her husband's bedside – to the children's nanny, Alice Yapp, to post. Miss Yapp, well versed in the servant's gossip about soaking flypapers, conveniently dropped the letter in the mud so that she had to bring it back for a clean envelope. In transferring it certain words caught her eye and she felt obliged to deliver it to one of Mr Maybrick's brothers. The letter began 'Dearest' and went on to say: 'Since my return I have been nursing M night and day and he is sick unto death . . . I cannot answer your letter fully today, my darling, but relieve your mind of all fear of discovery now or in the future.'

On the evening of 11 May, James Maybrick died. Several family members were at his bedside but Florence had collapsed and was lying semi-conscious in the dressing room. The servants, instructed to search the house, found a sachet of powder labelled 'Arsenic: poison for cats' in her room together with letters from Brierley and, of course, more flypapers. A bottle of meat juice, which Florence had taken to her room at one point, contained traces of arsenic. Florence claimed later that James had begged her to add some of the white powder he took every day to his food. Eventually she had given in to his entreaties and added it to the meat juice though, in the event, James never drank it. She had only realized later, she said, that it was arsenic.

A postmortem revealed a tiny amount of arsenic in James's stomach – hardly surprising when he was known to take it on a regular basis and when, quite apart from Florence's small store, enough arsenic had been found in the house to poison two dozen people. The amount of arsenic found in the body was not sufficient to cause death but none the less the doctors decided that he had been poisoned and Florence was charged with murder.

The medical evidence at the trial was shaky in the extreme; the defence called several doctors who said that James had died from gastro-enteritis and a number of witnesses who testified to his habit of taking arsenic as a pick-me-up. The moral evidence, however, was damning. Florence – an upstart American, which counted against her from the start – was guilty of betraying her husband and was therefore only too likely to be guilty of a murder 'founded upon profligacy and adultery', in the words of the prosecutor. Mr Justice Stephen took 12 hours to sum up, rambling frequently, often confusing the facts and mistaking the dates. His belief in Florence's guilt was clear enough: 'For a person to go on deliberately administering poison to a poor helpless sick man upon whom she has already inflicted a dreadful injury – an injury fatal to married life . . . must indeed be destitute of the least trace of human feeling,' he told the jury. 'You must remember the intrigue which she carried on with this man Brierley, and the incredible thought that a woman should be plotting the death of her

Florence Maybrick makes her statement in court

husband in order that she might be left at liberty to follow her own degrading vices.' Needless to say, the jury followed his lead and found her guilty.

Many of those concerned with the judicial system were worried by the unfairness of the trial and began pressing for changes in the system: this eventually led to the establishment of the Court of Appeal and the right of a person accused of murder to give evidence on his or her defence, which was not allowed at the time of the Maybrick trial. It was all too late for Florence. She served 15 years in prison and then, after a brief period as a celebrity, giving interviews and lectures, she sank into obscurity and poverty. For the last 20 years of her life she lived in a wooden shack in the woods of Connecticut, under her maiden name, feeding her many cats and collecting newspapers from dustbins for reading matter. No one connected her with the pretty, extravagant Florence Maybrick and her true identity was only revealed after her death at the age of 79.

Madeleine Smith

THE MAYBRICK case had echoes of the trial of Madeleine Smith in Edinburgh, Scotland, over 30 years earlier, on the charge of murdering her lover by poisoning him with arsenic. Madeleine, too, claimed that she used arsenic as a cosmetic, though she had told the chemist she needed it for rats, and the defence suggested that her lover might have been an arsenic-eater. Madeleine was luckier than Florence, for in her case the court, swayed by the morality of the day, assumed that if a young girl of good family strayed into an affair she must have been led astray by a vile seducer and was therefore a victim deserving of a certain amount of sympathy.

Without the colouring of 19th-century morals, the case looks rather different. There seems no reason to believe that Emile l'Angelier, a 31-year-old clerk from Jersey, was anything worse than a young man intent on marriage with a young woman from a superior background, while Madeleine was a shallow and selfish girl who fancied herself in love but was happy to send her lover packing when something better offered.

They had met early in 1855 when Madeleine was 19. She was the daughter of one of Glasgow's foremost architects and the family was well above l'Angelier's normal circle. However, Emile saw her several times in the town and was immediately smitten, so he managed to engineer an introduction from an acquaintance of the Smiths. Madeleine must have been taken with his graceful French manners and open admiration for soon they were meeting secretly, at first a few snatched moments in a bookshop near Mr Smith's office, or as she made her way to a music lesson. They began writing to one another and their feelings quickly warmed, but Mr Smith, a strict Victorian patriarch, soon became suspicious and Madeleine wrote: 'I think you will agree with me in what I intend proposing viz: that for the present the correspondence had better stop . . . by continuing to correspond harm may arise.' Her new resolve was shortlived and within a few weeks she was writing: 'I have loved before but never have I loved one better than you – When I set my affections on anyone I am true to them.' In July Emile told Mary Perry, a kindly grey-haired spinster who had befriended him at church and heard all about his secret love, that he and Madeleine were engaged.

Perhaps Mr Smith received more definite proof of his daughter's liaison or perhaps Madeleine plucked up the courage to tell him herself; in any case there was a stern family conclave and Madeleine was forbidden to contact Emile in any way. She gave her word of honour and agreed that she was 'in duty bound' to obey but quite soon she was finding a way round her father's prohibition. Emile's letters arrived addressed to one of the Smith's maids, Christine Haggert, and were removed before the mail was passed on to the family; Madeleine's letters were addressed to Mary Perry. Madeleine's bedroom was on the ground floor, the windows half above ground and half below the pavement, and Emile often visited her at night, when they would hold hands through the pavement railings and whisper sweet nothings. Sometimes they met at Mary Perry's house and at least once Emile was let into the Smith's house when the rest of the family were in bed.

In June 1856, when the Smiths went to their summer house, Madeleine had a room facing directly on to the garden and she could steal out at night to meet Emile. It was then they made love for the first time and Madeleine's joyful letters became sensuous and outspoken – quite shocking by Victorian standards – as she addressed him as 'My own beloved husband' and signed herself 'thy faithful wife' or 'Mimi l'Angelier'. Emile was racked with guilt, blamed himself for what had happened and said that nothing but marriage would efface it from his memory. Madeleine, too, often talked of marriage but knew very well that her parents would never permit it.

Later that year another man entered the picture and everything changed. He was William Minnoch, a well-to-do merchant of 34, slim and elegant, and socially acceptable. He had become friendly with Mr Smith and began to spend a good deal of time with the family, paying special attention to Madeleine. He was often mentioned in letters to Emile, who soon became jealous, but Madeleine reassured him that she had no regard for Minnoch and avoided him as far as possible. It was far from true: at the end of January 1857 she accepted Minnoch's proposal of marriage. She did not share the news with Emile. Instead, she wrote that after many sleepless nights she had decided to tell him that she no longer loved him and that in future they should consider themselves as strangers.

Emile was astonished, angry and wounded and he struck back by threatening to send her letters to her father. Madeleine turned hysterical, begging and pleading with him not to contact her family and bring her to 'open shame'. She protested, 'When I ceased to love you believe me it was not to love another. I am free from all engagements at present. Emile for God's sake do not send my letters to Papa . . . I will leave the house, I will die.' She begged him to come to her. At about the same time she was fixing her wedding day in June and buying arsenic.

One morning in February Emile's landlady, Mrs Jenkins, found him lying in bed looking very ill. He told her that he had been taken ill on the way home with pain and sickness. 'When I was taking off my clothes I lay down upon the carpet,' he said. 'I thought I would have died and no human eye would have seen me.' A few weeks later he was taken ill again and after many hours of vomiting he died on the morning of 23 March. On postmortem, 82 grains of arsenic were found in Emile's stomach, enough to kill 15 people. In his room were found over 200 letters from Madeleine and within a few days she was under arrest.

Her statement, read out in court, stated that she 'never administered, or caused to be administered, to M. l'Angelier arsenic or anything injurious'. She had last seen Emile, she said, about three weeks before his death. She had written to him on 20 March asking him to come and see her the following day, when she planned to tell him about her engagement to Mr Minnoch, but he never arrived.

Madeleine remained cool and composed throughout the trial, apparently confident that she would be acquitted, even when Mary Perry gave evidence that Emile had mentioned being unwell after taking cups of coffee or chocolate on his visits to Madeleine. 'It is a perfect infatuation I have for that girl. If she was to poison me, I would forgive her,' he had said. When Mary asked why he should think Madeleine might want to do him harm, he answered: 'I don't know, perhaps she might not be sorry to get rid of me.'

Madeleine had stated that she used the arsenic she bought on three occasions for cosmetic purposes, mixing it with water and applying it to her face and arms, a habit recommended by a school friend, Miss Guibilei. When Miss Guibilei was produced, she insisted that she had never recommended anything of the sort and had never had any conversation with Madeleine about arsenic.

The defence stressed that, though the letters proved that Madeleine had asked Emile to come to her, there was no knowing what other letters he had received at that time and what plans he might have made. After all, no one had seen him in the vicinity and there was no proof that he had been there. Then there was the question of the prisoner's character: how could a 'gentle loving girl' be suddenly transformed into the perpetrator of such a foul crime? Her outspoken letters had undoubtedly shocked the court but did they think that 'without temptation, without evil teaching, a poor girl falls into such depths of degradation? No – influence from without – most corrupting influence – can alone account for such a fall'. The jury brought in a majority verdict of 'not proven', only possible in a Scottish court, and generally believed to mean that her guilt was likely, but not absolutely certain.

Madeleine seemed unmoved; she only smiled at the announcement while a great cheer rose from the public benches. She certainly did not let the reflection on her good name spoil her life. Though she did not hear from Mr Minnoch again she married a London artist, George Wardle, in 1861.

Jessie Costello

OLD MRS AYERS, a pedlar of sweets who regularly toured the households of Peabody, Massachusetts, had succeeded in selling Mrs Jessie Costello a pound of fudge. Jessie ran upstairs to get some money and Mrs Ayers nearly suffered a heart attack when she heard her screaming at the top of her lungs. Jessie had found her husband Bill lying dead on the bedroom floor, even though he had been fit and well early that morning when he returned from an overnight vigil beside the body of a dead colleague from the Peabody Fire Department.

The autopsy showed that there was nothing surprising about Bill's death: his body contained a quantity of potassium cyanide. When it was found that only the day before Jessie had bought potassium cyanide from the pharmacy, along with oxalic acid, she was arrested. She explained that she bought both substances to make up a mixture that would put a good shine on her boiler and had no idea that potassium cyanide was dangerous. The pharmacist, however, clearly remembered telling her that it was poisonous and Jessie had replied that she knew about it and would take proper care.

Jessie was well-liked in the town; she was a woman with fascinating dark eyes and a ready smile, with an unblemished reputation as a loving wife and mother. On the face of it she was an unlikely murderer when she went on trail in July 1933. When doctors testified that the poison had been taken in capsule form, so that it might have been given under the guise of regular medicine, Jessie protested that she knew nothing about capsules and would have no idea how to fill them. Unfortunately for her, a neighbour remembered seeing Jessie filling medicine capsules when she was nursing a sick friend some time before.

The most damaging witness was patrolman Eddie McMahon of the Peabody police, who revealed to the astonished townsfolk that he had been carrying on an affair with Jessie ever since she had made eyes at him one day when he was directing traffic. After that they met secretly in quiet lay-bys, where they made love in parked cars, or in Jessie's home when her husband was working. When Eddie had appendicitis Jessie had visited him every night and as he recovered from his operation she had even shared his hospital bed with him for a few passionate moments. Jessie refuted his entire story: she scarcely knew the young patrolman and could not imagine why he should tell such lies about her, she said.

The defence tried to suggest, not too convincingly, that Bill had killed himself, even calling as a witness the manager of the local cinema, which shortly before his death had been showing a film called *Payment Deferred*, depicting a death by cyanide. This could, according to counsel, have put the idea into Bill's mind, for Jessie had given evidence that his good spirits were only a front and that he was, in reality, depressed and sickly.

According to the prosecution, Jessie had one eye on her sexy young patrolman and the other on Bill's insurance money; she had the means and the opportunity for murder. For the jury it was not enough. Unable to believe that such an upright citizen – and a handsome figure of a woman, into the bargain – could possibly commit such a crime, they found Jessie not guilty and she walked free from the courtroom. Eddie McMahon, the patrolman who had the bad taste to kiss and tell, lost his job with the police department and Jessie shed no tears for him.

Constance Kent

ON THE morning of 30 June 1860 three-year-old Francis Saville Kent was missing from his cot in the nursery of his house in Wiltshire, England. His nursemaid, Elizabeth Gough, had seen the empty cot when she awoke at about 5 am but assumed that the child's mother had taken him into her room, so the alarm was not raised until nearly 7 am. The house and grounds were immediately searched and the boy's body was found in an outside privy, with a deep stab wound in his side and his throat cut so deeply that his head was almost severed from his body. The time of death had been midnight or shortly afterwards. From the beginning it was assumed that the killer was someone in the household, though Mr Kent tried to suggest that it might be an outsider with a personal grudge against him. At the time, the most likely suspect seemed to be 16-year-old Constance Kent.

Constance was one of Samuel Kent's children by his first marriage. Her mother, who gave birth to 10 children in all, was frail and suffering from mental problems by the time Constance was a toddler and a young governess, Mary Pratt, was employed to look after the children. By the time Mrs Kent died, when Constance was eight, Mary Pratt was running the house and sharing Samuel Kent's bed. Soon afterwards she became the second Mrs Kent and by the time of the murder had four children – Francis, five-year-old Amelia, two-year-old Eugenie and baby Samuel – and was expecting a fifth. Mary Kents' children all slept on the second floor of the house with their parents but, though there were several other rooms available on the same floor, Constance and her two older sisters and younger brother shared the third floor with the servants. This was just one of the ways in which the second family was given preference over the first and at the time of the

Constance Kent

investigation there were a number of stories about harsh treatment meted out to the older children. The two eldest girls, it was said, were treated as unpaid servants and Constance was severely punished for any misbehaviour, locked up in the cellar or confined to her room on a diet of bread and watered milk.

Jealousy and resentment, then, were Constance's supposed motives. She had made several comments to friends, suggesting that her home life was unhappy, and everyone remembered the time when she had run away from home at the age of 12, dressed as a boy and taking her brother William with her; the children wanted to join their older brother Edward, who was working in the West Indies. Apart from the possible motive, there was the matter of the missing nightdress. The morning after the murder a bloodstained shirt had been found behind the boiler but in the general confusion it disappeared. Later, when it was found that one of Constance's nightdresses had disappeared, connections were made with the bloodstained garment, though reports suggested that it was the type of coarse garment worn by servants. Constance was arrested and spent a week in gaol until a hearing before magistrates decided that there was no case to answer.

Next it was Elizabeth Gough's turn to come under suspicion. After all, the boy slept in her room and it seemed unlikely that anyone else could have taken him without waking her. Mrs Kent had first seemed surprised that the nursemaid should think that Francis would be with her as she had never taken the child from his bed before. Now she changed her mind and admitted that she might have told Elizabeth not to be frightened if she came and took the child. The case against Elizabeth, too, was abandoned for lack of evidence.

At the inquest it had been reported that the boy had died from suffocation, rather than the cut throat, and that this explained the small amount of blood found at the scene. The findings lent weight to another theory which circulated widely in the county and was discussed in the newspapers. This pinpointed Samuel Kent as the murderer with Elizabeth Gough as his accomplice. The suggestion was that history was repeating itself as Kent found his way to the bed of Elizabeth Gough, as he had once carried on an affair with his children's governess. On one of his surreptitious night-time visits Francis could have woken up and called out, causing Kent, in a panic, to seize the nearest blanket to stop the child's cries and then press too hard, suffocating the child by accident. To avert suspicion from himself, he might then have decided to take Francis into the yard and cut his throat to make it look as though the attacker had come from outside. It was, after all, Kent who had insisted that the murderer must be someone who had quarrelled with him in the past.

Eventually the speculation died down, the Kent family moved out of the area and Constance was sent to a convent in France under the name of Emily Kent. Five years later she was at a convent in Brighton and training to become a nurse when she made a statement before a magistrate in which she confessed to the crime. She had done it 'alone and unaided', she said: 'Before the deed was done, no one know of my intention, nor afterwards knew of my guilt. No one assisted me in the crime, nor in the evasion of discovery.'

Her confession and subsequent guilty plea at Devizes Assize court were accepted and she was sentenced to death, later commuted to life imprisonment – but far from clearing up all the questions about the murder, her confession only added to the mystery. Constance's account of the killing hardly fits the facts. She said that a razor which she had taken from her father's room several days earlier was the only murder instrument, though evidence had shown that the wound in the boy's side could not have been caused by a razor. She said that she had made the second wound because she 'thought the blood would never come', though it seems impossible that a deeply slashed throat would fail to bleed if the child had been alive at the time. Though the doctor who had originally given evidence that Francis had been killed by suffocation obligingly changed his testimony and said that the razor wound was the cause of death, he could produce no good medical reason for the lack of blood.

Constance's only possible motive was in revenge for ill-treatment or neglect by her father and stepmother but she took care to deny this as 'entirely false', saying that she had experienced only the greatest kindness from both of them: 'I have never had any ill-will towards either of them.' Without motive nor convincing explanation of the method, Constance's guilt must be in doubt – but what would prompt an innocent girl to confess, so long after the event? There have been suggestions that in her secluded convent life she came under the influence of religious fanatics intent on saving souls who, knowing her background, managed to convince her that she had, in fact, committed the crime. It is just one more puzzle to add to all the other puzzles in the Kent case.

Adelaide Bartlett

IF ADELAIDE BARTLETT poisoned her husband she was certainly far more inventive than most poisoners, for Edwin Bartlett died from the effects of liquid chloroform. Liquid chloroform had never before been used in a murder and if anyone had been able to produce a credible theory as to how Adelaide managed to administer it to her husband, she would probably have been found guilty. As it was, Queen Victoria's surgeon, Sir James Paget, said afterwards that now that Mrs Bartlett had been acquitted, she should 'tell us in the interests of science how she did it'.

The public had been fascinated throughout the trial as the details of the Bartletts' marriage were revealed. Adelaide, the illegitimate daughter of an English aristocrat and his French mistress, was 19 when her family arranged a marriage with a 30-year-old grocer. Edwin was ambitious, good-natured and an active Methodist and though Adelaide said, 'My consent was not asked and I saw him only once before my wedding day', he seems to have had all the makings of a good husband. Keen that his young wife should continue her education, he sent her first to a finishing school and then to a convent.

When she returned to London the couple seemed to live together quite happily, though Edwin had very strange ideas about sex and marriage. He preferred his relationship with Adelaide to be platonic, so that he could put her on a pedestal and admire her. In fact he went further, believing that every man should have two wives: one to serve as a decorative companion, the other to look after his household and bedroom needs. Adelaide maintained that they only had sex on a single occasion, when she decided she wanted a baby. Though she duly became pregnant, the child was stillborn and the delivery was so long and painful that she decided not to try again.

In their 11 years together the Bartletts moved house several times and in 1883 they arrived in Wimbledon, where they became friendly with the minister of the local Wesleyan church, the Revd. George Dyson. From that moment, Edwin seems to have done everything possible to throw Adelaide and George together. He decided that the minister could teach her more history, geography and Latin and this meant that the two spent many hours closeted together. Sometimes George would spend all day with Adelaide, waiting for Edwin's return in the evening, and he dined with the couple at least three times a week. Edwin was quite happy to see his wife walking hand-in-hand with his friend and even encouraged them to kiss in his presence. He made George executor to his will and it was understood that if anything happened to him, the two of them would 'come together'. Of course, it is quite possible that they had already 'come together', but both always denied adultery, so perhaps their relationship went no further than sexual dalliance.

In 1885 the Bartletts moved back into town and Edwin fell ill. The doctor who was called found that Edwin displayed all the symptoms of mercury poisoning, though he denied ever taking mercury, a medicine used for syphilis. In addition, several of his teeth were in such an advanced state of decay that they needed to be extracted as soon as possible. The symptoms subsided, the teeth came out, but still Edwin remained depressed and lethargic, refusing to get out of bed and insisting that Adelaide should sit up with him at night, holding his foot for comfort. It was Adelaide who insisted on a second opinion because, she said, 'Edwin's relatives would soon accuse me of poisoning him.' The second doctor found little wrong with Edwin and encouraged him to go out more.

George Dyson visited the sickroom often and on 27 December Adelaide asked him to get her a bottle of chloroform, saying that it was the only thing that would ease Edwin's pains and help him to sleep.

Adelaide Bartlett

Dyson told local chemists that he needed the chloroform to remove grease spots and because he was a trusted minister they dispensed a far larger quantity than was normally allowed without prescription. Meanwhile, Edwin was feeling better and by New Year's Eve he was able to do justice to dinner of jugged hare and a supper of oysters and bread and butter, and to order a large haddock for breakfast. Then, in the early hours of the morning, he died. Adelaide told the doctor that she had fallen asleep in a chair by Edwin's bedside, holding his foot as usual, and awakened to find the foot stone cold. She had tried pouring brandy down Edwin's throat to revive him, but in vain.

George Dyson hastened round, not to console Adelaide but to find out what had happened to the chloroform. Heated words were exchanged and Adelaide was overheard shouting angrily 'Oh, damn the chloroform', while George accused her of telling him that Edwin was a sick man, likely to die before long. When the postmortem revealed a large quantity of liquid chloroform in Edwin's stomach George flew into a panic, while Adelaide confided in the doctor, telling him the whole story of the strange threesome. After insisting on a platonic relationship for many years, she said, and after 'giving' her to George Dyson, Edwin had recently decided to assert his marital rights in a most unwelcome manner. Adelaide had decided that she could discourage him by sprinkling chloroform on her handkerchief and waving it in front of his nose to make him drowsy. In the event she had not used it but had admitted her plan to Edwin and given him the bottle, which he put on the mantelpiece near his bed. This 'marvellous' story as *The Times* called it, added more spice to conjecture about the bedroom secrets of the Bartletts.

Adelaide was charged with murder, George was charged as an accessory and on 13 April 1886 they stood side-by-side in the dock at the Old Bailey. At the outset the Crown withdrew the case against George Dyson, who had earlier put all the blame on Adelaide, claiming that he had been 'duped by a wicked woman'. His acquittal was very unpopular with the public but Adelaide's counsel managed to turn it to her advantage by working hard to show how closely their actions were linked, so that the jury would be reluctant 'to send her to the hangman's cord, while he passed unrebuked to freedom'.

It was beyond dispute that Adelaide had had chloroform in her possession, that her husband had been killed by chloroform and that the bottle of chloroform had disappeared after his death, but the central question was asked over and over again: *how did the chloroform get into Edwin Bartlett's stomach?* There were suggestions that Edwin had taken it himself, perhaps intending to take his own life – though a man intending suicide does not usually order haddock for breakfast – or simply trying to put himself to sleep when all else failed. Alternatively, Adelaide might have added the chloroform to a glass of brandy, telling Edwin she was disguising an unpleasant-tasting medicine and encouraging him to bolt it down. This would explain the lack of burns in the mouth which liquid chloroform would normally cause but would almost certainly have made the patient vomit, which did not happen. The prosecution theory that Adelaide had first rendered her husband unconscious with chloroform then poured the rest down his throat seemed unlikely, for medical experts testified that pouring the liquid down the throat of an unconscious person would be an extremely delicate operation. Even when carried out by a doctor, the procedure would probably result in some of the liquid getting into the windpipe and there was no trace of chloroform in Edwin's windpipe.

The jury deliberated for over two hours and when they returned to the courtroom they announced that 'although we think that grave suspicion attaches to the prisoner, we do not think that there is sufficient evidence to show how or by whom the chloroform was administered'. They found Adelaide not guilty to cheers and applause from the public gallery.

Florence Bravo

THE MURDER of Charles Bravo is a mystery that has fascinated students of crime for more than a century. The only certainty is that he was poisoned but which of the women in his household administered the lethal dose will never be known. Charles was a good-looking young English barrister, thoroughly spoiled and accustomed to getting his own way, who married a beguiling young widow, Florence Ricardo, in 1875.

For those strait-laced times, Florence had a colourful past. When she was 19 she married the dashing Captain Alexander Ricardo of the Grenadier Guards, only to find that he was a drunkard who kept a succession of mistresses and was not about to change his dissolute way of life for the sake of his young wife. Florence, neglected and desperately unhappy, began to drink heavily. By 1870 the Captain had retired from the army and could devote himself full-time to women and the bottle, and Florence was at the end of her tether. Her parents suggested that the couple should go to Malvern to take the water cure which had become so fashionable. For the Captain it was a waste of time, but the trip was to change Florence's life. In Malvern she met Dr James Manby Gully, promoter of the famous water cure and medical advisor to such renowned figures as Dickens, Carlyle and Tennyson. Dr Gully was 62, strong, reliable and charismatic, and Florence fell head over heels in love with him. Shortly afterwards she separated from her husband, who obligingly drank himself to death the following year in Germany, leaving his widow a comfortable fortune.

Her liaison with Dr Gully, who bought a house close to hers in London, meant that she was no longer received in polite society and her family had cut her off, so Florence engaged a companion-

Florence Bravo

housekeeper, Mrs Jane Cox. Mrs Cox was the widow of a Jamaican engineer with little money and three sons to support, an unattractive, bespectacled woman whose efficiency meant that everything in Florence's household ran smoothly. The two women became close friends and confidantes and it was through Mrs Cox, who knew the Bravo family, that Florence met Charles. It may be that Florence was yearning for her lost respectability and Charles was certainly yearning for her substantial fortune. In any event, they decided to marry and settle in Florence's imposing London mansion. Florence put an end to her affair with Dr Gully and told Charles all about it. He, in turn, terminated his relationship with a young woman in Maidenhead.

So far as outsiders were concerned the marriage seemed to go well but both Florence and Mrs Cox were later to maintain that Charles was unreasonably jealous of his wife's past relationship with Dr Gully, throwing it in her face at every opportunity, causing bitter rows and occasionally even hitting her. Though Florence had brought most of the money to the marriage, all her property now belonged to her husband and he was mean with it. He persuaded her to give up her horses and her personal maid and his next planned economy was Mrs Cox.

On the evening of 18 April 1876 dinner in the Bravo household consisted of whiting, roast lamb, an egg dish and anchovies on toast. Charles drank several glasses of burgundy while Florence and Mrs Cox demolished two bottles of sherry between them. Florence, who had recently had a miscarriage, went to bed early and Mrs Cox sat with her. Charles was occupying the spare bedroom at the time and shortly after he retired a maid heard him calling desperately for water – though Mrs Cox, in the next room, claimed to have heard nothing. When the maid and Mrs Cox went into his room they found him vomiting out of the window and groaning with pain. Doctors who were summoned questioned the hapless Charles closely about what he had taken, but he insisted that his only medication had been laudanum rubbed on his gums to soothe his toothache. Though Mrs Cox told one of the doctors that Charles had admitted to her that he had taken poison and had asked her not to tell Florence, Charles denied it to the end. As the sickness and pain continued over the next three days, one of the doctors even told him that if he were not honest with them someone might be accused of poisoning him, but Charles still insisted that he had taken nothing but laudanum. He died in the early hours of the morning of 21 April and an autopsy showed that the cause of death was a large dose of antimony administered in the form of tartar emetic, which was easily dissolved in water and tasteless. The inquest, a sketchy affair, decided that the deceased had died from the effects of poison but there was no way of establishing how it had come to be in his body.

Many of Charles's friends were dissatisfied with the verdict and the newspapers began to run stories about the mysterious death of a young barrister. Florence received accusatory anonymous letters. Eventually a new enquiry was ordered and this time Mrs Cox caused a sensation by saying that Charles had told her 'I have taken poison for Gully – don't tell Florence'. She maintained that she had kept quiet about his actual words at first to protect Mrs Bravo's reputation. When Florence gave evidence, she confirmed that Mrs Cox had told her the reason for Charles's suicide after the first inquest. All the other witnesses told stories that contradicted the suicide theory: the maids had never heard the couple quarrelling and Charles's friends and family had seen no signs of depression or unhappiness.

The evidence of George Griffiths, formerly Mrs Bravo's coachman, caused a furore, for it proved that a large quantity of tartar emetic had been available at her home as recently as January. He had bought it to treat the horses, though only a small amount had been used, and he kept it locked in a cupboard in the stables. Griffiths had been dismissed for carelessness after a minor accident with the coach and said that before he left he poured away the remainder of the tartar emetic, but most of his listeners doubted that a discharged servant would have been that conscientious. At the end of the exhaustive 23-day inquest, the jury's verdict was that Charles Bravo had been murdered by the administration of poison but that there was insufficient evidence to decide on the guilty party.

There were plenty of rumours and questions but no answers. It could have been Florence who, trapped in a second unsatisfactory marriage with a husband who was closing the purse-strings on her money and depriving her of one luxury after another, slipped poison into his dinner-time burgundy or his bedroom water-jug. On the other hand, Florence seems to have lacked the strength of character and determination needed by a murderess. Mrs Cox had both and it could be that, faced with the prospect of losing her comfortable lifestyle and having to return without position or money to Jamaica, she decided to dispose of Charles before he could turn her out. Some investigators have even suggested a conspiracy between the two women, with hints of a lesbian relationship, which would explain why their evidence agreed on so many points that were disputed by the other witnesses. If this was the case then guilt must have driven a wedge between them, for after the verdict they went their separate ways: Florence went on drinking and died in 1878 and Mrs Cox returned to Jamaica after all.

Greta Peltz

GRETA PELTZ, a well-bred, well-educated 31-year-old American, found romance on a Caribbean cruise at Christmas, 1934. Her family doctor had suggested to a friend, Dr Fritz Gebhardt, that he should introduce himself to her on the voyage. He was an attractive, middle-aged company director, a world traveller with a strong personality. His first language was German and Greta, whose parents were German, spoke it fluently. Fritz set about courting Greta and she responded with delight.

She was not deterred by the fact that Fritz had strong Nazi leanings and frequently visited Germany for meetings with prominent Nazis. It came as a shock to find that he already had a wife and two children in Germany but he assured her that the marriage had been over in all but name for several years. His wife was Jewish and, because of new laws that had been passed, he would have no difficulty in having the marriage annulled, then he would be free to marry Greta.

Back in New York, Fritz wined and dined Greta and continued to make plans for their shared future. In May they went on a holiday to Lake George, registering as man and wife, and Fritz bought her a handsome aquamarine engagement ring. When they returned, Greta took a job in Fritz's office and moved out of her father's house and into an apartment two floors below her lover in Beekman Towers.

In November Fritz made one of his frequent trips to Europe. Greta hoped that he might bring back news that his marriage had at last been dissolved, but instead the break had given him time to think things over; when he returned he told her that he had decided that marriage was not for him after all. He wanted their affair to continue, but there would be no wedding. Greta was horrified; she wanted a husband and family, not a long-running affair, and her first instinct was to bring the relationship to an end. She would finish the work she was doing in the office, she said, then she would walk out of his life.

Fritz was not prepared to give up. Over the next three days he took her out for breakfast and dinner and tried to persuade her to change her mind. He loved her just as much as before, he assured her, so what difference did an official piece of paper make? He quoted her passionate love letters back at her: how could her feelings towards him have changed so quickly? When she still refused to visit his apartment or allow him to visit hers, he became angry. No one had ever walked out on him, he said, and he would not allow her to be the first.

Then, in the early hours of the morning of 12 November, the manager of the apartment block was woken by a phone call from Greta, who told him that she had just shot Dr Gebhardt. When the police arrived she was sitting on the stairs, her .32 calibre revolver in her handbag, still warm from firing. Fritz's body lay on the floor of his bedroom; he was in his nightclothes and had been shot four times. Greta asked for a lawyer, but refused to give any explanations or answer any questions.

At her trial Greta explained that after having dinner with her lover she had returned to her apartment alone. She had been in bed and asleep when Fritz had phoned her, asking for her help. He said that he was suffering a recurrence of a stomach complaint which caused him intense pain and which she had often treated for him in the past with the help of a special heating pad. He said that it was impossible for him to get out of bed and begged her to come.

She had climbed the back stairs to his apartment, still in her nightclothes, and let herself in. When she opened the bureau drawer to find the heating pad she saw, sitting next to it, the revolver she had bought six years earlier, when the area where she lived with her father had begun going downhill. Her brother had taught her to use it and had bought her a stock of ammunition, but Fritz had been worried at the thought of her keeping a loaded gun in her apartment and had taken it from her.

As she was reaching into the drawer for the pad Fritz came up behind her, seizing her by the elbows and holding her helpless. Realizing that she had been tricked, she told him coldly that, as he obviously did not need her, she would go back to her own apartment. 'You're not going anywhere. You're staying here as long as I want you,' he said, throwing her down on the bed. She threatened to scream but he reminded her that she was in his apartment, not the other way round, and that any screaming would cause a scandal. He then raped her brutally, calling her a 'damned whore' and leaving her groaning in pain.

When she dragged herself from the bed and tried to put on her clothes, he grabbed her again and this time tried to force her to have oral sex with him, boasting, 'I can make you do anything I want to.' Greta managed to break away from him and snatched the gun from the drawer. There was a struggle and she shot him to prevent him from violating her again. 'I was so ashamed I wanted to throw myself out of the window. I wanted to go downstairs and shoot myself.'

According to the defence, what she did after phoning the manager was return to her apartment and dress, then put the gun in her hand-bag while she was waiting for the police. The prosecution contended that, angry and humiliated by Dr Gebhardt's behaviour towards her, she had taken the gun to his apartment and shot him in a fit of rage. Greta faltered several times under cross-examination and there were several holes in her story: for instance, though she swore that the only ammunition she had for the gun had been bought by her brother several years before, the type of cartridges used in the shooting had only been manufactured since 1933. However, the defence was strong and highly emotional, with Greta frequently bursting into tears, and the jury was so affected by her account of the sexual abuse she had suffered that they brought in a verdict of not guilty.

Lizzie Borden

LIZZIE BORDEN was acquitted by the jury in Massachusetts, USA, on the charge of murdering her father and stepmother, though legend still holds her guilty and the popular rhyme states baldly:

> *Lizzie Borden took an axe*
> *And gave her mother forty whacks*
> *When she saw what she had done*
> *She gave her father forty-one.*

No one could argue that the Borden household in the little town of Fall River was happy or harmonious. Lizzie's father, 70-year-old Andrew Borden, had made a fortune, first as an undertaker, patenting a popular line in burial caskets, and later as a property speculator. Nevertheless, his meanness was well-known in the town and the Borden home, on 92 Second Street, was a shabby little whitewood house with fewer comforts than those of many of the local millworkers. His first wife had died two years after Lizzie was born and he had made a second marriage, to a fat, plain woman called Abby. She was deeply resented by Lizzie, who called her 'Mrs Borden', refused to eat at the same table and spoke to her only when it was unavoidable. Her anger reached boiling point when Mr Borden bought the house in which Abby's sister lived to save her from eviction and gave the deeds to his wife. Lizzie saw it as proof that Abby was after her father's money. Soon afterwards Abby's bedroom was ransacked and her watch and jewellery were taken. Mr Borden called the police but sent them away again when it became obvious that Lizzie was responsible. It was accepted by the family that she had committed the act during one of her 'funny turns', when she often acted out of character.

In the sizzling hot summer of 1892 strange things were happening in the household, even before the axe murders. Lizzie kept pigeons in the outhouses at the bottom of the garden and intruders twice broke in there. Mr Borden, thinking that they had designs on the pigeons, took the extraordinary course of killing all the birds. Then Lizzie went round the local pharmacists trying to buy prussic acid, only to find that no one would sell her the poisonous substance without a prescription.

The fourth of August was the hottest day of the year. Lizzie's older sister Emma had tried to escape the heat by going to stay with friends in the country. John Morse, brother of the first Mrs Borden, was staying for a few days but was out visiting other relatives. Once Mr Borden had left the house his wife busied herself with housework upstairs and the maid Bridget Sullivan set about washing the windows. Lizzie, who had breakfasted later than the others, was planning to do some ironing.

Shortly before 11 am, Mr Borden returned from town. Lizzie came downstairs to meet him and when he enquired where his wife was, Lizzie told him that during the morning she had received a note from a sick friend and had gone to visit. Mr Borden sat down on the horsehair sofa in the living room and picked up a copy of the *Providence Journal*, but he was exhausted by the heat and soon began to doze. Bridget was feeling ill – the after-effects of some mutton that had upset everyone in the house but Lizzie – so she went up to her attic bedroom for a rest, hearing the clock strike 11 as she mounted the stairs.

Only 10 or 15 minutes later she heard Lizzie calling frantically and hurried downstairs. 'Father's dead. Someone came in and killed him,' Lizzie told her. She would not let Bridget go into the sitting room but sent her for Dr Bowen, the family physician. The doctor was still out on his rounds so she left an urgent message and returned to the house, only to be sent out again to fetch Alice Russell, one of Lizzie's closest friends. Mrs Adelaide Churchill, the next-door neighbour, noticed the comings and goings and saw Lizzie standing by the screen door. She asked her what was wrong and was told: 'Someone has killed father.'

When Dr Bowen arrived he found Mr Borden's body lying on the sofa, his blood covering the floor and walls. The old man's head had been shattered by 10 hatchet blows, so that his face had been destroyed and one eyeball was hanging from its socket. The doctor reckoned that he had been struck while sleeping and that the first blow had killed him.

Mrs Churchill and Mrs Russell were comforting Lizzie in the kitchen, rubbing her hands and dabbing her forehead with a damp cloth, though she seemed remarkably calm and collected. When Mrs Churchill asked her where she was when her father was killed, she said, 'I went out to the barn to get a piece of iron.' Mrs Churchill then asked where her mother was and Lizzie gave the extraordinary reply: 'I'm sure I don't know, for she had a note from someone to go and see somebody who is sick. But I don't know that perhaps she isn't killed also, for I thought I heard her coming in.'

Mrs Churchill went upstairs with Bridget to look for Mrs Borden and as they climbed she glanced through the open door of the spare bedroom and saw the woman's ample body on the floor. She had been attacked from behind with a hatchet as she entered the bedroom and though the first blow must have killed her 18 more blows had been inflicted, leaving the room awash with blood. It seemed strange that Lizzie, when coming downstairs to greet her father, would have noticed nothing.

When John Morse returned to the house, after the police had arrived, he drew suspicion upon himself by his strange behaviour. A crowd of sightseers had already gathered around the house but, instead of hurrying inside to see what was wrong, he wandered slowly round to the back garden, picked some fruit from a tree and munched it thoughtfully before going inside. Then he produced an alibi so glib and exact that it seemed too perfect to be true. When it was checked, however, it was found to be correct in every detail.

The police realized that the murderer was either an intruder who had hidden in the house for some 90 minutes between the two killings without Lizzie or Bridget being aware of him, which seemed unlikely, or someone in the household. Bridget was soon discounted as a suspect, as there were several witnesses to her movements that morning; neighbours had seen her cleaning the windows, both outside and in, and she had even been seen vomiting from the effects of food poisoning. When Lizzie was questioned about her movements she told the police that she had spent 20 minutes in the loft of the outbuilding and had eaten three pears while looking for some weights for her fishing line, but the dust on the floor of the loft bore no footprints.

Enquiries were made about the note Lizzie said her stepmother had received but no note was found, no one admitted sending it and no one had seen it but Lizzie. An axe head, broken from its handle and with its blade smeared with ash from the stove, was found in the basement but there was no proof that it was the murder weapon. A reward was posted for information leading to the arrest of a bloodstained outsider who might have left the Borden household that morning. Interest quickened when a Dr Handy claimed to have seen a 'wild man' in Second Street at around the time of the killings, but faded again when he was identified as 'Mike the Soldier', a well-known local drunk.

At the inquest, Lizzie changed her story and contradicted herself several times. She now said that she was not upstairs when her father arrived home but in the kitchen. 'I thought I was on the stairs but now I know I was in the kitchen,' she said unconvincingly. She now denied that she had ever said she heard her stepmother returning to the house. The authorities were in two minds about charging Lizzie with murder. Though she seemed the only possible killer and the public prosecutor was convinced of her guilt, he was not convinced that there was enough evidence to obtain a conviction. All the same, Lizzie was arrested and stood trial in June the following year.

By then the press vilification of Lizzie, which had at first set people all over America howling for her execution, had caused a backlash in her favour. Now she appeared as a quiet and God-fearing woman – secretary of the local Christian Endeavour Society, member of the Women's Christian Temperance Union, Sunday school teacher – incapable of such bestial deeds. Flowers and good-luck messages poured in from all over the country and suddenly she became the hounded and persecuted victim of the unfeeling state.

Lizzie, now a rich woman, had hired George Robinson, the best lawyer in Massachusetts and a former governor of the state. One of the three trial judges had been elevated to the bench during his governorship and therefore owed him a favour. Certainly things went Lizzie's way when the judges refused to admit the transcripts of her muddled answers at the inquest, or accounts of her attempts to buy prussic acid, into evidence. Though blood from the two killings had covered the rooms where they took place, no one had noticed any blood on Lizzie at any time and it seemed impossible that she could have changed and washed without Bridget noticing what was going on, yet Bridget said that she had seen and heard nothing. Though Alice Russell had seen Lizzie burning a dress in the stove shortly before the police were due to search the house – because, she said, it was faded and had splashes of paint – she was sure there was no blood on the dress. On the other hand, she had see no paint on it either!

George Robinson appealed to the emotions of the jury by pointing to the respectable, lady-like woman in the dock and saying, 'To find her guilty, you must believe she is a fiend. Gentlemen, does she look it?' The jury could not believe it and at the end of the 10-day trial they found her not guilty. Her supporters threw a celebration party where Lizzie was able to chuckle over the newspaper clippings they had saved for her. Her new popularity did not last long. She bought a larger house on the more genteel side of Fall River and lived there as a recluse, giving up all her good works. For a few years Emma shared the house with her but eventually they quarrelled and Emma left. Lizzie stayed on, alone but for the servants, until she died in 1927,

Lizzie Borden with her counsel in court

aged 67. Bridget, whom some still suspected of covering up for Lizzie's crimes, returned to Ireland, allegedly with a slice of the Borden legacy.

No one else was ever arrested or even seriously suspected in the Borden case. Five plays and many books have been written about it, giving various explanations of how Lizzie could have carried out the crime. In her book *A Private Disgrace*, American writer Victoria Lincoln puts forward the theory that Lizzie murdered during an attack of temporal epilepsy – the cause of the 'funny turns' well-known to her family – which could result in loss of memory afterwards and explain Lizzie's contradictory statements and coolness when she was accused of murder.

Alma Rattenbury

'I KNOW who did it . . . I did it with a mallet. Ratz had lived too long,' Alma Rattenbury babbled to the police who came to the Villa Madeira in Bournemouth, England, to investigate the brutal attack on 67-year-old Francis Rattenbury, known as Ratz. It was 2 am and Alma was in a state of almost manic excitement, capering about, trying to kiss the police constable, putting one record after another on the gramophone and turning the volume up to full blast. She went on muttering, half incoherently: 'I would like to give you £10 . . . no, I won't bribe you.' At about 3 am, when she was told that her husband's condition was critical, she said: 'I did it . . . he lived too long . . . I'll tell you where the mallet is in the morning. I shall make a better job of it next time . . . I made a proper muddle of it. I thought I was strong enough.' Soon after that her doctor arrived and gave her a shot of morphia so that she could get some sleep.

In the morning the police interviewed the Rattenbury's chauffeur, 18-year-old George Stoner, who said that he had been in his room at about 10.30 pm when he heard Alma calling to him. In the drawing room he found Francis Rattenbury in the armchair, with blood running from his head. Alma had been crying: 'Help me to get Ratz to bed, he has been shot.' He had asked Alma how it happened and she said she didn't know. At 8.15 am, once Alma was up and dressed, Detective Inspector Carter charged her with the attempted murder of her husband and she made and signed a statement as follows:

'About 9 pm on Sunday, 24 March 1935, I was playing cards with my husband when he dared me to kill him as he wanted to die. I picked up the mallet. He then said, "You have not got guts enough to

Alma and Francis Rattenbury with their son on the sands at Bournemouth

do it." I then hit him with the mallet. I hid the mallet outside the house. I would have shot him if I had a gun.'

Alma was then arrested and taken to the police station. As she left the house her companion Irene Riggs, her young son John and George Stoner were all standing in the hall. 'Don't make fools of yourselves,' she told them, and George was heard to say, 'You've got yourself into this mess by talking too much.'

Over the next few days, the strange story of the Rattenburys and their chauffeur was revealed. Alma and Francis had married in 1925; he was a distinguished architect some 30 years her senior. Though the marriage was happy enough at first, they grew apart with the years. Alma was impulsive and romantic, and had achieved some success in writing popular sentimental songs. Ratz was a solitary and rather morose man, prone to fits of melancholy, often talking morbidly about suicide when he had drunk too much whisky in the evenings. He was becoming increasingly deaf and Alma decided that it would be advisable to hire a young man who could act as chauffeur and handyman.

In September 1934 George Stoner, the good-natured and somewhat backward son of a local bricklayer, joined the household. He gave his age as 22, though in reality he was not quite 18. He drove Alma to the London shops, cinemas and theatres and soon he was sharing her bed. It was the shy young man's first experience of sex and he fell deeply in love. When Alma discovered his real age and attempted to end the affair they quarrelled violently and he vowed that he could not live without her. He was often jealous but Alma reassured him that it was six years since she had had sex with her husband and that Ratz had told her that she should lead her own life.

In the spring of 1935 Alma told her husband that she had to go to London for a minor operation and would need £250 to cover expenses. Ratz glumly produced the money, which Alma spent on a five-day spree with Stoner in London, in the course of which she bought him silk pyjamas and shirts, two suits, a coat, underwear and handkerchieves.

She even gave him the money to buy a diamond ring which he could present to her as a token of his love.

The two lovers returned from their trip on Saturday 23 March and the next day Ratz sank into one of his black moods. At teatime he read aloud passages from a book in which the hero considers suicide and Alma tried to cheer him by suggesting that they should take a trip to Bridport next day to visit a business associate. Later that Sunday night someone battered Francis Rattenbury so viciously that he died four days later without ever regaining consciousness.

By this time the police had learned about the strange triangle at the Villa Madeira and George was arrested. He asked detectives, 'You know Mrs Rattenbury had nothing to do with this affair?' He confessed that he had watched through the french windows and saw Alma kiss her husband goodnight, then he had waited, crept in when Mr Rattenbury was asleep and hit him. He then went upstairs and told Alma, who rushed down. 'You know, there should be a doctor with her when they tell her I am arrested, because she will go out of her mind,' he added.

Now both suspects had confessed, both claiming complete responsibility. Yet, when they appeared at the Old Bailey, charged with murder, they both pleaded not guilty. Alma had now changed her story. She said that George had been angry and jealous about the Bridport trip and had cornered her in the dining room, threatening to kill her if she went. She had calmed him down but when he joined her in the bedroom later he was 'looking a bit odd'. He told her that she was not going to Bridport the next day because he had hurt Ratz; he had hit him over the head with a mallet. It had previously been shown in court that George had borrowed a mallet from his grandfather on the Sunday morning, because he needed to drive in some tent pegs.

Alma described how she had tried to rub her husband's cold hands: 'I tried to speak to him and then I saw his blood, and I went round the table and trod on his false teeth and that made me hysterical.' Then she began drinking whisky and after that everything was a blank. She had conveniently forgotten her interviews with the police and her confessions of guilt; her statement was 'absolute double-Dutch' to her, she said.

Alma was represented at the trial by the best lawyers money could buy, while George had to rely on the inexperienced counsel provided by legal aid. He was adamant that nothing must be done to suggest that Alma was in any way involved with the crime. He did not go into the witness box – perhaps because his counsel thought that his evidence would only damage his case, or perhaps because George felt that he might incriminate the woman he loved. His counsel was reduced to suggesting that an addiction to cocaine meant that he was not responsible for his actions. Unfortunately, the prosecution was able to demonstrate that George did not even know what cocaine looked like.

George was found guilty and sentenced to hang. Alma was found not guilty but as she left the court the waiting crowd booed her. Three days after her acquittal, Alma took a train to Christchurch and sat for a while by the river. She wrote a note on the back of an envelope: 'One must be bold to do a thing like this. It is beautiful here, and I am alone. Thank God for peace at last . . .' A farmworker saw her walk towards the river, crouch down, then topple in. She had plunged a knife six times into her chest and three of the wounds had pierced her heart.

George Stoner, in the death cell at Pentonville, sobbed when he heard of her death. A week later he wrote to his lawyer saying that he was innocent of the crime but would never have told the full story if Alma had lived. He said that he had fetched the mallet for perfectly normal reasons and had put it in the coalshed. That night he had found Alma in bed in a terrified state. There was a loud groan from downstairs and Alma went rushing down. He followed and found Mr Rattenbury with terrible head injuries. The mallet lay on the floor and he had kicked it under the sofa. Later, after Alma was arrested and he learned about the statements she had made, he had done everything possible to incriminate himself.

George's appeal was turned down but the Home Secretary recommended a reprieve and he served only seven years in prison before being paroled. He served in the armed forces in the Second World War and took part in the D-Day landings, then, after the war, settled down to respectable married life.

It is hard to judge, in the confusion of contradictory statements, whether the verdict was right or wrong. In his summing up, the trial judge said that it would be unfair to form any conclusion on the basis of a statement made while Alma was under the influence of morphia; however, she made several confessions admitting responsibility, with no suggestion that anyone else was involved. Until shortly before the trial, she was still refusing to blame George. A number of people who had known Alma in the past, when she lived in Canada, believed that she took drugs and her behaviour after the attack seems more in keeping with the influence of drugs than with alcohol. Moreover, she was known to be subject to attacks of excitability 'as though she had taken something'. If she was high on drugs on the night of the murder her husband's constant complaining might have sent her into a fury, and while not fully in control of her actions, she might have seized the mallet and set about him.

Alma's suicide was widely seen as an act of despair by a woman who could not bear to go on living while her lover was sentenced to hang. However, if she were so deeply in love she would have seen that George had the money to furnish the best defence rather than leaving him to the mercies of legal aid. It could be that, having been persuaded to change her story on the grounds that she was a mother whose children would be orphaned if she was executed, she was now unable to face the idea of living with her guilt.

Alice Crimmins

ACCORDING to Alice Crimmins, she opened the door of her children's bedroom in her ground-floor apartment in Queens, New York, on 14 July 1965 to find that although their beds had been slept in, five-year-old Eddie and four-year-old Alice were missing. She immediately phoned her estranged husband Eddie, who was fighting her for custody of the children, to ask if he had taken them. It was Eddie who rang the police to report the children's disappearance. Detective Gerard Piering, who arrived to investigate, took an instant dislike to 26-year-old Alice. With her figure-hugging toreador pants and strawberry blonde hair, her rubbish-bin full of empty liquor bottles and her address book full of phone numbers of past and present boyfriends, she was not his idea of a caring mother and she seemed surprisingly calm about the missing children.

Alice told him that she had given the children a meal at about 7.30 pm, and had put them to bed at 9 pm. She remembered shutting the window because there was a hole in the fly-screen, yet in the morning she had found the window wide open. At midnight she had taken little Eddie to the bathroom but young Alice, known as Missy, had not woken. After she had put Eddie back to bed she had fastened the hook and eye latch which was fitted on the outside of the door to stop Eddie getting up and raiding the refrigerator in the night. She had heard no sound from the bedroom after that, though she did not go to bed herself until between 3.30 and 4 am, so the children must have been taken after that time.

Later in the day, a young boy discovered Missy's body on a vacant lot about seven blocks away. She had been strangled with her pyjama top, which was still knotted around her neck. Little Eddie's body was

283

found a week later in the undergrowth on the embankment of an expressway, some 2 km (1¼ miles) from his home. The body was badly decomposed and it was impossible to tell the cause of death. For months detectives followed up leads that ended nowhere and at the end they were left with Alice as the murder suspect. At first Eddie was also under suspicion but when he produced an alibi and passed a lie-detector test with flying colours, he was more or less ruled out of enquiries. Alice, who had refused to take the test, became the favoured suspect. She was known to lead a promiscuous lifestyle, with various different men sharing her bed in the Queens apartment, and the children's needs often seemed to come second to her own. The latch on the outside of the children's door was probably fitted to prevent them from interrupting Alice's sexual antics rather than to protect the contents of the refrigerator. There had been one occasion when she had left them alone over the weekend while she went to the Bahamas on a boyfriend's boat, though she maintained that this was unintentional: she had been asked to a party on board and had found herself way out in the ocean before she realized what was happening. Her current lover, Joe Rorech, at first admitted that she had talked to him about the custody hearing, saying that she would rather see the children dead than let Eddie have them. Later he said that, when they spent the night together in a motel, she had admitted to killing her little daughter and begged him to forgive her.

A breakthrough in the case came when detectives traced a neighbour with an incriminating tale to tell. Sophie Earomirski first told her story in an anonymous letter but was eventually located and persuaded to testify. At 2 am on 14 July 1965 she had seen a man and woman walking along the road near Alice's apartment. The woman was carrying a bundle wrapped in blankets and leading a little boy by the hand. When the man told her to hurry, she said that she had to wait for the dog because it was pregnant. When the man threw the bundle into the back of a car, the woman – identified by Mrs Earomirski as Alice Crimmins – said, 'My God, don't throw her like that.'

Alice was indicted and charged with Missy's murder. At her trial, pathologist Dr Melton Helpern said that the food in Missy's stomach was at an early stage of digestion, indicating that she had died within two hours of her last meal. As Alice had fed the children at 7.30 pm, it was 'patently absurd to think that death might have occurred in the pre-dawn hours'. Damaging evidence was given by Joe Rorech and by the 'woman at the window', Mrs Earomirski. Her evidence led to discussion about the pregnant dog: Alice's dog Brandy was indeed pregnant at the time but the defence contended that no one had known that on the night of the murder. Alice herself was questioned at length about her many lovers, both before and after her children's death. Though the judge cautioned the jury that they were not trying Mrs Crimmins's morals, her strenuous love-life counted heavily against her.

Alice was found guilty of first-degree manslaughter and sentenced to between 5 and 20 years' imprisonment, but the sentence was later quashed and a new trial was ordered. At the second trial two new witnesses appeared. One was a woman who lived in the same district as Alice and had been travelling in a car driven by her husband on the early morning of 14 July when she saw a man and woman, accompanied by a dog and a small boy. The man had been carrying a large bundle. The other, for the defence, was a young man who remembered walking along the road at the time in question with his family: his wife and young son, his daughter who was carried under his arm like a sack and their plump dog, who might well have appeared pregnant to a casual observer. This time Alice was found guilty of the murder of her son and the manslaughter of her daughter. The appeals continued and eventually the murder conviction was dismissed but the manslaughter conviction was upheld.

Alice was paroled in 1977 but criminologists still debate the case, for the evidence against Alice was never strong. No convincing motive was ever put forward for the killings. If, as was suggested, the children got in the way of her love life, she could have gained her freedom by handing them over to Eddie. The comment that she would rather see them dead than in his custody seems more like the throw-away comment of an angry mother engaged in a dispute with an ex-husband than a threat to murder. Joe Rorech, who said that she had confessed to him, was a man with a lively imagination who later came up with a story about a high-powered political intrigue involving Alice and leading to the abduction and killing of the children by mobsters. As for the 'woman in the window', she may well have seen a salesman's family passing by and embroidered the scene in her imagination after hearing about the crime. If the woman carrying a bundle was Alice, with Missy's body under her arm, then the man accompanying her must have been her accomplice, but no accomplice was ever produced. It may be that, in common with a number of other women tried for murder, her loose morals were her downfall.

Edith Thompson

EDITH THOMPSON was hanged at Holloway Prison, London, on 9 January 1923, at the same time that her lover Frederick Bywaters went to his death at Pentonville. Frederick, who had killed Percy Thompson in the street three months earlier, faced his end bravely but Edith, who had always protested that she had had nothing to do with her husband's death, collapsed and had to be carried to the scaffold. It was Edith's letters to her lover – passionate, fantastic, foolish letters – that had convicted her, making it seem that the crime had been planned in advance, a sinister conspiracy to dispose of an inconvenient husband. Yet the circumstances of the crime suggest an impulse killing, with no careful thought or planning.

Percy and Edith Thompson had married in 1915 and their life together was routine and uneventful; Percy worked as a shipping clerk and Edith was manageress at a firm of wholesale milliners. Temperamentally they were unsuited, for Edith was a thorough-going romantic, given to self-dramatization, while Percy was down-to-earth and unimaginative. However, their life together jogged along uneventfully until the summer of 1921 when handsome, virile Frederick Bywaters, a ship's clerk on the SS *Morea*, was one of a party of young people who joined them for a holiday on the Isle of Wight, invited by Edith's younger brothers.

Freddy was only 19 at the time, eight years younger than Edith, but there was an immediate attraction between them and before the end of the holiday they were exchanging secret kisses. Percy, too, liked the young man and invited him to lodge with them at their home in Ilford until his ship sailed again. The romantic attachment between Freddy and Edith developed, with Percy apparently unaware of what was

Frederick Bywaters and Edith Thompson with her husband Percy (right)

happening. It was a three-cornered argument on 1 August that brought things into the open. A minor disagreement between husband and wife had developed into a full-blown row, during which Percy hit Edith and threw her across the room so that she knocked over a chair and hurt her arm. Freddy came running in from the garden to protect Edith and angry words were exchanged, with Freddy telling Percy that he was making Edith's life hell and should give her a divorce. Percy retorted that she was his wife and that he intended to keep her.

After that, Freddy left the house and went to stay with his mother but he continued to see Edith, usually for brief meetings in teashops, though shortly before his ship sailed in September they managed to share a bed for the first time. It was during the periods of separation that Edith wrote the fateful letters, several dozen of which were produced at the trial. She wrote to him as 'darlint', a diminution of 'darlingest' and her letters were long and effusive, full of gossip and chatter and outpourings of love. She deliberately stirred up Freddy's feelings of jealousy and the tone became more sinister as the months passed: 'Yes, darlint, you are jealous of him – but I want you to be – he has the right by law to all that you have the right to by nature and love and yes, darlint, be jealous, so much so that you will do something desperate.'

She talked openly of trying to dispose of her husband by putting poison or ground glass in his food. She lamented that Percy had become suspicious when his tea tasted bitter 'as if something had been put in it' and that ground glass did not have the desired effect: 'I used the light bulb three times, but the third time he found a piece, so I've given up until you come home . . . I used a lot – big pieces too – not powdered, and it has no effect.' In another letter she wrote, 'he says . . . when he was young he nearly suffocated by gas fumes. I wish we had not got electric light, it would be easy. I am going to try glass again occasionally – when it is safe'. She sent Freddy all sorts of newspaper cuttings about cases concerning death by poisoning and hoped that the proposed crime would not affect his feelings for her:

'This thing that I am going to do for both of us – will it ever – at all, make any difference between us, darlint? Do you understand what I mean? Will you ever think any the less of me?'

In the autumn of 1922 Freddy was back in England and the illicit meetings resumed. The couple met in a London teashop on the afternoon of 3 October and that same evening Edith and Percy went to a West End theatre with some friends. They arrived back in Ilford near midnight and were walking home from the station, talking about a dance they might attend in two weeks' time, when Freddy jumped out of the shadows and grabbed Percy by the arm.

There was a brief altercation, then Freddy pulled out a knife and stabbed Percy several times. A witness heard Edith screaming: 'Oh, don't! Oh don't!' and as Percy slumped bleeding to the ground, Freddy fled into the shadows. Edith, seeing that there was nothing she could do for her husband, ran for help, meeting a young couple with the frantic request, 'Oh, my God, will you help me, my husband is bleeding.' A doctor was summoned but by the time he arrived Percy was dead and Edith demanded, 'Why did you not come sooner and save him?'

The search for the assailant soon led to Frederick Bywaters and the incriminating pile of letters was found in his possession. When she learned of his arrest, Edith sobbed, 'Oh God, why did he do it? I didn't want him to do it.' From the beginning both Freddy and Edith insisted that she knew nothing of his movements that night, and that there was no murder plot between them. According to Freddy, he had never meant to kill Percy. He had jumped out at him in a fury, accusing him of being a cad and demanding that he should divorce Edith: 'I loved her and I could not go on seeing her leading that life. I did not intend to kill him. I only meant to injure him. I gave him an opportunity of standing up to me as a man but he wouldn't.' He said that Percy threatened to shoot him and, thinking that he had a gun, Freddy pulled out his knife – a knife that he always kept in his pocket, like many sailors – and, in fear of his life, stabbed Percy.

Edith's counsel tried to keep the damaging letters out of court as inadmissible evidence but the attempt failed. The prosecution selected all the passages that related to possible murder attempts, though among the thousands upon thousands of words written by Edith she had imagined many different ways out of the love tangle, including divorce, elopement and a suicide pact. Murder was just one of the fanciful ideas she toyed with. Freddy, when questioned about the letters, said that he had never considered that she was serious about poisoning her husband: 'She had been reading books and she had a vivid way of declaring herself,' he explained. 'She would read a book and imagine herself a character in the book.' Edith said that she had only been trying to excite her lover's interest and make him think that she was willing to do anything for him, to keep his love. The evidence of the pathologist seemed to support her story, for no trace of glass or any toxic substance was found in Percy Thompson's body. Later, Edith's counsel was to say that if she had not insisted on going into the witness box against his advice, she would have been acquitted. It was her vanity and her obvious sexuality that put the noose around her neck.

The judge, Mr Justice Shearman, was strongly biased against the defendants and particularly against Edith, an adulterous married woman who had indulged in a 'sordid intrigue'. He reminded the jury that this was 'a vulgar, common crime' and left them in no doubt that the two defendants had plotted the murder together. When the guilty verdict was announced, Freddy exclaimed: 'I say the verdict of the jury is wrong. Edith Thompson is not guilty. I am no murderer. I am no assassin.' Edith, hearing them both sentenced to death, cried: 'I am not guilty. Oh God, I am not guilty.'

An appeal, on the grounds that the judge's summing up had been biased and that the verdict went against the weight of the evidence, was rejected and though several thousand people signed a petition supporting a reprieve for Edith, no appeal was granted. Bywaters protested Edith's innocence to the end. Though he accepted that he must pay the price for his crime, he wrote of Edith: 'For her to be hanged as a criminal is too awful. She didn't commit the murder. I did. She never planned it. She never knew about it. She is innocent, absolutely innocent. I can't believe they will hang her.' But they did.

Elvira Barney

WHEN Elvira Barney was found with her dead lover and a .32 Smith and Wesson revolver in the bedroom of her exclusive mews cottage in London's Knightsbridge, her attitude towards the police was typical of her personality and lifestyle. When a detective asked her to accompany him to the police station she slapped him across the face, crying, 'I'll teach you to put me in a cell, you foul swine!' Then she telephoned her parents, Sir John and Lady Mullins, warning afterwards: 'Now you know who my mother is, perhaps you will be more careful what you say.'

Elvira came from a wealthy family and grew up spoiled and arrogant, one of the 'bright young things' of the 1920s, who drank too much, drove recklessly, threw extravagant parties and indulged in promiscuous sex. At the age of 23 she married John Sterling Barney but a year later they separated and Elvira rejoined the society circuit in search of a good time. Several lovers later, she was living with 24-year-old Michael Scott Stephen at 21 Williams Mews, Knightsbridge. Stephen described himself as a dress designer but at the time his only occupation was sponging off rich women. The couple scandalized the neighbours with their noisy parties and even noisier quarrels.

It was one of those quarrels that was to result in the death of Michael Stephen. In the early hours of the morning of 31 May 1932 Elvira phoned her doctor, crying hysterically: 'For God's sake come at once. There's been a terrible accident.' By the time he reached the mews Michael was dead, shot at close range. Elvira was kissing him repeatedly and moaning: 'He can't be dead . . . I love him so . . . He wanted to see you to tell you it was an accident . . . Let me die, let me die. I will kill myself.' The doctor had trouble controlling her and had to put his foot on the revolver lying on the floor to prevent her from seizing it.

Though she was in great distress, the story Elvira told the doctor was the one she was to tell the police later and it was a version of events from which she never departed. She said that she and her lover had arrived home, half drunk, at 2.30 am from a party at the Café de Paris. They had made love but had quarrelled afterwards: Michael was angry because she had not responded as he wanted and she was still annoyed about an argument over money earlier in the day. When Michael got dressed and announced that he was leaving she begged him not to, saying that if he did she would kill herself. Michael had rushed to the armchair and grabbed the revolver from behind the cushion. Elvira said she was nervous of the revolver, though she had had it for years, and used to hide it in various places. 'You won't do it with this,' Michael said. Elvira had tried to wrest the gun from him and in the struggle that followed, it went off. At first she did not realize that Michael was hurt, as he stepped into the bathroom and shut the door. Then he half-opened it and told her to get the doctor. Before he died he kept saying that he wished the doctor would hurry: 'I want to tell him it was an accident; it was not your fault.'

After she had made her statement Elvira was released from custody, only to be arrested three days later. By then the police had heard from neighbours about the violent nature of Elvira Barney's relationship with Michael Stephen, the rows and the threats, culminating in the night of his death, when Elvira had been heard to shout, 'I'll shoot you.'

At her trial, the forensic evidence against Elvira was strong. There were no smoke or scorch marks on the victim's clothes or hands, though his hand would have been blackened if it had been touching the gun when it was fired. If the gun had been fired at point-blank range, while they struggled as described by Elvira, there would normally be scorch marks around the bullet hole. Instead, the angle of the bullet suggested that it had been fired from further away, which would indicate that Elvira had pulled the trigger. Moreover, the Smith and Wesson gun had a very heavy action with a pull amounting to 6.4 kg (14 lb) and was, in the opinion of gun-maker Robert Churchill of Leicester Square, one of the safest revolvers made. Finally, a bullet hole had been discovered in the bedroom wall and if two shots had been fired it was far less likely to have been an accidental shooting.

Mrs Hall, a neighbour, had heard Elvira screaming 'I'll shoot' twice before she heard a gun-shot and then Michael had shouted 'What have you done?' Elvira was crying: 'Chicken, come back to me. I will do anything I can for you.' Mrs Hall also described an incident about three weeks before when Michael had arrived in the early hours of the morning and was calling to Elvira, asking her for money. She sent him away but he came back again later and this time Elvira had appeared at the window naked and fired a shot at him, saying, 'Laugh, baby; laugh for the last time.'

Mrs Hall's court testimony was by no means as damning as her earlier statement to the police, as 'I'll shoot' (instead of 'I'll shoot you') might well have been a threat of suicide rather than murder. When cross-examined by Elvira's counsel, Sir Patrick Hastings, Mrs Hall agreed that on the morning after the 'Laugh baby, laugh' incident she had seen Elvira and Michael leaving the flat together and they had seemed very friendly. She had told Michael that he was a perfect nuisance in the mews and should clear off but he had said that he did not want to leave Elvira because he was afraid that she might kill herself.

Hastings contended that the shot Mrs Hall thought had been fired at Michael in the mews had in fact been fired within the house, and accounted for the bullet hole in the bedroom wall. As far as the claims that the gun had such a heavy action that it could not have gone off by accident, Hastings refuted this by pointing it towards the court ceiling and pulling the trigger several times in quick succession – though he later admitted that it had given him a sore finger. For the defence he called only two witnesses. First came a doctor who had examined Elvira after her admission to Holloway Prison and found that she had extensive bruising on her arms and cuts and abrasions on one of her hands, all consistent with her story of struggling with her lover over a revolver.

Next came Elvira herself, looking older than her 27 years, seeming nervous and subdued. In low, dignified tones she admitted that both her marriage and her affair had been unhappy. She had supported Michael almost entirely and one of the chief problems between them was his gambling and a woman friend who had encouraged him in it. About the night of Michael's death she told the same consistent story. She had no idea whose finger was on the trigger when the gun went off. She insisted that she had never had any motive for shooting Michael and only shortly before his death had made a will leaving everything to him.

After the closing speeches, the judge reminded the jury that they could find the defendant guilty of murder, or manslaughter, or not guilty of any offence at all. They found Elvira not guilty of murder and not guilty of manslaughter and crowds outside the Old Bailey cheered her as she left.

Shortly afterwards she wrote her story in a Sunday newspaper. It began 'I write in tears' and continued: 'People think of me as an exotic woman who was on trial for her life. They forget that my greater tragedy is with me yet. The man I loved more than anything else in the world is dead and now that I have come back to the freedom which I once shared with him, I am reminded in a thousand different ways of all that he meant to me.'

In spite of her 'greater tragedy', Elvira's character had not changed. Shortly after the trial Sir Patrick Hastings took his family on holiday to France. As he drove up a steep hill on the Boulogne to Paris road he narrowly escaped death when a car came speeding round the corner on the wrong side of the road. To his astonishment, he saw that the driver was Elvira Barney.

She went to France and changed her name, but not her lifestyle: it was still a long round of parties, bars and fashionable restaurants, as well as new lovers. Four years after the trial, she was found dead – and alone – in a hotel bedroom in Paris. She was 31 years old.

Marguerite Fahmy

THERE WAS never any doubt that Marguerite Fahmy shot her Egyptian playboy husband Prince Ali Kemal Fahmy Bey in their luxury suite at the Savoy Hotel, London, but the defence centred on the motives and intentions behind the shooting. Marguerite was represented by one of England's most famous legal brains, Sir Edward Marshall Hall, who won the sympathy of the jury by painting a picture of his client as an unfortunate Western woman who had made the mistake of marrying an Oriental whose veneer of civilization was thin and who had abused and degraded her.

The beautiful Marguerite and the exotic Ali made splendid head-lines and the trial, exposing high-society scandal and the bedroom secrets of the wealthy, was one of the most celebrated of the 1920s. The shooting happened at 2.30 am on 10 July 1923, in the middle of a dramatic storm, with thunder crashing and lightning zigzagging the sky. Night porter John Beattie was taking luggage to a room on the fourth floor when he heard the unmistakable sound of three gun-shots. Beattie ran back down the corridor and as he rounded the corner he saw Marguerite throw down a pistol. Ali was lying in the corridor outside his suite, bleeding profusely from a head wound. Marguerite's white evening dress was spattered with his blood. 'What have I done? I've shot him,' the hysterical Marguerite exclaimed over and over again and when the duty manager arrived she clung to him, crying, 'I have been married six months and I have suffered terribly.'

Ali had been captivated by the sophisticated French divorcée 10 years his senior when he first saw her in Cairo, and he had offered to put on a 'fête' on his yacht in her honour. Marguerite was travelling with another man at the time and had turned him down. This only

Marguerite Fahmy

sharpened the interest of the handsome young millionaire who was accustomed to getting anything he wanted and when they met again in Paris the following year he set out to woo her with diamonds, emeralds and expensive cars. When he had to return to Egypt he showered her with effusive letters, calling her 'torch of my life' and referring to her 'bewitching charm' and 'exquisite beauty'. Eventually Marguerite could resist no longer; she joined him in Egypt, first as his mistress but soon accepting his proposal of marriage. As a condition of the marriage settlement Marguerite agreed to convert to the Islamic faith – Ali would lose his inheritance from his mother if he married outside the faith – but she would not be obliged to wear Muslim dress and she would keep the right to divorce her husband. It was a precursor of things to come that, once the ceremony was under way, Marguerite found that Ali had had the divorce condition left out of the agreement.

The couple set off on what should have been an idyllic honeymoon, sailing up the Nile to Luxor on board Ali's luxurious yacht, with its crew of 25. However, the problems began almost immediately. According to Marguerite, her husband was not interested in normal sex and was always pressuring her into acts of sodomy. They quarrelled constantly and often came to blows. Ali wrote gleefully to her sister saying that he was 'engaged in training her' and that with women 'one must act with energy and be severe'. After one argument, when Ali demanded the return of jewellery he had given her and swore on the Koran that he would kill her, she sent a letter to her Paris lawyer, to be opened in the event of her death, stating that she formally accused 'in the case of my death by violence Ali Fahmy Bey of having contributed to my disappearance'. When they arrived in Luxor, Ali locked her in her cabin and instructed the servants to make sure that she did not leave the yacht.

When Ali took a post at the Egyptian embassy in Paris his wife had a little more freedom but the marital rows were now so frequent that hotel guests and theatre patrons were treated to the sight of the ostentatiously wealthy couple screaming insults at one another, with complete disregard for everyone around them. Once when Marguerite had spent an afternoon at the cinema with a friend and arrived home after Ali, he punched her hard enough to dislocate her jaw. He accused her of seeing other men, she accused him of homosexual liaisons.

In July 1923 the couple went to London for a holiday, booking into a spacious and splendid suite at the Savoy Hotel. One of the first things that Marguerite did was consult the hotel doctor, for she had developed painful haemorrhoids as a result, she claimed, of Ali's unnatural lovemaking. After a week of treatment brought her no relief, the doctor suggested an operation. This caused another rift between the warring couple: Marguerite wanted to return to Paris for the operation, while Ali wanted her to have it in London.

That night they went to the theatre, to a successful production of *The Merry Widow*. The light-hearted operetta did little to improve the atmosphere between them and afterwards the argument raged on over supper in the Savoy Grill. Twice Marguerite refused to dance with her husband, though she did dance with his secretary, and once she shouted that she was going to smash a bottle over his head. When the band leader asked if there was a particular piece of music she would like to hear, she told him she was not in the mood because 'my husband has threatened to kill me tonight'. The band leader, his respectful manner unruffled, said that he hoped to see her again tomorrow.

It was after they had retired for the night that John Beattie was wheeling his trolley past the suite. Suddenly the door burst open and Ali ran out in his night clothes, closely followed by Marguerite. 'Look at my face. Look what she has done,' he told Beattie, who could see a red mark on his cheek. Marguerite had said something in rapid French, pointing to her face, but he could see no marks. Beattie asked them to go back inside and close the door and as he walked away he heard Ali whistling to Marguerite's little dog, which had followed them into the corridor. Seconds later, he heard the shots.

In the witness box at the Old Bailey, Marguerite described the misery of her marriage and her fear of her husband. She explained that Ali had given her the pistol and she had never fired it before the day of her husband's death. In the afternoon, when Ali had become particularly violent and threatened to kill her, she had fired it out of the window to scare him off. Knowing nothing about firearms, she had assumed that, once fired, the gun was no longer dangerous.

On the fatal night, Ali had told her that he would only provide her travel expenses to France if she earned the money. He then began to rip off her clothes. The fight had erupted into the corridor but when Ali had hustled her back into the suite he had advanced on her, saying, 'I will revenge myself.' She had picked up the gun, which was lying where she had left it earlier, but her only thought was to get away from her husband. She had managed to escape into the corridor but he pursued her and seized her by the neck, trying to choke her. She pushed him away but he crouched menacingly in front of her, saying, 'I will kill you.' Hardly knowing what she was doing she pointed the gun, trying to frighten him. She was not even aware that she had pressed the trigger until she heard the gun go off and then she had no idea how many times it fired. Then, when she saw him lying on the ground, she knelt beside him, saying, 'My dear, it is nothing, speak to me.'

The prosecutor, Percival Clarke, asked why she did not leave her objectionable husband once they arrived in Paris where, after all, she had her own flat and influential friends. He would have sent someone to fetch her back from her flat immediately, she explained, and as for her friends 'I did not want my friends to know all about my sorrow'. When he suggested that she must have hated her husband bitterly, she replied: 'I did not hate him, I only hated what he wanted me to do.'

Marshall Hall, in his summing up, relied heavily on raising the jury's repugnance towards the 'treacherous Egyptian beast'. 'Madame Fahmy', he said, 'made one great mistake – possibly the greatest mistake any woman of the West can make. She married an

Oriental . . . The curse of this case . . . is the Eastern feeling of possession of the woman, the Turk in his harem, this man who was
entitled to have four wives if he liked for chattels, which to we Western people, with our ideas of women, is almost unintelligible, something we cannot deal with.' He finished his address with an
impassioned plea: 'Members of the jury, I want you to open the gates
where this Western woman can go out, not into the dark night of the
desert but . . . back into the light of God's great Western sun.'

In the end it was Ali and his 'Oriental ways' that were tried and
found guilty, while Marguerite was declared not guilty of murder
and not guilty of manslaughter. It may be that if evidence about
Marguerite's past character had been introduced in court, instead of
being ruled inadmissible by the judge, the trial might have ended
differently. As the prosecutor had suggested, she was a 'woman of the
world'. Though she had been born to a poor working-class family, had
an illegitimate child at the age of 15 and proceeded to earn her living
from prostitution, she later underwent a metamorphosis at the hands
of a high-class brothel-keeper. Now well-groomed, well-spoken and
fashionably dressed, she was able to attract wealthy admirers. She
married a younger man, mainly to legitimize her daughter, but was
soon divorced and became the mistress of one rich man only to move
on to an even richer one. If these facts had been revealed to the jury,
they might have been less ready to believe in the 'poor, quaking
creature' of Marshall Hall's description and might have formed the
view that she had married Ali for his money and then, not finding
marriage to her liking, had calculated that she would do far better
financially as a widow than as a wife who had left her husband.

Hannah Kinney

HANNAH KINNEY, who was acquitted on the charge of poisoning her husband in December 1840, may have been not guilty of murder – or she may have escaped execution because she was good at putting up a convincing front, so that a number of witnesses were willing to testify that the marriage was happy and Hannah was never seen to scowl.

When Hannah married George in 1836 in Boston, Massachusetts, she already had an interesting past. She was married for the first time at 17 but her husband walked out on her after his business failed, claiming that she had taken lovers. While she was waiting for her divorce to come through she lived in the same Boston boarding house as George Kinney and the two became good friends. At the same time she met up with her cousin, Enoch Freeman, a Baptist minister in Lowell, Massachusetts and married him in 1835. A year later he died, suddenly and unexpectedly. There were unkind rumours in the parish at the time, especially as Hannah had never been liked; she did not, according to many members of the congregation, conduct herself in a manner suitable for a minister's wife. Hannah hastily moved back to Boston and married George Kinney.

She seemed to be dogged by misfortunes, for George's hosiery business collapsed soon after their marriage and she was forced to support the family by running a millinery shop and taking lodgers. George turned moody and began drinking too much. When this led to an argument he would leave home for several days at a time. He finally admitted that he had run up huge debts through gambling and was suffering from a venereal disease.

In August 1840 George took to his bed. Several different doctors were called in, prescribing a range of medicines containing morphine, laudanum and opium. He was also taking a quack remedy for syphilis, some home-made pills of unknown content. On 9 August, shortly after drinking a cup of herb tea, George died. Later a friend who had tasted the tea to check that it was not too hot testified that he was sick afterwards.

Arsenic was found in the body and Hannah was put on trial for murder, though no evidence was brought to show that she had ever bought arsenic. According to the defence, she had nothing to do with administering the poison. Instead, George could have taken the arsenic himself, either intending suicide as a way of escaping from his heavy debts and unfortunate lifestyle, or as a medicine. Men of the time frequently took arsenic as a cure for syphilis and he might have overdosed himself, or died from the effect of arsenic taken as medication and combined with the barrage of doctor-prescribed medicines.

A number of friends and neighbours gave evidence that George Kinney never voiced any criticism of his wife and as he lay dying he said what a good woman she had been, putting up with his difficult ways and supporting the family. To some of them, Hannah had confided that George had died in just the same way as her second husband Enoch and the prosecution saw this as incriminating, but Hannah's lawyers pointed out that it was unlikely that a murderess would make a comparison of her two victims so publicly.

The defence, claiming a 'complete absence of motive', pointed out that 'if this woman is a murderer she is a moral monster, such as the world never saw'. The jury took less than five minutes to decide that she was no such thing.

Elizabeth Fenning

IN 1815, a 21-year-old servant, Elizabeth Fenning, was tried and convicted of 'administering arsenic to Orlebar Turner, Robert Gregson Turner and Charlotte Turner, with intent the said persons to kill and murder'. On 15 July she was hanged at Tyburn in London, still protesting her innocence.

Elizabeth worked as a cook in the Turner household, which consisted of Orlebar Turner, who ran a stationery business, his son and daughter-in-law, two apprentices and two servants. Everyone seems to have found Elizabeth pleasant and hard-working, though she had been in trouble when her mistress saw her going into the bedroom of one of the apprentices late at night. It was Elizabeth, not the young man, who was threatened with dismissal and at her trial it was suggested that her resentment turned to hatred of the family.

The murder method was said to be a dish of dumplings made by Elizabeth on 21 March. They had looked rather unappetising, heavy and dark instead of white and fluffy, but the family tucked into them just the same, along with beef and potatoes. After only a few minutes, all three of them were taken ill with intense stomach pains and vomiting.

The doctor, John Marshall, was called in and found the three members of the family, as well as Elizabeth Fenning herself, all suffering from a serious gastric upset. When he looked round the kitchen, he was shown the pan in which the dumplings had been cooked and found traces of a white powder that later proved to be arsenic. Orlebar Turner remembered that there had been a clearly-labelled packet of arsenic in his desk drawer in early March – he usually kept a small supply to deal with vermin – but it had gone missing since then.

Elizabeth Fenning in Newgate Prison, awaiting execution

When Elizabeth was questioned she said that she knew nothing about the packet of arsenic and that she had made the dumplings the way she always did. If anything was wrong with the food it must be that the milk she had used to make the sauce was tainted. However, testimony from Robert Turner showed that he had eaten only the dumplings, without any sauce, and he had been just as ill as the others.

One of the apprentices, Robert Gadsdon, gave evidence that was damning to Elizabeth. He said that he had seen the prepared dumplings in the kitchen before dinner but Elizabeth had told him not to eat any, as they would do him no good. He had eaten a portion just the same and had been very sick. He added that the defendant usually made excellent dumplings; the previous batch, eaten by Elizabeth, the maid and himself had been quite different in taste and texture.

After the cook's conviction Orlebar Turner, who was not convinced of her guilt, considered petitioning for her reprieve but was warned by the judge that Robert Turner might then fall under suspicion. Two reliable witnesses had made statements saying that Robert had, for some time, been showing signs of mental disturbance and that shortly before the dumpling incident he had asked them to lock him away. 'If I am at liberty, I shall do some mischief; I shall destroy myself and my wife,' he told them. Perhaps, after all, that is exactly what he tried to do.

Jessie M'Lachlan

AT WEEKENDS, when accountant John Fleming left Glasgow, Scotland, for the country, his father James – a bad-tempered and hard-drinking old man – stayed behind. His only company at these times was his bottle and the 25-year-old maid, Jessie M 'Pherson, but this suited the old man well enough as he chose to spend most of his time in the servants' quarters and had an eye for a pretty maid.

When John Fleming arrived home on Monday 7 July 1862, his father told him that he had not seen Jess since Friday and that the door to her room was locked. When it was eventually opened, Jess's partly clothed body was found lying on the blood-soaked bed. She had been hacked to death with a cleaver. Though there were no signs of a break-in, the maid's best clothes and some of the family silver were missing. There were bloodstains on the kitchen floor, though efforts had been made to wash them away, showing that the body had been dragged from there into the bedroom.

James Fleming said that he had heard nothing untoward throughout the weekend. He had not reported the girl's disappearance because he assumed she had gone off with her boyfriend, though it was shown that the boyfriend had called twice during the weekend, expecting to find her at home. When spots of blood were found on two of his shirts, he was arrested.

Then a second suspect appeared, in the shape of 28-year-old Jessie M'Lachlan, a close friend of the dead girl. She was identified as having pawned some of the missing silver, and though she claimed that this was at James Fleming's request, he denied it. When it was found that bloody footprints in the bedroom matched hers, she was arrested. James Fleming was released, in spite of the many inconsistencies in his story. In the days when class distinctions were still treated with reverence, a working-class maid was a much more acceptable defendant on a murder charge than a member of a respected professional family.

From the beginning it was obvious that Jessie was not telling the whole truth and the circumstantial evidence weighed heavily against her, though not nearly as heavily as the judge's summing up, which was strongly biased against her and unwilling to concede a point in her favour. It was only after the guilty verdict had been announced that Jessie made a statement which, she said, was a true account of the crime.

She stated that she had arrived to visit her friend on Friday evening only to find her bleeding from a serious wound across her forehead. Jess told her that the old man had been trying to force his attentions on her for some time and that, during the evening, they had had a row and he had attacked her. The girl's condition had deteriorated overnight and, realizing she was dying, Jessie had been preparing to go for the doctor when James Fleming, alone with her friend in the kitchen, had set about her with the meat cleaver. He said that he had done it because, if a doctor had been called, he would have been blamed for her death. He would make it look like a burglary so that no one would suspect the truth, but if Jessie told anyone what she knew, he would accuse her of committing the crime.

The judge dismissed it as 'a tissue of wicked falsehoods' and sentenced her to death, but afterwards there was such an outcry that this was commuted to life imprisonment. There was still a strong feeling that she had not been given a fair trial but, all the same, Jessie spent 15 years in gaol – a harsh sentence if all she had done was attempt to conceal a murder committed by another.

Candace Mossler

IN THE early hours of the morning on 30 June 1964, several tenants in a block of luxury apartments at Key Biscayne, Florida, were disturbed by a dog barking. It was Rocky, the boxer belonging to multi-millionaire Jacques Mossler, whose barking had caused complaints before. From inside the Mossler apartment they heard a scuffle and thuds, then they heard a man's footsteps running down the corridor. One tenant, just returning home, saw a tall man with long dark hair hurrying from the building.

The evidence of the tenants was to pinpoint the time of Jacques Mossler's murder. He was found in the living room with 33 stab wounds in the upper part of his body. He had also suffered several blows to the head from a blunt instrument, possibly a heavy glass swan that was found lying nearby.

Jacques had been living in Florida for about nine months, while his wife and family remained in their 28-roomed mansion in Houston, Texas. Sixteen years earlier he had married a glamorous divorcée 24 years his junior. Candace had two children, Jacques had four and they adopted four more. Candace was later to claim that Jacques went in for a wide range of sexual perversions but the marriage only seemed to run into trouble when her nephew, Melvyn Powers, came to stay in 1961. After 18 months he was still there and when Candace was unwilling to fix a date for his departure, Jacques had him thrown out.

When Candace and her nephew were tried for her husband's murder, the prosecution alleged that Candace had started a passionate affair with her nephew while under her husband's roof and continued it after he left. While Jacques was away in Europe in the autumn of 1963, it was said, the two were constantly seen together, with Melvyn introducing Candace as his fiancée and telling friends that she was about to get a divorce.

A few weeks before Jacques' death, Candace had taken four of the children to stay with him in Florida. At the end of June she was suffering from migraines and several times she drove to Miami to obtain medication from the emergency department of Jackson Memorial Hospital. It was here that she went in the early morning of 30 June, strangely enough taking the children with her and spending time in a hotel lounge before she went to the hospital. According to the prosecution, all this was in order to give herself an alibi while her lover went to the apartment and killed Jacques.

Detectives noticed that Candace showed no distress over the horrific death of her husband. Though there was no sign that the contents of the apartment had been disturbed she told the police that some of her jewellery had been stolen, along with money from her husband's wallet. When asked who might have killed her husband, she said that he had made a number of enemies in his business dealings and even named some of them. In addition, she mentioned that she suspected Jacques of having homosexual lovers.

At the trial, there was a good deal of talk about the relationship between Candace and her nephew and several men testified that either Candace or Melvyn had offered them money to murder Jacques Mossler. There was evidence that Melvyn had arrived in Miami on the afternoon of 29 June; a friend testified that he had left Houston wearing dark clothes and when he returned the next day he had been wearing light clothes, with trousers that seemed to be made for a much shorter man. A car borrowed by Candace from one of her husband's companies, and which fitted the description of the car driven away from the apartment block by a dark young man on the morning of the murder, was found at Miami's airport, covered with Melvyn's fingerprints, with a car-park entrance ticket stamped at 5.19 on the morning of 30 June. In addition, Melvyn's palm print was found on the kitchen counter, which had been thoroughly cleaned by a servant on the afternoon before the murder.

The lawyers made a meal of the proceedings, dragging them on for 14 weeks and using every trick in the book to win a point. The defence lawyers produced witnesses to discredit prosecution witnesses, did their best to produce confusion over every piece of evidence and exploited the idea of Jacques Mossler's homosexuality (for which there was never any proof), suggesting that he might have been killed in a homosexual quarrel, or murdered by the jealous lover of one of his boyfriends.

It took the all-male jury two and a half days to debate the evidence before bringing in a verdict of not guilty. Candace kissed them all in turn and drove away with Melvyn in an open car, waving like royalty. The two remained together for a time, though in 1971 Candace married a Texan, only to divorce three years later. She died in a Miami hotel room in 1975 and when the contents of her house in Houston were auctioned, hundreds of people came to purchase a souvenir of the woman at the centre of what was known – in spite of the acquittal – as the 'Candy Murder Case'.

Chapter Five

PARTNERS IN CRIME

Introduction

CONSPIRATORS come in all types: two clever schoolgirls, a housewife and her hit man, the leaders of a weird religious cult, a pair of small-town thieves looking for excitement. When more than one person is involved, murder is seldom spur-of-the-moment, something that happens in a flash of passion. Instead, the plot is laid, the victim is ambushed and the murderers are bound together in a deadly secret.

There is a chilling premeditation about their crimes and it is often impossible to identify the prime mover – which of the partners in crime hatched the idea and had the vicious drive to carry it through, convincing a lover or fellow criminal that murder was the best way to accomplish their common aims. Sometimes it is a woman's infatuation for an evil man that draws her into a cycle of violence and murder but just as often, in the cases that follow, the woman is the stronger partner, manipulating her man with sly skill and working with venomous cunning.

Once in the dock, the ties that bind the two together often break and the partners turn on one another, each protesting that it was the accomplice who masterminded the plan or did the deed. But in law, the partner who stands by is just as guilty as a co-conspirator who pulls the trigger or wields the brick.

Pauline Parker and Juliet Hulme

THE NEW ZEALAND teenagers Pauline Parker and Juliet Hulme lived in a world of their own. They were completely wrapped up in one another, spending long hours writing highly-coloured 'novels' and making plans for their joint future, and they could not bear to be separated. Eventually their parents began to realize that their friendship was so passionate as to be unhealthy.

Pauline was the daughter of Honora Mary Parker and Herbert Rieper, a wholesale fish merchant. The couple had never married but had lived together for 23 years and had three living children, 18-year-old Wendy, 16-year-old Pauline and a Down's syndrome child who lived in an institution. Juliet was a highly intelligent 15-year-old, the daughter of an English research scientist who had brought his family to New Zealand in 1948 because Juliet suffered from tuberculosis and the climate would be beneficial for her.

Now Mrs Hulme was having an extra-marital affair and Mr Hulme was planning to return to England to take up a well-paid job in atomic research. He intended to take his 10-year-old son Jonathan with him, leaving Juliet with her mother, but both parents were so worried about the over-close friendship between the two girls that they decided this would be a good opportunity to separate them for a while. Mr Hulme would take Juliet and Jonathan for a holiday in South Africa, where he was planning to spend some time, then, when he travelled to England with Jonathan, Juliet would return to her mother. The girls were horrified. No one was going to split them up, it was unthinkable. If Juliet was going to South Africa, then Pauline must go too. Both sets of parents were adamant that this was out of the question.

On the afternoon of 22 June 1954, the two distraught teenagers ran

Juliet Hulme (left) and Pauline Parker, after being remanded in Christchurch, New Zealand

up to a refreshment kiosk in a park on the outskirts of Christchurch. They were spattered with blood and sobbing about an accident. One of them said that her mother had tripped on a board and banged her head as she fell and rolled over. 'I'll never forget her head banging,' exclaimed the other girl. Mr Kenneth Ritchie went off along the path, in the direction the girls had indicated, where he found the badly battered body of Mrs Parker. Even at a glance, it was obvious that this was no accident; later, 45 separate head injuries were identified. Mrs Ritchie, left to mind the kiosk, had shown the girls where they could wash and heard them laughing as the water flowed.

The girls were taken into custody immediately and they soon admitted to the killing. They had planned ahead, taking along a brick in a stocking as a weapon. As they walked through the park, Pauline pointed out a pretty stone to her mother and then, as Mrs Parker bent to look, she wielded the brick inside its stocking, knocking her mother to the ground, then hitting her again, passing the improvised weapon to Juliet so that she could take a turn. Juliet maintained that at first she had thought they might use the brick to frighten Mrs Parker into allowing Pauline to accompany her to South Africa, but that after the first blow, she said, 'I knew it would be necessary to kill her. I was terrified, hysterical.' Pauline admitted that she had planned the murder days ahead. She could not say how many times she had hit her: 'A great many, I imagine,' she said coolly.

At the trial, Pauline's diary was the main exhibit for the prosecution. The entries were explicit and chilling. 'Anger against Mother is boiling inside me as she is the main obstacle in my path,' she had written, and 'Why could not Mother die? Dozens, thousands of people are dying every day. Why not Mother, and Father too?' On 21 June she wrote: 'We decided to use a brick in a stocking rather than a sandbag . . . Feel quite keyed up.' On 22 June the entry read: 'The Day of the Happy Event.'

The defence tried to show that the girls were insane and called two doctors, one of them the Parker family physician, who believed that they were both paranoid and suffered from delusions; by their lights they believed that what they had done was right. Two experts on mental illness, however, both gave the opinion they were both completely sane and of above-average intelligence. They had known exactly what they were doing, they had known that it was wrong and what the possible consequences might be. One of the prosecution doctors was convinced that they had a lesbian relationship.

All through the trial the girls were calm; they smiled often and sometimes exchanged a few words. Only once did either of them show emotion: when the revelations from Pauline's diary seemed to indicate that she had had sex with a boyfriend, Juliet's face twisted in fury. When they were found guilty and sentenced to be detained during Her Majesty's pleasure they seemed unconcerned. Pauline was sent to a prison near Wellington and Juliet to Auckland, so the two friends were, at last, separated after all.

Ruth Snyder and Judd Gray

ONE SUNDAY morning in March 1927, seven-year-old Lorraine Snyder awoke in her home on Long Island, USA, to hear a strange tapping in the corridor outside her bedroom – the only sound in an otherwise silent house. She found her mother lying bound and gagged, able only to tap on the floor with the heel of her shoe. As Lorraine removed the cheesecloth gag from her mother's mouth, Ruth Snyder told her to get help from their neighbour, Louis Mulhauser. When he arrived and freed her from her bonds, she babbled out a story about being attacked by an intruder and asked anxiously what had happened to her husband. Mr Mulhauser found Albert's dead body lying across the bed; he had two large wounds in his head and there were also strands of picture wire round his neck.

When the police arrived, Ruth told in more detail her story of being attacked by a big, dark-skinned man with a thick moustache, who had dragged her from her room and trussed her up. After that she must have fainted, for she knew no more until shortly before Lorraine found her. The furnishings in the downstairs rooms were in disarray, with chairs overturned, cushions scattered and curtains torn down. To the practised eye, it looked like an amateur's attempt at re-creating the scene of a burglary, rather than a burglary itself. Ruth at first claimed that her jewellery was missing but, when it was found stuffed under her mattress, she suddenly remembered that she had put it there for safe keeping.

From the beginning, the police disbelieved the burglary story. At the postmortem it was shown that though Alfred had been beaten over the head with a blunt instrument, the blows were not forceful enough to kill him and he had been chloroformed and then strangled.

It seemed hardly likely that a murderous robber would have spent so much time on one of his victims, while leaving Ruth alive to identify him. Then there was the matter of Albert Snyder's insurance policies: quite recently Ruth had raised her husband's insurance from a modest amount to $45,000 and a double indemnity clause meant that if he died by violence the payout would double. When enquiries revealed a close relationship between Ruth and a corset salesman, Judd Gray, they were both taken in for questioning about Albert's murder and the true story was eventually revealed.

Ruth was bored and unhappy in her marriage to a quiet, reliable man 13 years her senior when she met 32-year-old Judd in June 1925. After their first meeting he took her back to his office and they made love, beginning an affair that would lead to murder and execution. Judd called Ruth 'Momsie', she called him 'Lover Boy' and they met frequently, renting hotel bedrooms for a few hours and becoming more and more infatuated with one another. At the same time, Albert seemed to become very 'accident-prone'. He narrowly escaped death when repairing his car with the engine running; after Ruth had given him a glass of whisky he fell asleep and only woke in time to realize that the garage doors were shut and he was inhaling poisonous fumes. Another time he was almost gassed as he was taking an afternoon nap, as Ruth had turned on a gas tap 'by mistake'.

There was no mistake and no last-minute reprieve for Albert Snyder in the early-morning hours of 20 March. When the Snyders returned late from a bridge party, Judd was already hiding in the house. Ruth had seen to it that Albert drank more than usual and once he was fast asleep she tiptoed out of the bedroom and joined her lover. Earlier she had brought a sash weight, the chosen murder weapon, up from the basement and equipped herself with picture wire, chloroform and cotton wool, just in case. Judd crept into the bedroom and brought the weight down on Albert's head but his victim awoke and began to struggle, so that the weight fell to the floor. Albert cried out to his wife to help him but her only answer was to pick up the sash weight and

Ruth Snyder listens to evidence in court

bring it down on his head with all her strength. Still Albert did not die, so she stuffed chloroform-soaked cotton into his mouth and one of them – later each was to blame the other – finished him off with the piano wire. Afterwards the two murderers burned Ruth's nightdress and Judd's shirt – Ruth fetched him a fresh one from her husband's supply, walking past the body to do so – and then they ransacked the rooms to make it look like a burglary.

When arrested, Ruth protested that, though she and Judd had planned the murder together, she had taken no part in the actual killing and in fact had tried to stop him at the last moment. Judd admitted his part in the murder but said that it was all Ruth's fault: 'She had this power over me. She told me what to do and I did it.'

Many men must have indulged fantasies about this masterful woman, for while in the death cell Ruth received over 160 proposals of marriage. 'Momsie' and 'Lover Boy' both went to the electric chair in Sing Sing, dying within a few minutes of one another. A newspaper reporter secreted a camera in his clothes and photographed Ruth's death for posterity.

Bonnie Parker and
Clyde Barrow

HOLLYWOOD has immortalized the legend of Bonnie and Clyde, making them into attractive youngsters, rather naive and confused, trying to escape from the hopelessness of the Depression years. In fact they were tough, vicious killers. They robbed and shot their way across five states of the USA, firing on anyone who got in their way. Genuine gangsters viewed them as 'kill-crazy punks' who gave gangsterism a bad name.

Clyde Barrow, one of eight children, was born on a Texas farm in 1909. He was frequently in trouble as a child and was only nine when he was sent to an approved school as an incorrigible thief and truant. He had a sadistic streak too and neighbours remembered that he took a delight in torturing farm animals. He was 21 when he met 19-year-old Bonnie, a small, fair-haired girl from a devout Baptist family, at the house of a friend. Bonnie took him home to meet her mother who was delighted to see her taking an interest in a young man. Though Bonnie had married at 16, her husband had soon deserted her and had since been gaoled for robbery.

Clyde spent the night on the couch of the Parker house and in the morning he was arrested for five car thefts and two burglaries. Bonnie screamed and cried, beat the wall with her hands and begged the police not to take him. When he was given a two-year gaol sentence, Bonnie smuggled in a gun so that he could make his escape. It was all in vain, for he was recaptured a few days later after an attempted burglary and sentenced to 14 years' imprisonment. This time, the only way he could get out early was by persuading another prisoner to cut off two of his toes with an axe. He was given parole and arrived back at Bonnie's house on crutches.

Once Clyde was able to walk properly he made a brief attempt at honest work, but he was unable to settle down and quite soon he and Bonnie took off together to pursue their criminal career. By this time Bonnie was completely under Clyde's influence, so she was willing to follow wherever he went. In no time she found herself in gaol after an unsuccessful robbery, so she was not present at the first murder committed by Clyde and his associates in April 1932, when they shot a Texas jeweller and made off with $40. After three months she was released without charge and became a useful member of the gang, which was soon getting plenty of publicity. The newspapers called Clyde the 'Texas rattlesnake' and Bonnie was described as his 'quick-shooting woman accomplice'. A raid on a filling station at Grand Prairie, Texas, gave them their biggest haul of $3000 and, with their pockets full of money, they went on a motoring jaunt around Missouri, Kansas and Michigan, staying at luxury hotels and eating in classy restaurants.

Once the cash was exhausted they went back to holding up stores and banks, always in a haphazard, spur-of-the-moment fashion, shooting at the slightest excuse, even when their haul was only likely to be a few dollars. In Sherman, Texas, Bonnie Parker offered the store-keeper a $5 bill for a loaf of bread and a tin of salmon, then produced a revolver and told him to put up his hands. When the store-keeper grabbed a meat cleaver and told her to get out she shot him three times in the stomach.

Bonnie was the getaway driver after the next murder: Clyde and a new member of the gang, 17-year-old W.D. Jones, were trying to steal a brand-new car when the owner rushed out of his house to try to stop them. Clyde shot him in the neck and the three robbers made their escape in the stolen black coupé they were using at the time. It was Christmas Day, 1932.

In March of the following year Bonnie and Clyde were hiding out in

Bonnie Parker playfully 'gets the drop' on Clyde Barrow in a snapshot taken by Clyde's brother Buck somewhere in rural Texas

a Missouri apartment, where they were joined by Clyde's brother Buck and sister-in-law Blanche. Neighbours who had seen guns taken into the house alerted the police and they decided on a raid. Clyde was standing by the garage when he saw one of the policemen jump from the car and he did not wait to ask questions; he blasted the officer with a shotgun. Bonnie, still in her nightdress, began firing a rifle from an upstairs window. In the chaos that followed Blanche ran screaming down the road, her pet dog in her arms. The robbers dived into their car and made off at top speed, amid a volley of police gunfire, rescuing Blanche two blocks away. Both Clyde and W.D. were slightly injured but the policemen fared worse: two were dead and another seriously wounded.

In the apartment the police found a stack of rifles and machine guns as well as rolls of film which, when developed, showed the outlaws in various jokey poses. One showed Bonnie threatening Clyde with a shotgun and in another Bonnie was standing with one foot on the car bumper, holding a revolver and smoking a large cigar. The photographs were published in newspapers up and down the country and Clyde became so angry when reports kept referring to her as his 'cigar-smoking moll' – for he insisted that she had only borrowed the cigar from Buck for the photo – that he threatened the editor of one newspaper with reprisals if this was mentioned again.

Now nowhere was safe for the fugitives and disaster overtook them when their car plunged into a gorge near Wellington, Texas, and caught fire. Clyde and W.D. were thrown clear but Bonnie was badly burned. For a time they hid out in a tourist camp in Arkansas while Bonnie received medical treatment, paid for by several robberies of grocery stores. In July they were at another tourist camp, in Missouri, when they were again surrounded by police and had to shoot their way out. Buck was shot in the head and Blanche was blinded by flying glass so the gang were forced to go to ground in a wood, where the police soon caught up with them. In the gun battle that followed Buck was shot in the hip, shoulder and back and the police found Blanche crouching over him sobbing, 'Don't die, Daddy, don't die.'

Buck died six days later and Blanche received a 10-year gaol sentence. Bonnie and Clyde had escaped once more but their time was running out. They spent the next three months desperately dodging the law but on 23 May 1934 their Ford V–8 sedan was ambushed by six officers. Over 160 shots were fired and the bodies of Bonnie and Clyde were so riddled with bullets that they danced like marionettes.

Even before the bodies could be removed crowds gathered, snipping scraps of bloodstained clothing or locks of hair as souvenirs. Eventually the outlaws' car was towed to the nearest town with the remains of Bonnie and Clyde still in it, and a procession of sightseers' cars following behind. Already their legend was well-established.

Bonnie had predicted their end in her poem 'The Story of Bonnie and Clyde', which she had sent to the *Dallas Evening Journal*. The last verse ran:

> *Some day they will go down together,*
> *And they will bury them side by side.*
> *To a few it means grief,*
> *To the law it's relief,*
> *But it's death to Bonnie and Clyde.*

Christine and Lea Papin

TWO MURDERS of such wanton brutality that they shocked the whole of France were committed for no better reason than an argument over a faulty iron. There had already been trouble over the iron in the Lancelin household in the quiet provincial town of Le Mans. One of the maids, Lea Papin, had dropped and damaged it and the money for its repair had been deducted from her wages. Then, on the morning of 2 February 1933, Lea and her sister Christine were preparing to do the ironing when the iron failed to work. They tried plugging it into one socket after another and turning it on and off, but only succeeded in fusing the lights. The maids, knowing that they would be in serious trouble when their mistress returned from shopping, waited fearfully in the room they shared.

Madame Lancelin and her daughter Geneviève were surprised to find the house in darkness and angry to discover that the lights were out of action. They knew exactly who to blame and went straight upstairs, calling for the Papin sisters. The four women met on the first-floor landing and Christine told the story of the iron. Madame Lancelin began shouting angrily, advancing on the two girls ready to mete out a few slaps. What happened next was almost beyond belief. Christine snatched up a pewter pot from a nearby table and felled Madame Lancelin with a blow. 'Tear her eyes out,' Christine shrieked to her sister and Lea leapt on Madame Lancelin, gouging the woman's eyes with her fingers. Geneviève stood shocked into immobility and before she could recover sufficiently to go to her mother's aid Christine knocked her to the ground, banging her head against the floor and scratching out her eyes with her fingernails.

That was only the beginning of the horror. As the two women, blinded and screaming in pain, lay helpless on the landing, Christine ran to the kitchen and, in the darkness, scrabbled about for a hammer and a knife. The two maids then battered and slashed at the screaming Lancelins, pausing several times to change the hammer and knife between them. When the screaming was over and the bodies lay still, the two maids washed the blood from their hands in the kitchen sink, bolted the back and front doors and went up to their room to strip off their blood-soaked clothes. There, sexually aroused by their sadistic violence, they made passionate love.

Monsieur Lancelin was expecting his wife and daughter to join him for dinner with friends and, when they did not arrive, he tried several times to phone his home. Anxious when neither his family nor the maids answered the phone, he went back to the house to find the door locked and the house in darkness except for a faint glow, like a candle, from the servants' room. He called the police, who forced an entry. In court, the police, inspector graphically described the dreadful scene that met their eyes. 'The corpses . . . were frightfully mutilated. Mademoiselle Lancelin's body was lying face down, head bare, coat pulled up and her knickers down, revealing deep wounds in the buttocks and multiple cuts in the calves. Madame Lancelin's body lay on its back. Her eyes had disappeared. She no longer seemed to have a mouth and most of her teeth had been knocked out.' The walls were covered in blood and the murder weapons lay on the floor, along with pieces of bone, teeth and an eye.

When the police went up to the attic they found the two sisters naked and hugging one another in one bed. They did not attempt to deny their guilt but related the story without emotion. They had not planned to kill their employers, they said; it had been a reaction to Madame Lancelin's aggressive behaviour and they had no regrets. 'If it was to be our skin or theirs,' said Christine, 'I would rather it was theirs.' Throughout the questioning they were co-operative and subdued, with just an occasional flash of something like pride at their murderous achievement. It was obvious to the interrogators that

28-year-old Christine was the dominant sister with Lea, six years younger, subservient in many ways.

While awaiting their trial, which did not take place until September, the sisters were imprisoned separately and for them, this seemed to be the most distressing part of the whole business. They had only been separated once before when their alcoholic father, their only remaining parent, deserted them. Christine was old enough to go into service but Lea went to an orphanage. As soon as she was old enough, she joined her sister and since then they had always taken positions together. They had no friends, either male or female, and spent all their spare time in their room, completely wrapped up in one another. Separation was torture for them and Christine was inconsolable, throwing herself on the floor of her cell and screaming for her sister. When the prison authorities allowed them to meet for a short time, Christine hurled herself on Lea, hugging and kissing her with such force that they had to be torn apart.

When the trial opened on 30 September admission to the courtroom was by ticket only and every seat was taken. Huge crowds gathered outside, chanting 'death to the Papins', and the mood was so angry that a strong cordon of police surrounded the Palais de Justice throughout the proceedings. The prosecution tried hard to elicit the real reasons behind the frenzied attack but they could not persuade the sisters to admit to any hatred or resentment felt towards their employers. They had been fairly paid and fairly treated; there was nothing about their treatment in the Lancelin household to lead to smouldering anger. They had had several positions before and their references were always satisfactory. None of their employers had found them difficult, bad-tempered or inclined to violent behaviour. The defence called a psychiatrist to give evidence that the sisters were unbalanced and not responsible for their actions but the weight of medical evidence was on the other side. Prosecution doctors argued that both women were completely normal, with no sign of mental disturbance.

The jury had no difficulty in finding both sisters guilty of the double murder but decided that Lea Papin had acted under her sister's influence. When Christine Papin heard herself sentenced to die on the guillotine her knees gave way and she had to be helped to her feet. Lea only smiled slightly as she heard herself sentenced to 10 years' penal servitude. Later Christine's sentence was commuted to penal servitude for life, the usual outcome for a woman convicted of murder, but she only lived for four years. The mental instability which had in all probability undermined her personality for years quickly asserted itself and she died insane. Lea, on the other hand, served her sentence quietly and caused her gaolers no problems. Freed from her sister's domination she became an ordinary, unremarkable girl once more. After six years she was released and was never heard of again.

Elizabeth Duncan,
Gus Baldonado and Luis Moya

ELIZABETH DUNCAN looked much like any other American matron nearing 60 – bespectacled, hair carefully permed, conservatively dressed and totally harmless. The reality was quite different, for Elizabeth Duncan was a very dangerous woman, without conscience and with an all-consuming hatred of her new daughter-in-law. Elizabeth was much married, so much so that she lost count of the number of husbands – they were anywhere between 15 and 20, it appears, many of the 'marriages' bigamous. However, the abiding love of her life was her son Frank. She was a devoted, possessive, jealous mother; even when Frank established himself as a successful lawyer she followed him round like a clinging wife. She was in court for every case, standing up and applauding when the case went Frank's way.

Marriage did not feature in Elizabeth's plans for her beloved son but, ironically, it was her actions that brought him and his future wife together. When, at the age of 29, Frank finally decided that it was time to have his own apartment and live his own life there was a furious row and Elizabeth promptly responded with an act of emotional blackmail: she took a handful of sleeping pills. When Frank, suitably contrite, came to visit her in hospital, he met a pretty young nurse, Olga Kupczyk, and the scene was set for a tragic drama. Frank and Olga began dating secretly and in due course Olga became pregnant. When Frank broached the subject of marriage with his mother she flew into such a rage, issuing all sorts of wild threats, that Frank thought it prudent to pretend that he had dropped the idea. Thinking that the main danger was another suicide attempt, he married Olga secretly but continued to return each night to the apartment he shared with his mother.

Elizabeth Duncan was quick to discover Frank's secret and she immediately started hatching schemes to dispose of her unwanted daughter-in-law. She talked them over with her elderly friend Emma Short who might, she thought, take a major role in her plan. Emma could invite Olga to tea to discuss her problems with her mother-in-law, then Elizabeth could leap out of hiding and strangle the unsuspecting Olga. Then she would wait until late at night, drag the body out to her car and throw it into the sea. Amazingly, Emma Short's only objection to the plan was that she disliked the idea of sharing her apartment with a dead body for such a long time. Later she was to say that she did not 'approve' of Elizabeth's murder plans, yet when her friend set off to town with the intention of hiring a hit man to do the job for her, Emma went along for moral support.

Elizabeth took her custom to a run-down café owned by a Mexican family in the least salubrious area of Santa Barbara, California. She knew that several members of the family were on the wrong side of the law: she had seen them in court as Frank defended them. On her second visit she met two young men, Gus Baldonado and Luis Moya, who were willing to take on the job for $6000. Elizabeth, not in the least discouraged by the fact that she did not have anything approaching $6000, talked them into taking a small cash advance and promised the rest when they had fulfilled the contract.

One dark November night in 1958 Olga, who was preparing for bed, responded to a knock on the door. There stood Moya, who told her that her husband was outside in the car, the worse for drink. Trustingly, Olga went with him but as she leaned towards the recumbent form in the back of the car, Moya beat her over the head with his gun and Baldonado pulled her inside. The murder was botched from the start for Olga soon came round and, as a healthy young nurse, she was able to fight hard. By the time she finally sank into insensibility, both young men were covered in blood. They began to panic and, anxious to get rid of the body, they stopped at the first likely spot, a deep dip at the side of the road. Olga was still alive and they tried to finish her off with a bullet, but once again their plan went wrong and the gun failed to fire, so instead they battered her to death with a rock.

At first the police were baffled by Olga's sudden disappearance but when they heard about Elizabeth Duncan's resentment of her daughter-in-law – she had been heard shrieking threats at the young woman – they began asking questions. The answers they received came from Emma Short, who had been present in the café when the murder contract was arranged. Elizabeth was questioned and quickly lied herself into the courtroom. She was found guilty, along with her two hit men, but the executions did not take place until 1962. Frank Duncan, the emotional ties to his mother still strong, fought tirelessly for a reprieve until the very moment she stepped into the gas chamber.

Elizabeth Duncan on the witness stand

Sheila Garvie and Brian Tevendale

SHEILA and Max Garvie had been married for nine years. They lived at West Cairnbeg farm in east Scotland with their son and two daughters; they were well-off, Max was a leading light of the local flying club and of the local branch of the Scottish National Party, and they seemed happy enough. Behind the contented facade, though, the marriage was stale and Max was the first to start looking for excitement. He became fascinated by pornography, began visiting nudist camps and making new perverse sexual demands on his wife which prompted her to confide in friends about his unwelcome behaviour.

In 1967 they met 22-year-old Brian Tevendale and his married sister Trudy Birse, and they began spending every weekend at the farm as an inseparable foursome. The group used every sexual permutation they could think of. Not only did Sheila and Brian make eager bedmates but Trudy found Max's sexual demands perfectly acceptable. Sometimes the couples would change partners in the middle of lovemaking or one of the men would take both women to bed at the same time. They even invited Trudy's husband, a policeman, to join them. Max, who was bisexual, found Brian just as attractive as Trudy.

Max was delighted with the arrangement but Sheila and Brian became so wrapped up in one another that they decided to go away together. Once Max discovered their plans he hired some 'heavies' to give Brian a beating, making it clear that he would not stand for his wife's desertion.

On the evening of 14 May 1968 Max Garvie left in his car for a political meeting at Stonehaven and disappeared. At first Sheila

Brian Tevendale (left) and Sheila Garvie (right) in a wedding picture where only the bride did not know of the murder

refused to admit that he was missing: she was expecting him back any day, she said. It was his sister who reported his disappearance to the police five days later. Sheila and Brian spent most of their time together, with Sheila looking far happier than any woman with a missing husband had a right to look, and gossip was rife.

Then Sheila's mother contacted the police and told them about a conversation in which her daughter had hinted that Brian Tevendale might have killed Max. The following day Max's body was found in an underground tunnel, shot through the neck, his head battered with a blunt instrument, possibly a gun butt. Sheila Garvie, Brian Tevendale and a young friend, Alan Peters, were all arrested and charged with murder. The trial began in November, when the revelations about the sexual goings-on at West Cairnbeg farm caused a wave of public revulsion. There was a strong feeling that those involved deserved to be convicted, even before detailed evidence about the murder was given.

Like so many partners in crime, Sheila and Brian tried to lay the full blame on one another. According to Brian, Sheila had shot her husband during a struggle: she had refused his demands for anal intercourse and he had pulled a gun and threatened to shoot her if she did not give in. She had lunged for the gun and in the tussle that followed, it went off. When he arrived at the farm, Max was already dead and all he had done was help her to get rid of the body.

According to Sheila, this account was complete fiction. She had had nothing to do with the shooting, which had happened while she was in bed, though she felt 'morally responsible' because of her relationship with Brian. Alan Peters backed up her story, saying that he and Brian had arrived at the farm together and that Sheila had not been present when her husband died.

Both Sheila Garvie and Brian Tevendale were convicted of murder and sentenced to life imprisonment but the jury brought in that peculiarly Scottish verdict of 'not proven' in the case of Alan Peters.

Gabrielle Bompard and Michael Eyraud

GABRIELLE BOMPARD and Michael Eyraud were a greedy and unpleasant couple who decided that murder would be more lucrative than their usual petty thefts. Gabrielle was a 22-year-old prostitute who picked up men in high-class bars and hotel lobbies in Paris. Michael was a married man more than twice her age, who had never made a success of any honest job he attempted. When the two became lovers in 1889, they supplemented Gabrielle's income by robbing her clients, who would find it embarrassing to report the circumstances of their loss to the police.

As the summer drew on, Gabrielle spotted a better prospect in Monsieur Gouffe, a 50-year-old bailiff who was a little too fond of alcohol and was always bragging about the amount of money he was taking back to store in his office safe. Gabrielle made a great fuss of him, going out to dinner on his arm, telling him that she was unhappy with Michael and would welcome the attentions of a new lover. Once she had gained his confidence she invited him back to the one-room apartment she had rented for the purpose in a fashionable street.

Gabrielle and Michael had laid their plans carefully. They had chosen the room because there was an alcove behind the bed, masked by a curtain. Inside the alcove Michael had rigged up a system of pulleys and ropes fastened to the ceiling, the idea being that he could hide behind the curtain and pull on one end of the rope. The other end, attached to a hook, was left hanging down at the side of the curtain, where it would not be seen.

Gabrielle welcomed Gouffe with champagne and led him to the

341

bed. As she kissed him and stroked his hair she undid the belt of her robe and pushed it open, revealing her naked body. While Gouffe had eyes for nothing else, she took the belt from her robe and, in apparently coquettish mood, looped it round his neck, knotting it carefully. As Gouffe lunged for her, Michael reached from behind the curtain and attached the hook to the knotted belt. He then hauled on his end of the rope and Gouffe was jerked into the air, eyes popping and feet kicking.

When they were sure that he was dead, they went through his pockets to find his office keys. They then tied the body in a sack and stowed it in a trunk and, excited by their success, made love. Michael then took the keys and let himself into Gouffe's office but failed to open the safe and fled empty-handed when he was almost caught by the patrolling night watchman. The lovers were still faced with the problem of disposing of a body and the following day they took it on a train bound for Lyons and dropped it off in the river. They then set off for Marseilles and eventually, when they had borrowed enough money for the trip, they travelled to America.

It was several months before the trunk was found and by then the decomposing body was unrecognizable. Scientists were able to establish, from measuring the bones, that the dead man had walked with a limp and suffered from water on the knee, and they could establish his age from his teeth. The information they gained matched the details of the missing Gouffe and identification was completed by comparing the hair of the corpse with that taken from Gouffe's hairbrush. Details of the find were circulated throughout Europe and an assistant in a London store recognized the trunk, which Gabrielle and her lover had bought when travelling in England. He was able to give a good description of his French customers and this was soon matched with the description of the pretty young woman with a voluptuous figure who had been seen several times with Monsieur Gouffe.

Meanwhile the two murderers had reached San Francisco, where Gabrielle left Michael in favour of a young American, telling him that Michael was threatening her life and she needed his protection. However, she found it impossible to settle in America and begged her new lover to take her back to France. Once there, she learned that the police were searching for her and that it was only a matter of time before she was arrested, so she decided to give herself up, claiming that the murder had been planned and executed entirely by Michael Eyraud, who had forced her to take part in his scheme. The hunt for Michael was intensified and he was arrested in Cuba, protesting that Gabrielle's account of the murder was all lies. The crime had been entirely her idea, he said, and she was trying to frame him to conceal her guilt.

The jury found them both guilty but while Michael was to die on the guillotine, Gabrielle was sentenced to 20 years' imprisonment. 'Why not the woman too!' Michael cried when he heard the sentence. Gabrielle escaped death because French society of the time was reluctant to execute a woman and after serving 10 years she was released to sink into obscurity.

Augusta Fulham and Henry Clark

AUGUSTA FULHAM and Lieutenant Henry Lovell William Clark met at a regimental dance in 1910 and the attraction between them was immediate. Henry, or 'Harry', was a 42-year-old physican in the Indian Subordinate Medical Service with a reputation for drinking too much and carrying on affairs with women among the British expatriate community in Meerut. He had little time to spare for his wife, a nurse several years older than himself, or his four children. Augusta was the good-looking 36-year-old wife of a civil servant and was equally bored with her quiet, retiring husband.

Their affair, with its secret assignations and passionate love letters, provided just the excitement that Augusta craved, though it was a blow when Harry was posted to the hospital in Agra and could only manage an occasional visit to Meerut. It was not enough for Augusta and she coolly decided that the only way to improve the situation was to poison her husband. She persuaded Harry to supply her with suitable poison and he sent a supply of 'tonic powders' containing arsenic. Over the next few weeks Augusta added them to Edward Fulham's food.

When Edward became ill and failed to respond to treatment, his doctor suggested sending him to hospital. His condition improved dramatically but as soon as he returned home, he suffered a relapse. This time, when the doctor insisted on another spell in hospital, Augusta arranged for him to go to Agra, where he would be at Harry's mercy. The day after he arrived Edward told his daughter that he had a feeling that he was going to die. She then watched Harry Clark give him an injection and soon afterwards her father was dead. It was Harry who signed the death certificate, giving the cause of death as heatstroke.

Once Edward was dead only Harry's wife stood in the way of Augusta's plans for a blissful future and she began to press Harry, who was drinking more heavily than ever, to arrange to dispose of the problem. Soon Mary Clark was suffering from gastric upsets. None of the food she was served seemed to agree with her, so she decided to prepare her meals herself in future and her health improved rapidly.

On the night of 17 November 1912, Mary Clark was battered to death in the bedroom of her bungalow in Agra by intruders. Her husband raised the alarm when he returned from an evening out – where he had managed to establish a cast-iron alibi – and discovered the body. Inspector Cecil Smith, head of the local police, was immediately suspicious: nothing had been stolen and without robbery as a motive, it seemed more likely that Mrs Clark had died at the hands of hired killers. When questioned, the Clark's cook became panicky and contradicted himself over and over again, finally confessing that Harry had planned the murder, hiring four young Indians, who had been admitted to the bungalow by the cook, once Mrs Clark had retired for the night.

Inspector Smith soon uncovered the gossip about Harry's affair, so Augusta was questioned and her house searched. Under her bed was a locked tin box which, she said, Harry had given her for safe keeping. Inside were several hundred of the letters she had written to Harry over the past few months. They were full of passionate protestations of love, as well as many references to the plan to murder her husband and the need to get rid of Mary Clark. Augusta was dumbfounded by the discovery of the letters: when Harry had entrusted the box to her, a few days before his wife's murder, he had simply told her that he wanted to keep his private papers out of the house during the investigation. She had thought that her incriminating letters had been destroyed long ago, but Harry could not bear to part with them.

Under questioning Augusta collapsed and told the Inspector what he needed to know and both she and Harry were arrested. Harry remained loyal and wanted to marry Augusta, who was expecting his child, before the trial but she rejected him bitterly, saying that but for him she would still be free and happy. 'He is the cause of all my trouble,' she said. 'He has poisoned and wrecked my life.'

At the trial Augusta gave evidence against her lover while he made a full confession, trying to spare her as much blame as possible and maintaining that they had never intended to kill Edward Fulham, only to make him ill so that he would return to England to recuperate. However, once he had realized that Edward was dying and was beyond help, he had given him a last injection 'out of pity, just to put an end to his misery'.

Both prisoners were convicted and Harry was hanged on 26 March 1913. Augusta was reprieved because of her pregnancy but, though her child was delivered safely, she died in May of the following year.

Mary Creighton and Everett Applegate

IN THE summer of 1935 Mary Creighton received a series of unpleasant anonymous letters written on cheap yellow paper, threatening that if her lodgers, Everett and Ada Applegate, did not leave the neighbourhood there would be serious consequences. Mary took them to the police but there was little they could do and in time the letters ceased.

Mary was a good-looking woman in her mid-thirties, well-known in the local community and married to a quiet, self-effacing man. Their good friends the Applegates had moved into their home on Long Island, USA, the previous November, when they were forced to move out of a relative's house and had nowhere else to go. Both families were short of money so it made sense to share expenses, though the Creighton's house only had two bedrooms and it meant the two teenage girls, Ruth Creighton and Agnes Applegate, sharing a bed in the attic and young Jackie Creighton sleeping on the porch.

In September 1935 the massively fat Ada, aged 36, was suffering from sickness and stomach pains. The doctor suggested gall bladder trouble and sent her to hospital, where her condition improved – but within five hours of returning home the pain and vomiting recurred and Ada died two days later. Though her doctor was surprised by her death, he decided that it was due to 'coronary occlusion'. This might well have been the end of the matter if a concerned citizen had not furnished the police with details of Mary's past history. While living in New Jersey she had been tried, along with her husband, for the murder of her brother Raymond by arsenical poisoning. They were

347

acquitted, but soon afterwards Mary was rearrested and put on trial on the charge of poisoning her mother-in-law. Once again, nothing could be proved against her but it was enough to rouse suspicions on Long Island. Ada's body was exhumed and the preliminary medical examination suggested arsenical poisoning.

The Creightons were taken in for questioning and when Mary signed a statement her handwriting was compared with that of the anonymous letters and found to be remarkably similar. She admitted that she had written the letters herself because she wanted the Applegates out of the house. Everett had been paying unwelcome attentions to her and, besides, he was a bad influence in a household which included young girls. District Attorney Martin Littleton called on a distinguished New York psychiatrist, Dr Richard Hoffman, for help in questioning Mary Creighton. He also asked him to visit the Creighton household and make a report, paying special attention to 15-year-old Ruth Creighton in view of Mary's remarks.

Ruth quickly admitted that she and 'Uncle Ev' had been lovers since the previous June, shortly before the anonymous letters started arriving. Her mother knew about it because she had caught them in bed together, she said. Mary, on the other hand, claimed that she knew nothing about the relationship, though she admitted to having sexual relations with Everett herself. She had had high words with Ada on one occasion, when Ada made snide comments about Ruth's morals. Everett confirmed what Ruth had said and was immediately arrested for statutory rape.

Meanwhile, Mary had made the first of three separate confessions, in which she sometimes took the blame herself and sometimes turned it all on Everett. First she said that Everett had given her some white powder to put into an eggnog she was making for his wife. He knew all about the trials for murder in New Jersey and threatened to tell if she did not obey him. In the second confession she said that she had bought rat poison for legitimate reasons then, when Ada was running Ruth down, she put some of the poison into her food on an impulse, without Everett's knowledge. In the third statement, she said that the first time she had seen the white powder was when she saw him mix it into a drink and she had then watched him lift up his wife and give it to her. Everett, in his statement, admitted being involved in the murder but said that it was Mary who had given the poison to his wife, virtually forcing the last drink down her throat when Ada protested that she wanted no more. At the same time he maintained that he had never had an affair with Mary, as he did not find her physically attractive.

At the trial, both changed their stories. Everett denied any involvement with the murder of his wife, while Mary testified that she had been afraid of Everett, because he knew about her past. For this reason, she had written the anonymous letters, hoping to get rid of him, but when she failed, she had been in his power. He had told her to obtain the rat poison and she had given it to him, then she had been forced to watch helplessly while her friend Ada drank milk and eggnogs laced with arsenic. Her confessions, she said, had been tricked out of her by detectives who told her that her daughter Ruth was in custody and would 'burn with her' if she did not admit her guilt.

The prosecution expected Ruth's testimony to discredit both defendants, yet once on the stand she acknowledged the affair with Everett but said that her mother knew nothing about it. She admitted that she had originally told the District Attorney that her mother had caught her in bed with 'Uncle Ev' several times. A good deal of court time was spent investigating the relationship between Ruth and Everett, but Everett's counsel pointed out that his client did not need to kill his wife to seduce Ruth or her mother as he had already had intimate relations with both of them for some time. Of course, he admitted, no one could excuse Everett's behaviour: 'But are you going to convict him for murder because of that? Are you going to say he is no good anyway and better off dead because he violated this young girl? If that is how you are going to judge him then why have this trial, why come to court? There are trees and telegraph poles outside. You could finish it quicker that way.'

Mary's counsel pointed out that the Creightons had always had a happy marriage before Everett came into the house; she had been a good wife and mother and a good friend to Ada. She had been forced into a sexual relationship with Everett but there was no proof that she had poisoned Ada or ever had any desire to do her harm.

The jury believed none of it and both defendants were convicted of first-degree murder. They were executed at Sing Sing on 16 July 1936, but while Everett Applegate walked to the electric chair, Mary Creighton was paralysed with fear when the time came and was pushed in a wheelchair on her last journey.

Catherine Hayes,
John Billings and John Wood

IN MARCH 1726 a nightwatchman patrolling the banks of the Thames in London, near where the Tate Gallery now stands, had a bad shock when he shone his lantern on a shadowy object, only to find that it was a dismembered human head. The custom at the time was to display a murder victim to the public for the purpose of identification, so the head – duly washed, with hair neatly combed – was set up on a pole in the churchyard of St Margaret's, Westminster. Several people who saw the head thought that it had belonged to John Hayes of Tyburn Road, the street which then led to the village of Tyburn at Marble Arch and is now the shopping centre of Oxford Street.

At first his wife, Catherine, flatly denied the possibility, saying that her husband, a successful moneylender, was on business in Portugal. When she was eventually persuaded to view the head she broke down in floods of tears, kissing the face and lamenting for her beloved husband. It was not long before the grisly facts of John Hayes's murder came to light and revealed Catherine as a vicious, cold-blooded killer.

John had married Catherine, a servant on his father's farm, secretly and against the wishes of his parents, who thought her neurotic and unreliable. When the couple moved from Worcestershire to London Catherine began taking in lodgers and in 1726 two young men, John Billings and John Wood, were living in the house. Both had become Catherine's lovers when her husband was away from home and she must have decided that life would be far more exciting if he was out of the way permanently. She fed the young men all sorts of tales about John Hayes's stingy nature and godlessness, even saying that he had been responsible for the deaths of their two children in order to talk them into killing him.

One evening all four went drinking at the Brawn's Head Inn, New Bond Street, but the three conspirators made sure that John Hayes drank far more than the rest of them. Back at the house, the young men waited until Catherine gave the signal that her husband had collapsed on the bed in a drunken stupor, then Billings struck the first blow with a hatchet and Wood joined him in battering the unconscious man to death. Catherine told the young men to cut off her husband's head and put it in a bucket. At first the plan was to boil off the flesh so that it would be unrecognizable but they decided that this would take too long, so instead they emptied the blood from the bucket down the sink, then Billings and Wood carried it to the bank of the Thames and threw the head into the river. When they got back, the three conspirators chopped the remainder of the body into pieces, packing some of them in a box and wrapping the remainder in a blanket, then they threw them into a pond in Marylebone Fields.

Once the head was identified, all three were questioned and Wood quickly broke down and confessed. He later died in prison and his friend Billings was hanged. Catherine's fate was far worse: at that time a woman who killed her husband was convicted of 'petty treason' and sentenced to be burned at the stake. The custom was for the executioner to strangle the prisoner before the flames reached her, but in Catherine's case the executioner misjudged the timing and got his hand burned in the fire, dropping the rope before the job was done. As a result, the watching crowds saw Catherine trying to push away the faggots as the flames licked her body, and heard her agonized screams as she was burned alive.

Catherine Hayes

Maria and Frederick Manning

THE HANGING of Maria and Frederick Manning for the murder of Patrick O'Connor took place in front of Horsemonger Lane Prison, London, on 13 November 1849 and drew a crowd of thousands. Spectators treated the execution as an entertainment, renting standing space on specially erected platforms and bringing along their binoculars for a better view. The novelist Charles Dickens had been persuaded to attend, against his better judgment, and he was horrified by the scene. Afterwards he wrote to *The Times*:

> When the day dawned, thieves, low prostitutes, ruffians and vagabonds of every kind flocked on the ground, with every variety of offensive and foul behaviour. Fightings, faintings . . . tumultous demonstrations of indecent delight when swooning women were dragged out of the crowd by the police, with their dresses disordered, gave a new zest to the general entertainment . . . I am solemnly convinced that nothing that ingenuity could devise to be done in this city, in the same compass of time, could work such ruin as some public executions and I stand astounded and appalled by the wickedness it exhibits.

The crime for which the Mannings paid the ultimate penalty was sordid and stupid, for they had little hope of escaping detection. Their victim was Patrick O'Connor, a former suitor of the Swiss-born Maria Manning, whom he had met on a cross-Channel boat when she was in service as lady's maid to Lady Blantyre. Maria already had an admirer, railway guard Frederick Manning, and for a while she vacillated between the two men, eventually choosing Frederick as the better match. After the marriage in 1846 the couple moved to the West Country to manage a public house but Manning proved a poor landlord and was soon dismissed, returning to London to open a beershop in Hackney. It was becoming clear to Maria that she had married the wrong man and she renewed her friendship with Patrick O'Connor, who had a good job as a customs officer and money in foreign railway bonds. At one point she left her husband and went to live with Patrick, but was eventually persuaded to go home again.

Frederick must have been convinced that Patrick and his money could be of use to them, for Patrick was often invited to the Manning home and introduced to the lodger, a medical student named Massey, as a 'dear friend of the family'. At the same time Frederick was asking Massey all sorts of strange questions about the effects of chloroform and laudanum and whether a drugged person would be capable of writing a cheque, whether an airgun could kill a man and what was the weakest part of a human being's skull. Perhaps Frederick began to worry that he had asked too many questions and was drawing attention to himself, for Massey was given notice to quit his lodgings – though not before he had noticed the delivery of a load of quicklime.

Two days after the Mannings had bought a large shovel, they invited Patrick to dinner. Friends saw him talking to Maria at the back door of her house while he smoked a cigar, the last time that he was seen alive. Maria conducted him downstairs to the kitchen then, as she laid one arm affectionately round his neck, she produced a pistol and shot him in the head. Even at such close range she did not manage to kill him outright and when Frederick came into the kitchen he found Patrick moaning. He later explained coolly: 'I never really liked him, so I battered his head with a ripping chisel.' When he was dead, the Mannings buried him under the flagstones of the kitchen floor, covering his body with quicklime, then sat down to enjoy a well-cooked goose for dinner.

Next day Maria went round to Patrick's lodgings with the keys she had taken from his body and stole money, two gold watches and some railway shares. Frederick managed to sell some of the shares by impersonating Patrick, but was so panicky about being recognized that he refused to dispose of the rest. Maria was furious and decided that it was time to leave her useless husband and look after herself. Taking both money and shares she departed for Edinburgh, leaving two trunks in the left luggage office of London Bridge station, labelled as belonging to Mrs Smith, a passenger to Paris. When Frederick realized what had happened he fled to the Channel Islands, with only the money raised from a quick sale of his furniture.

Patrick O'Connor's friends and workmates missed him at once and began making enquiries. As he was last seen at the Mannings' house the police soon arrived to make a search and found the newly moved flagstones, with the body beneath. The hunt for the Mannings began and Maria was quickly arrested in Edinburgh, where she had been trying to cash the rest of the stolen railway shares under the name of Mrs Smith. Frederick was apprehended a week later in Jersey, where he had been moving from one boarding house to another and trying to dull his panic by drinking several bottles of brandy a day.

'Is the wretch taken?' were Frederick's first words about his wife. He blamed her for everything; she was the one who shot Patrick, she had dug the grave, she had taken the money. 'She is a very violent woman,' he explained. 'I have been afraid for my own life.' Maria's main motive was revenge, he said. Patrick had persuaded them to take the London house, which was more expensive than they could afford, promising to rent a room himself, but he had gone back on his promise.

At the trial the two Mannings were separately represented and each tried to blame the other, though it was easier to believe that the strong-minded, controlled Maria was the moving spirit behind the murder plot rather than the cringing, pleading Frederick. When the verdict came in, Maria berated the court: 'You ought to be ashamed of yourselves! There is no justice and no right for a foreign subject in this country.' Was it likely, she demanded, that she would have killed a man who held her in the greatest respect and would have married her the moment she was free? If she was disposed to murder anyone, she would have chosen her husband, who had made her life 'a hell on earth'. In her fury, she threw handfuls of rue – at the time it was the custom to sprinkle herbs around the dock to 'sweeten' the court – at the judge.

Maria made strenuous efforts to obtain a reprieve, even appealing directly to Queen Victoria, still saying that her husband was responsible for the murder and that she was not in the house at the time and knew nothing about it until the next day. All her efforts failed and she mounted the scaffold in a black satin dress. It was the most popular fabric of the time, but Maria's appearance that day put it out of fashion for at least 20 years.

Myra Hindley and Ian Brady

THE NAME of Myra Hindley still raises an outcry of horror and anger every time it appears in the headlines, as the question of her release from prison is raised yet again. Capital punishment had been abolished in Britain a few months before the 'Moors Murderers' were convicted of their monstrous crimes against children for their own twisted sexual pleasure, so Myra Hindley and Ian Brady escaped the gallows – but some criminologists believe that if the sadistic murders had been discovered earlier, the campaign to preserve the death penalty might have been irresistible.

Before she became infatuated with Ian Brady Myra was a religious girl, a convert to Roman Catholicism, fond of children. As a teenager she was keen on dancing and swimming and was generally well-liked. She had a strong personality and was often the dominant partner in a relationship but there was no warning of the perversions to come. Ian Brady, on the other hand, seems to have been twisted from childhood, when he enjoyed torturing cats and killing birds. By the time he was 20 he had quite a history of petty crime and a spell in Borstal behind him but he had settled into a job as a clerk in Gorton, Manchester. In 1961 Myra joined the firm as a typist and was immediately attracted to the tall, reserved young man with the deep-set, brooding eyes. She did her best to attract his attention but it was a year before he started asking her out.

As soon as she became involved with Ian her family noticed changes in her. She was no longer interested in religion, she became secretive and began locking her things away, and she no longer enjoyed mixing with people. It was hardly surprising: Ian was 'educating' her, introducing her to the books on torture and killing that he enjoyed. He was a great admirer of Hitler and together they listened to Nazi marching songs on the gramophone.

No one knows when he first broached the idea that Myra should entice a child into her car, a child who would later be killed. When first 12-year-old John Kilbride then 10-year-old Lesley Ann Downey went missing, no one connected their disappearance with the couple who kept themselves to themselves. Everything changed when the two murderers, perhaps needing an extra boost to the excitement of killing, tried to involve David Smith, Myra's brother-in-law. For some time Ian had been introducing Smith to his ideas: they had practised shooting revolvers out on the moors, read pornographic books together and planned an armed robbery on a bank. The robbery was never carried out and it seems likely that Ian was only testing out his friend to see how far he was prepared to go. He boasted to Smith that he had committed three or four murders and fancied that he had a receptive audience and that Smith would be a willing convert.

One night in October 1965 Myra arrived at Smith's door, asking him to see her home because the street lights were out and she was nervous to walk alone. When they reached her council house, Myra asked him in to collect some miniature bottles of liqueur Ian had for him. While he was waiting for them, he heard Myra calling 'Dave, help him!' Thinking Ian was being attacked, he ran into the living room to find Ian standing over a prone young man, bringing an axe down on his head and shoulders over and over again. When at last his victim was dead, Brady said cheerfully: 'That was the messiest yet. It normally only takes one blow.'

Myra brought plastic sheeting and blankets and they set about wrapping up the corpse and cleaning up the blood. Then Smith helped Ian to carry the body upstairs to the spare bedroom, where it would remain until they could borrow a pram to get it to the car. Afterwards Myra made tea and reminisced, laughing merrily, about the time she had been sitting in the car on Saddleworth Moor with a body in the boot. She had been waiting for Ian to finish digging a grave, but a policeman had stopped to ask if she was in difficulties.

Smith left in the early hours of the morning, dazed and shocked, and a few hours later he went to the police, carrying a breadknife and a large screwdriver for protection, in case Brady saw him and decided to attack. When they heard the story the police went to Myra's house and though Myra tried to stall them, claiming that the key to the locked back bedroom was at her office, Ian eventually admitted, 'There was a row last night' and gave them the key. In the bedroom, just as Smith had described, was the body of Edward Evans, a 17-year-old engineering apprentice. In Myra's car they found a detailed plan for disposing of Evans's body and the selected spot for burial.

In a thorough search of the house, police found left-luggage tickets for Manchester Central Station hidden in the spine of Myra's prayer book. The contents of the two suitcases retrieved from the station included photographs of a naked child, a gag in her mouth, her eyes full of terror and bewilderment. She was identified as Lesley Ann Downey, who had disappeared on Boxing Day 1964 after visiting a fairground. Tape recordings found with the photographs were to reveal new horrors: the murderers had recorded the cries and pleading of the little girl as she was violated and killed. There were photographs of Myra in several identifiable spots on Saddleworth Moor and an exercise book containing a number of names, including that of John Kilbride. Questioned about whether this was the child who had disappeared on 23 November 1963, Ian answered that it was another boy, someone he had known in Hull.

The police began the grim job of digging on the moor and on 16 October 1965 they discovered the naked body of a child in a shallow grave, along with clothes and a plastic necklace identified by Mrs Ann Downey as belonging to her daughter. John Kilbride's grave was located from one of the photographs Ian took of Myra standing proudly at the spot. His clothes and spectacles had been buried with him.

Throughout the trial Ian tried to shield Myra and she protested her

The search for the Moors Murder victims with – inset – three missing children: (top left) *John Kilbride,* (top right) *Keith Bennett,* (bottom left) *Pauline Reade*

innocence, but no one believed her. Some listeners thought that she had been completely under Ian's spell, others thought that she was the dominant partner; either way, they believed her guilty. The tapes recording Lesley Ann Downey's ordeal were played in court, while some of the jurors wept openly. At first the child was heard pleading 'Don't undress me, will you', and 'I want to see my mummy . . . Honest to God I have to go because I am going out with my mamma. Please, please help me, will you.' Later she was crying and screaming in pain: 'Please take your hands off me a minute please . . . I can't breathe . . . Please God. Why? What are you going to do with me?' Myra was heard telling her to stop crying and keep quiet: 'Shut up or I will forget myself and hit you one.'

Ian Brady was found guilty of three murders, Myra Hindley of two; in the case of John Kilbride she was found guilty of harbouring and assisting Ian Brady, knowing that he had killed the boy. Ian was sent to Durham gaol, Myra to Holloway and at last the two soulmates were separated. Though at first they maintained a frequent and warm correspondence and begged to be allowed to see one another, in time the bond was loosened and broken.

Though Ian became resigned to living the rest of his life in prison, Myra has constantly sought freedom. In 1973 she involved a prison officer, Patricia Cairns, with whom she had a lesbian relationship, in an escape attempt, resulting in a six-year prison sentence for Cairns. Since then she has worked hard to convince everyone that she is a reformed character, turning back to Catholicism and earning a BA Honours degree from the Open University. In 1987, perhaps hoping to gain sympathy for her cause, she responded to a letter from the mother of another missing child by admitting knowledge of the killing of 12-year-old Keith Bennett, who disappeared in 1964, and 16-year-old Pauline Reade, missing since 1963. Myra was able to take the police to Pauline Reade's grave on the desolate moor but Keith Bennett's body was never found.

It remains to be seen if she will ever succeed in gaining her parole, as feelings on both side run high. Lord Longford and other reformers have worked hard on her behalf, but each time the subject of her release comes up Lesley Ann Downey's mother spearheads the campaign to make sure that Myra Hindley remains in prison. As she says, she herself has a sentence that will be with her for the rest of her life.

Mary and Earl Smith

MARY SMITH earned her nickname of 'Shoebox Annie' in San Francisco, California, where she was a practised thief. She would wrap a lidless box securely and cut a slit in the paper across the top of the box so that she could then invert it over some choice item displayed on a shop counter and walk away with the item concealed in what looked like a pre-wrapped parcel.

She did well enough and as her son Earl grew up she trained him in her ways. When he was a child her favourite ruse was sending him to buy a list of goods, leaving a dud cheque signed by his mother as payment. If he was caught he would burst into tears and confess that he had signed the cheques and his mother would kill him if she found out. The shopkeeper would sympathize with the boy's distress and let him off with a caution. As a teenager, Earl was no longer satisfied with being his mother's messenger and began mugging strangers for the contents of their wallets. He was caught and spent the next three years in a reformatory.

By 1920 Mary and Earl were living in Montana and upgrading their criminal activities. They decided that they were less likely to be caught if they disposed of the people they robbed, so that there was no one to give evidence against them. They could never be convicted of murder, said Mary, if there was no body for the police to find, so they installed a copper tank beneath their home and filled it with corrosive acid.

Earl, smartly dressed and using an assumed name, won the confidence of a rich oil speculator, Ole Larson, and invited him back to the house to sample his mother's cooking and discuss a mutually advantageous deal. Larson was never seen again and, though the trail clearly led to the Smiths' door, the police were baffled by the lack of physical evidence and were unable to make an arrest.

The next unwary victim to accept the Smiths' hospitality was a wealthy young married woman who fell under Earl's spell. When the police came to investigate her disappearance they discovered the woman's clothes, jewels and furs but no sign of her. This time they were far more rigorous in their questioning but Mary simply shrugged and said that as far as she knew, the woman was still alive and well. 'If you think she's dead, where's the body?' she taunted them. Once again, the police were unable to take any action. Mary and her son, knowing that they were now a marked couple in Montana, moved to Seattle, where they continued to make a good living from thieving and trickery.

In 1930, a young naval officer, Lieutenant James Bassett, advertised his blue sports car for sale. Earl answered the advertisement and asked Bassett to take him for a test drive, then invited him home to collect the cheque. Mary was ready for them, with water boiling in the kitchen – not to make the tea but to wash away any bloodstains after Earl had battered the lieutenant to death with a hammer. Together they dragged him into the bathroom, undressed him and cut the body into pieces, putting the pieces into the bath so that the blood could drain out while the gruesome pair enjoyed their dinner. They then put the pieces into sacks, took them out into the country in the lieutenant's own car and buried them one at a time in a field.

James Bassett's family soon reported him missing and his description was circulated, along with the details of his car, which had disappeared with him. A few days later the police spotted the car and who should be driving it but Earl Smith, with his mother in the passenger seat. Lieutenant Bassett's watch and empty wallet were found in the car but, with no evidence that he was dead, it was still impossible to accuse the Smiths of murder. Instead they were charged with grand larceny. Earl, who by now had a long criminal record, was given a life sentence while Mary was sentenced to eight years.

They would both have escaped a murder charge if Mary had been able to keep her tongue still. Instead, she boasted about the last killing to her cellmate, telling her the whole story of dismembering and burying the body. She admitted that they had been frightened that night because they thought they had been seen when they were preparing to bury the body, but no one had ever come forward. 'So everything was all right,' she told her companion cheerfully.

The cellmate informed against her and when the police made enquiries they found people who had seen Mary and Earl burying parcels in a field. Lieutenant Bassett's body was located at last. After the guilty verdict, Earl committed suicide in his cell but Mary escaped the death sentence and spent the rest of her life in prison.

Betty Jones and Karl Hulton

BETTY JONES, who had left the quiet Welsh village where she grew up at the earliest opportunity, was working in London as a stripper under the name of Georgina Grayson in 1944. When she met Karl Hulton, who called himself Ricky Allen and told her he was a Chicago gangster, she thought that this was her chance to see some real excitement at last. She liked the idea of being a 'gangster's moll' and told him she wanted to do something dangerous. When Ricky showed her his gun she was both scared and fascinated.

Using a stolen army truck as a vehicle, the two embarked on a series of robberies. The first victim was a woman driver who was forced out of her car by Betty. Ricky then hit her over the head and knocked her to the ground, kneeling on her while Betty went through her pockets. They left the girl lying bleeding by the road. Another girl, who accepted a lift from the couple, was hit over the head with an iron pipe, half strangled and thrown unconscious into the river.

On the night of 6 October, Betty flagged down a private hire car driven by 34-year-old George Heath. According to the statement she gave to the police later, Ricky had waited until they were on a quiet road, then told the driver to stop so that they could get out. As the driver leaned over to open the door, she 'saw a flash and heard a bang'. Then Ricky had taken over the driving and, once George Heath had stopped breathing, Betty searched his clothes for money and valuables, taking his watch, cigarette case and matching lighter as well as money and petrol coupons. After that, Ricky had dumped the body in a ditch, where it was found next morning. They then went for a meal.

The killers might never have been traced if they had disposed of the car immediately but Ricky was found driving it the following day.

He gave Betty as his alibi for the previous evening and she was asked for a statement. Later that day she told a friend, a reserve policeman, about the investigation and added: 'If you'd seen someone do what I've seen done, you wouldn't be able to sleep at night.' When the conversation was reported, Betty was taken in for questioning. Soon, both Betty and Ricky were giving their versions of the murder. Ricky maintained that robbing the cab driver had been Betty's idea; when he protested that he did not want to go ahead, she told him to give her the gun so that she could do it herself. When the police took him to the spot where the body had been found, he said, 'I wouldn't have been here but for that girl.' He claimed that he had never meant to shoot Heath and that the gun had gone off accidentally while he was distracted by his girlfriend's chatter. According to Ricky Betty had helped him to carry the body over to the ditch, but although police evidence confirmed that the body had not been dragged across the grass Betty always denied helping him.

In court, 18-year-old Betty said that she had only gone along with Ricky because he had often threatened her and she was frightened of him. However, other witnesses said that they had seemed perfectly at ease with one another and Betty had not shown any sign of fear. The jury found both defendants guilty, though in Betty's case they added a recommendation for mercy. Both were sentenced to death by hanging but two days before the execution date Betty's sentence was commuted to life imprisonment. She remained in prison for nine years.

Martha Beck and Raymond Fernandez

DELPHINE DOWNING, a widow with a three-year-old daughter, contacted a lonely hearts club in the hope of finding a congenial man for friendship with a view to marriage. She felt that she had found him through her correspondence with Charles Martin; he sounded like a kind, caring man who would make a good father. When he came to visit her at her home in Michigan, USA, he brought with him his sister, the rotund and smiling Martha. Delphine was surprised but pleased, thinking that he was concerned for her reputation. A man whose intentions were not respectable would hardly bring his sister along.

In the weeks that followed Delphine allowed herself to be charmed by Charles, who thoughtfully took over management of her financial affairs. She may well have been taken aback by Martha's obvious jealousy once she realized that her brother was sleeping with Delphine, but she assumed that Martha would get used to the idea in time.

Neighbours used to seeing Delphine every day were surprised when she suddenly disappeared without a word. Charles told them that she had gone away for a while, leaving him and Martha to look after her house. One of the neighbours, not as impressed by the odd couple as Delphine had been, notified the police. They arrived as Charles and Martha were returning from an evening at the cinema and asked to look round the house. In the cellar they found a patch of recently laid cement and when they dug down the bodies of Delphine and her daughter Rainelle were uncovered.

369

When the couple were questioned they were revealed as Raymond Fernandez, who had long made his living from swindling women who answered 'lonely hearts' advertisements, and his mistress Martha Beck. Raymond, born in Hawaii of Spanish parents, moved to Spain in the 1930s, gained a reputation as a war hero during the Civil War and married a Spanish woman. In 1945 he worked his passage to the USA on an oil tanker. His defence lawyers were later to maintain that an accident on this voyage, when a hatch cover fell on his head, had changed his personality for the worse. Arriving in America, he soon found his niche as a confidence trickster. By 1947, with something like 100 victims already behind him, he went on holiday to Spain with Mrs Jane Thompson, travelling as a married couple. After a quarrel, Mrs Thompson was found dead in her hotel room. Spanish police were anxious to question Raymond about her death but he had already left for America, where he produced a fake will and took possession of Mrs Thompson's apartment.

It was in this apartment that he first met 26-year-old Martha Beck. Her name had come from a lonely hearts club but, as a divorcée with two children to support and very little money, she was no use as a potential victim. The vastly overweight Martha had little in the way of physical attraction to offer either, but she and Raymond soon recognized one another as soulmates. Martha's appetite for perverted sex was as insatiable as his and she threw herself wholeheartedly into his business as a swindler, convincing him that, working as brother and sister, they could find even more gullible women to deceive.

From the beginning, Martha's jealousy got in the way. Raymond's success in conning money out of his women friends meant that he had to win their love, but Martha could not bear the thought of him making love to another woman. In August 1948, he made a bigamous marriage in Illinois with Myrtle Young, but the bride found herself sharing a bed with Martha rather than with her new husband. When Myrtle refused to stand for this any longer Martha gave her a large dose of

Raymond Fernandez (third from left) *and Martha Beck* (right) *are examined in the Municiple Court, Michigan*

barbiturates and, while she was still in a befuddled state, put her on a bus to Arkansas where she collapsed and died.

In December the couple were in Albany, New York, where Raymond persuaded 66-year-old widow Janet Fay into signing over all her assets and a substantial insurance policy to him. Martha admitted to hitting Mrs Fay over the head with a hammer in a fit of jealousy, then Raymond finished the job by strangling her with a scarf. They put the body in a trunk which they stored in Raymond's sister's cellar while they arranged to rent a home in Queens, New York. They moved in, complete with trunk, and buried the body in the basement, covering it with cement. A few days later they left the house.

As far as Delphine Downing was concerned, it was never known for certain which of the two actually committed the murder. Delphine had been given barbiturates and then shot. It may have been Martha who fired the shot, in another of her jealous rages. On the other hand, Raymond at one point in the investigation claimed that he had shot her to hasten her death, as she was already dying from the drug overdose. Little Rainelle had cried so inconsolably after her mother's death that Martha drowned her in the bath.

The couple were charged with the three murders – Janet Fay and Delphine and Rainelle Downing – though they were suspected of 17 more. A long battle ensued over where the couple were to be tried as, though they had been arrested in Michigan, the first murder had been committed in New York. The choice was a significant one, for in Michigan the most the killers could expect was a life sentence, while New York still had the death penalty. New York won.

Their trial began on 9 June 1949 and when Martha was brought into the court she broke away from her guards, ran to Raymond and kissed him, exclaiming, 'I love you and I always will.' Their only hope was to convince the jury that they were not responsible for their actions – Raymond because of his head injury, Martha because of a disastrous childhood, when she was reputedly raped by her brother. Every detail of their sordid sex life was revealed in evidence and the courtroom was crowded with spectators who wanted to catch a glimpse of the 'monster' and his 'fat ogress'.

The trial lasted 44 days and at the end of it Raymond Fernandez and Martha Beck were both found guilty of murder in the first degree. On 8 March 1951 they both went to the electric chair at Sing Sing. Shortly before the execution Raymond sent Martha a loving message and she said: 'Now that I know Raymond loves me, I can go to my death bursting with joy.'

Delfina and
Maria de Jesus Gonzales

IN THE early 1960s the white slave traffic was booming on Mexico's west coast. Teenage girls looking for work answered advertisements for employment as maids and were abducted, never to be seen again. Enquiries kept leading back to a smoothly dressed woman with a mole on her cheek who had been seen several times in the company of girls who subsequently disappeared.

Faced with yet another missing teenager in January 1963, the police department in Guadalajara decided to devote extra resources to stopping this trade in human flesh once and for all. A watch on local brothels was mounted and the woman with the mole, Josefina Gutierrez, was arrested. Realizing that the game was up and determined not to shoulder the blame alone, she told them that she collected victims for two sisters, Delfina and Maria de Jesus Gonzales, who owned a ranch in a remote spot near the town of San Francisco del Rincorn. They entertained customers there and also provided girls for the brothels of the area.

The Ranch El Angel was difficult to find and by the time the police arrived the sisters had heard they were planning a raid and had gone into hiding, leaving the ranch in the charge of a group of armed 'minders'. Inside the police found 13 young girls, all weak from ill-treatment and drugs. They had a terrible tale to tell. When a girl was first 'recruited' she was beaten and gang-raped, then turned over to a succession of customers. She was regularly fed drugs to make her more amenable and flogged unmercifully if she did not obey every command. If she became pregnant, the foetus was forcibly aborted by the simple expedient of a vigorous beating administered to the stomach.

Some of the girls had become mentally unbalanced from their suffering, others were riddled with venereal disease, but at least they were alive. They told the investigators that once a girl lost her looks, fell ill or became so hopelessly addicted to drugs that she was no longer useful, she was killed and quickly buried behind the ranch. A team of diggers was brought in to turn over the ground near the ranch and they uncovered the remains of more than 80 girls, together with many aborted foetuses. There were also 11 male bodies which belonged to migratory Mexican workers who were returning home from seasonal work in the US, their pockets full of money. They were easy prey when they stopped in at the ranch to hire a girl for the night; their drinks were drugged, their money was taken and by morning there was a fresh grave outside.

The evil sisters had been plying their trade for 10 years, paying protection money to various influential citizens so that they were always tipped off when a raid on one of the brothels was about to take place and could thus remove the young prisoners in advance. This time there was no protection: their hiding place was soon discovered and the Gonzales sisters were brought to trial. They tried to evade responsibility, telling the court that all the bodies belonged to girls who had died from natural causes while in their care – they were poor, undernourished girls who were already suffering from disease when they arrived – but the testimony of their pathetic victims made nonsense of their story. They were convicted and sentenced to 40 years' imprisonment. The investigation did not end with their trial and a number of local worthies were ultimately to pay the price for their co-operation.

Carol Bundy and Douglas Clark

THE KILLINGS that became known as the 'Sunset Strip Slayings' first hit the headlines on 12 June 1980, when the bodies of stepsisters 15-year-old Gina Narana and 16-year-old Cynthia Chandler were found alongside a Los Angeles freeway. Both had been shot in the side of the head. Twelve days later two more bodies were discovered in different places. Both 24-year-old Karen Jones and 20-year-old Exxie Wilson were prostitutes who worked Sunset Strip in Hollywood: Exxie Wilson's head had been cut off and removed. The body of 17-year-old Marnette Comer was half-mummified by the time it was found in late June and an unidentified corpse was discovered a month later on Sunset Boulevard.

All were the victims of 32-year-old Douglas Clark and his girl-friend Carol Bundy, a 37-year-old nurse and mother of two. They had met at a country and western bar and he had moved in with her immediately, teaching her all sorts of new ways to enjoy sex. He brought girls back to her apartment – one of them only 11 years old – and had sex with them in front of Carol, who recorded the event with pictures.

Douglas had always entertained fantasies about murdering women during the sex act and once he decided to turn his fantasies into reality it was often Carol who enticed girls into the car where he would force them to have oral sex, then shoot them in the head at the moment of climax. He took Exxie Wilson's head home and stored it in the deep freeze until he was ready to take it out and use it for sex acts. Carol stood the head on the kitchen counter and gave it a full make-up. 'We had a lot of fun with her,' she said later. 'I was making her up like a

Barbie.' Afterwards they scrubbed the face clean and packed it in a box, then dumped it in an alleyway.

It was Carol who gave the game away. At the country and western club she met up with an ex-lover, John Murray, and as the evening wore on and she got slightly drunk she started hinting at the things she had witnessed. Murray put two and two together and guessed that her new boyfriend was the 'Sunset Strip' killer. Afraid that he might go to the police, Carol decided that he, too, must be killed. His body was found a few days later, with nine stab wounds and without a head. The head was never recovered; Carol said she had thrown it into a ravine to delay identification.

Two days after Murray's body was discovered Carol broke down in front of a friend and confessed what she had done, crying that she had been trained to save lives, not to kill. The friend, horrified, went to the police and the lovers were both arrested. The gun that had killed five of the six victims was found, along with undergarments collected from the girls as souvenirs.

Douglas Clark was charged with six counts of first-degree murder and Carol Bundy with two murders, that of John Murray and the unidentified girl found on Sunset Strip. Douglas tried to convince the jury that the murders had been carried out by John Murray and Carol, and that she had killed her partner in crime so that he could not testify against her. No one believed him and he was sentenced to die in the gas chamber.

At first Carol pleaded insanity but changed her plea to guilty early in the trial. She was sentenced to 27 years to life on the first count of murder and 25 years to life on the second, the terms to run consecutively.